Genetic Counseling, the Church, and the Law

Task Force Members

Albert S. Moraczewski, O.P., Ph.D.,
Chairman of the Task Force
Vice President for Research
Pope John XXIII Medical-Moral
Research and Education Center
St. Louis, Missouri

Gary M. Atkinson, Ph.D.
Associate Professor of Philosophy
William Woods College
Fulton, Missouri

Robert C. Baumiller, S.J., Ph.D.
Associate Professor
Department of Obstetrics
and Gynecology
Georgetown University
Washington, D.C.

Margaret Dewey, O.P., M.S., M.A.
Ground Work for a Just World
Lansing, Michigan

Patrick J. Kelley, J.D.
Attorney at Law
Husch, Eppenberger, Donohue,
Elson & Cornfeld
St. Louis, Missouri

Rev. Anthony R. Kosnik, S.T.D.
Dean of Theology
Sts. Cyril and Methodius Seminary
Orchard Lake, Michigan

Rev. Edward J. Mahoney, Ph.D.
Director
Continuing Education Division
Diocese of Burlington
Burlington, Vermont

Patricia Monteleone, M.D.
Professor of Pediatrics
Cardinal Glennon Memorial
  Hospital for Children
St. Louis, Missouri

William Sly, M.D.
Professor of Pediatrics
St. Louis Children's Hospital
St. Louis, Missouri

Maurice Zeller, C.SS.R., S.T.D.
Rector
Holy Redeemer College
Waterford, Wisconsin

Genetic Counseling,
the Church
and the Law

Edited by
Gary M. Atkinson, Ph.D.
and
Albert S. Moraczewski, O.P., Ph.D.

A Report of The Task Force on Genetic Diagnosis and Counseling
Pope John XXIII Medical-Moral
Research and Education Center
St. Louis, Missouri

Nihil Obstat:
> Rev. Robert F. Coerver, C.M., S.T.D.
> Censor Deputatus

Imprimatur:
> +John N. Wurm, S.T.D., Ph.D.
> Vicar General of St. Louis

December 17, 1979

The Nihil Obstat and Imprimatur are a declaration that a book or pamphlet is considered to be free from doctrinal or moral error. It is not implied that those who have granted the Nihil Obstat and Imprimatur agree with the contents, opinions or statements expressed.

Library of Congress Catalog Card Number: 79-92084

ISBN 0-935372-06-7

Dedication

To Pope John Paul II whose person symbolizes resistance to genocidal forces and whose writings place science and technology in the service of the human race through their subordination to morality and the teachings of Jesus Christ.

CONTENTS

FOREWORD

Anyone dealing with broad social issues needs to be acutely conscious of the *weltanschauung,* the world view, which forms the context within which the discussion takes place. This is nowhere more true than in the area of applied genetics: genetic screening and counseling, antenatal diagnosis, selective abortion, contraception, and sterilization. The discussion of such topics quickly forces us to face fundamental theoretical and practical questions: what is the nature and value of the human person, and what may we do or not do in preventing or alleviating serious genetic diseases. Conditions such as cystic fibrosis, Huntington's Disease, Tay-Sachs, or neural tube defects are among the most painful problems confronting human beings. If one knows that there exists a high probability, say 25% or 50%, of transmitting a genetic defect to one's offspring, where does one's responsibility lie? Does it go so far as not getting married? If a woman is already married, what steps (if any) should she or her husband undertake to see to it that she does not become pregnant? If she is already pregnant and it is known for certain that the child in her womb is afflicted, what steps may she take then? It has been estimated that approximately 10% of the population has or will develop an inherited disorder. Furthermore, the average person is estimated to carry between four and eight defective genes which, if conjoined with the same defective genes in the spouse, can produce defects in the offspring.

There is no point in denying the fact that the currently accepted attitude among many genetic counselors is in general favorable toward sterilization of one of the spouses and abortion if a child suspected of having a genetic defect has already been conceived. It is often stated that it is better not to bring a child into the world at all than to do so when it will be burdened with some serious handicap. If one were to attempt to provide an explanation of why such an attitude should be so predominant, perhaps the best hypothesis is that it results from a specific fundamental view of the nature and value of the human person. Such a view may be summed up by saying that the key values of human living are the having of pleasurable experiences, the avoidance of painful experiences, and the exercise of one's freedom and reason independently of any accountability to a personal God in the making of decisions regarding one's own welfare. Since the existence of a severely afflicted child is counter to these values, both

xi

for the child itself and for the parents, family, and wider society, the only reasonable thing to do from that perspective is to prevent that existence by any means available. Indeed, so serious is the problem of genetic defect that even the value of freedom and autonomy (for the parents) may, according to that viewpoint, be somewhat compromised in order to safeguard individuals from unnecessary suffering.

The severity and burden of many of these genetic diseases must not be underestimated. A visit to an institution where severely handicapped children are maintained will dispel any romantic feelings about these dreadful conditions. Nonetheless, the magisterium of the Church has consistently held that a human fetus may not be directly aborted even for the highest motives such as wanting to free the infant from a lifelong burden of pain and suffering. Furthermore, married couples may not directly interfere with the natural consequences of sexual intercourse. An individual, male or female, may not undergo surgical sterilization with the direct intention of preventing future conceptions. All this may seem heartless in the conditions cited, and not only heartless but harmful to the welfare of the species. Such a harsh position appears to make a mockery of the Church's claim to be a servant of human persons and a bearer of good news and hope.

The Church's teaching can be seen to make sense only when viewed from a different perspective regarding the significance and direction of human existence. For the Church is constrained to proclaim in season and out of season the saving truth disclosed by the person of Jesus Christ: that God loves us, loves each one of us unconditionally, without regard to our status, and that we are to love one another as Jesus himself has loved us. Such a general truth, so "noble" in the abstract, must be taught in the concrete situations of daily life, especially in those contexts where one might doubt the truth of that message.

The central issue is over how far one's vision of the human person extends. As Christians we believe that the only way of going beyond the world of human existence disclosed to the senses and unaided reason lies in the Person of Jesus Christ. Jesus holds the key to the mystery of suffering and death, a mystery now disclosed to us through his own suffering, death, and resurrection. He embraced our human condition to teach us how to live in the real world. Suffering, pain, disappointment were part of his life. This is an indication that suffering and pain are not irredeemably evil. While we are immersed in space and time, the realities of life are not to be viewed solely as they are disclosed to our senses. As we move horizontally in time, we are at every moment in touch vertically with another dimension, that of eternity. Hence, the reality of each day has to be seen in its totality — the present *and* its connection with the eternal now. In the latter dimension the pain and agony of the present take on a redeeming meaning. That suffering is united to the redemptive suffering of Our Lord.

A reassuring truth, developed with strength and clarity in St. Paul's Letter to the Ephesians, is the fundamental unity of all believers with one another and with Jesus Christ. Nevertheless, this ontological unity requires an operative, day-to-day unity to make it meaningful for us. St. Paul mentions that when one suffers or rejoices all do. When one of our brothers or sisters is burdened with some handicap — genetic or otherwise — we are called to share that burden. This perhaps is a challenge most of us have *not* met. Greater efforts needs to be expended by believers to aid in concrete ways those who are suffering. Because it is a common human trait to shun the unfortunate, the grossly deformed or handicapped, the Christian should be especially ready to shoulder responsibility to improve the lot of the suffering. In this regard, the Church must be ever aware of the need of sensitizing the believer to the human problems associated with genetic defects. But more than this is involved. Because society has a serious obligation to provide care and support for handicapped children and their families, the Church should assist in this task by collaborating with and encouraging research into the diagnosis and treatment of genetic defects as well as by providing adequate facilities for seriously handicapped children.

It is important to recall that we as human beings have a mandate to "subdue the earth," which means that we are to employ our skills to make this world a more suitable place for *all* to live. Such endeavors include improving our health and our environment, which means eradicating diseases to the extent that our wisdom permits. Not every disease is crippling, but those conditions which prevent or impede the individual from exercising and enjoying his or her humanity are to be our special concern. Much progress has been made in correcting many diseases — diabetes, tuberculosis infectious diseases, etc. — but many others elude our current skills. Among the latter, of course, are those which are the topic of this study.

With the prevailing attitude of sterilization and abortion, research into therapy for these conditions is less likely to be pressed. If we eliminate the problem by eliminating the patient, then the incentive to understand and control these conditions is diminished. On the other hand, if we, confronted with the ravages of these crippling and sometimes dehumanizing genetic defects, are pushed to find the true solution, such a pursuit will increase our understanding of the mysteries of human genetics which will eventually lead to preventing or correcting these defects. In the meantime, what do families and individuals do in the face of probable or actual disease of genetic origin? What are the moral concerns of the genetic counselor, of the Catholic health facility, of the Church, of society in dealing with such agonizing problems? This study endeavors to examine these and related questions in the light of the Church's official teaching, which always presumes that the human condition, with all its pain and uncertainties, is embraced by the loving care of God.

The Task Force

PREFACE

About the Pope John Center

The Pope John XXIII Medical-Moral Research and Education Center was founded in 1973 to provide the Church with carefully documented research studies dealing with the long-range ethical implications of modern medicine and their significance in relation to biotechnological advances. The Center seeks to engage highly competent scientists, physicians, theologians, and ethicists for specific projects. Without adopting a narrow sectarian point of view, the Pope John Center strives to view the relevant ethical and theological issues in the light of Catholic teaching.

About This Report

Antenatal diagnosis and genetic counseling have become increasingly prominent in medical care during the past decade. As the techniques for diagnosis of genetic diseases have improved in accuracy and safety, their usage in medical practice has become more widespread. With an increased number of genetic disorders identified (over two thousand), the question of treatment has become more pressing. Unfortunately, at this time the number of conditions which can be adequately treated and corrected is a tiny fraction of the total. Because of the degree of suffering and disability which many of these genetic disorders entails, there has been a growing tendency to resort to abortion when a fetus is antenatally diagnosed as being afflicted with a serious defect. Similarly, couples who have been identified as being at high risk of conceiving a child with a notable genetic disorder are faced with a complex reproductive decision. Numerous moral issues arise for the potential parents, for the genetic counselor, for the Catholic hospital and for the Church.

To deal with such complex issues more effectively, the Pope John Center assembled an interdisciplinary Task Force on Genetic Diagnosis and Counseling (GENTAF). This group — identified on a previous subsequent page — met four times to identify the issues, divide the task and to react to one another's reflections. The individually written reports of the Task Force members ultimately were amalgamated into a single report by the two co-editors in order to avoid duplication, fill up lacunae, and unify the viewpoints. Such a process required that difficult decisions be made when conflicts of opinions arose among members of the Task Force. Ultimately, the deciding factor was compatibility with the teaching of the Church's Magisterium as judged by the editors.

Among the ethical issues associated with genetic counseling, and controversial because of their practical appeal when a couple is identified as at risk for conception of a child with a serious genetic defect, are contraception and sterilization. The Editors have not included the multiple arguments and conflicting views affecting these procedures because the Center has recently published a separate work, (Atkinson and Moraczewski, 1979) which discusses those topics at greater length.

The Editors believe that the God-given rights of women as persons should be reflected in the use of literary forms. However, while every effort has been made to observe the equal dignity of male and female in use of pronouns in this study, at times the Editors have been elected for the sake of readability to use the masculine pronoun in a generic sense.

ACKNOWLEDGEMENTS

To this study many persons have contributed mightily. Our gratitude goes in the first instance to the Task Force members (GENTAF). For the meetings they attended, for their untiring patience in dealing with complex issues, and for their gracious willingness to permit their individual contributions to be amalgamated into this final report, we express our sincere appreciation. What good may be found in this study is largely attributable to their individual contributions; what defects may be present are the total responsibility of the editors.

We are grateful especially to the St. Ann Foundation, whose generous grants financed the major part of the research and writing of this study. Without its help and encouragement, this study could not have been initiated or completed.

Various persons have read the manuscript in whole or in part and offered very helpful suggestions and comments. Among these we especially thank The Reverend Donald G. McCarthy, Ph.D. and Miss Mary J. Cosgrove, Esquire.

We acknowledge the timely advice of Monsignor Elmer H. Behrmann.

Miss Mary Ellen Honich, who tracked down elusive references, ably assisted us in library research. The final draft reads more smoothly due to the editing of Ms. Rita Adams, Ph.D. With unlimited patience and calm perseverance, Mrs. Carol Kuehler typed the final revisions of the complete manuscript.

To all of the above and to those we may have inadvertently overlooked, our grateful thanks and prayers.

The Editors
St. Louis, Missouri
September 1979

General Introduction

The past twenty years have witnessed a remarkable advance in our understanding of the chemical and chromosomal bases of human inheritance. This growth of the pure science of human genetics has led to technological developments in the applied sciences of genetic diagnosis and therapy. It has also contributed to the deepening awareness on the part of the general public of the human suffering caused by genetic defects.

A number of factors may be cited to explain this rapidly increasing significance of genetic medicine:

1. The increase in understanding of genetic defects and the ways in which these are transmitted
2. The growth of the relative importance of genetic causes of human disability, at least in the developed countries, as infections and other environmental causes of illness are brought under control
3. The acquisition of techniques for diagnosing affected individuals *in utero* (antenatal or prenatal diagnosis) and for detecting the carrier status of prospective parents
4. The development of prenatal and postnatal methods of therapy for a number of genetic conditions
5. The legal availability of selective abortion for those fetuses diagnosed as affected by genetic disease
6. The increasing significance of the legal issues involved in genetic counseling, such as the requirements of confidentiality and full disclosure
7. The advent of screening programs to detect the carrier status of members of populations believed to be at risk for giving birth to affected children.

Most of these factors will be discussed in this study. For convenience and clarity this study is divided into three parts and an appendix. As a point of departure, Part I, "Genetic Medicine — An Overview," is primarily introductory to the area of genetic diagnosis and counseling. Chapter 1 provides a brief description of the different types of genetic disease, the methods of antenatal diagnosis and their application to genetic screening and sex selection. Chapter 2 examines alternative theories of counseling and the role of the counselor in the clinical setting in order to facilitate an awareness of the current status of the art and a sympathetic appreciation of the human burdens associated with genetic disease. Eleven case histories are introduced to promote this understanding and to serve as illustrations of the nature of genetic disease.

Part II discusses the social, philosophical and theological context in which contemporary genetic issues are being raised. Because our image of the world and our concept of the human determine the priority assigned to basic human values, Part II also examines briefly the impact modern science has had on human self-image and on the way in which the world is perceived. In addition three different philosophical approaches to what constitutes the human are also examined in Chapter 3. The fourth chapter considers the biblical and magisterial teachings with regard to the meaning of the human. This chapter ends with a short consideration of the human viewed from the perspective of Christian personalism.

In light of the discussions of Part I & II, Part III looks at Christian concerns and responses to the presence of genetic disease. Chapter 5 identifies many of the important moral and social issues which arise as a consequence of potential or actual genetic defects. In the following chapter the responses of the individual Christian, client and counselor, are considered. The responsibility of the Church as a community, together with the responsibility of its Bishops, and its health care institutions are identified and examined in Chapter 7. Because the burden of diagnosing, treating, and caring for those who have been afflicted with a genetic disease is more than the Church is able to manage adequately, the final chapter examines the Christian expectations and realization of civil society's responsibilities in the matter of genetic disease.

The Appendix is a legal analysis of genetic counseling and tort liability. The first section discusses "wrongful life" and "wrongful birth" cases in terms of the professional's scope of duty. In the second section of the Appendix, the standard of care and the special problems of deliberate concealment or disclosure of diagnosis in genetic counseling cases will be treated.

At the outset it should be recalled that the moral reflections contained in this work are done against a background of Christian faith and values. Papal Teachings are explicitly invoked and applied to the moral problems. Some authors on the topic similarly do so in varying degrees (for example: Ashley and O'Rourke, 1978; Curran, 1978; May, 1977; McFadden, 1977). Other authors do not appear to have this concern but their works can be helpful (for example: *The Encyclopedia of Bioethics,* 1978; Lebel, 1978; Roy, 1978). Because of the complexity of the issues, often it is advisable to consult more than one author on the subject in question.

PART I

Genetic Medicine:
an Overview

Chapter 1

Genetic Defects: their Nature and Diagnosis

The explosive advance of modern biology has been due in part to a deeper and more detailed understanding of the way in which the directions (genes) for the growth and development of living organisms are contained in their cells. This first chapter provides a quick overview of fundamental genetics and genetic diseases. These two sections are followed by a discussion of the various technologies available for the diagnosis of genetic diseases. This discussion includes consideration of the present status and future prospects of these technologies as well as some thoughts about the moral dimension and application of the techniques to genetic screening and sex selection.

Fundamental Genetics

A genetic defect is a disorder that results directly or indirectly from an alteration of the information contained in the genetic material. Every normal human being receives, at the time of conception, the total complement of genetic information required for development into a mature member of the human species. This information is contained in vastly complex linear molecules called deoxyribonucleic acid (DNA). The long molecule of DNA is composed of segments called genes which "specify" or "code for" a single protein. The proteins specified by the genes are either structural components of individual cells or enzymes which facilitate biochemical reactions. The genes are arranged in discrete packages called chromosomes which vary in size and probably in the number of component genes. At certain stages of cell division, the chromosomes contract into a tight form that can be visualized under a microscope. In this state a normal human cell can be seen to contain forty-six chromosomes, arranged in twenty-three pairs, and each can be identified by size and characteristic staining reaction. Each pair consists of one chromosome of paternal and one of maternal origin. The sex of an individual is determined by the sex chromosomes. There are two types of sex chromosomes: a medium-sized chromosome called the X chromosome and a small chromosome called the Y chromosome. The Y chromosome carries the male-determining genes. Normal individuals have two sex chromosomes: the female has two X chromosomes, whereas the male has an X and a Y. The other forty-four chromosomes are called autosomes. Thus, the normal human being possesses twenty-two pairs of autosomes and one pair of sex chromosomes. If the two chromosomes of a pair look alike, they are called homologues and the pair is said to be homologous. The pairs of autosomes are homologous, so that the female possesses twenty-three homologous pairs, whereas the male possesses only twenty-two, the XY pair of sex chromosomes being nonhomologous. Most genes are present in two copies, one being the paternal (sperm-derived) and one the maternal (egg-derived) member in each chromosomal pair. Exceptions are the genes carried on the X and Y chromosomes of the male. Females have two copies of the X chromosome, though only one of them is active or functional in any one cell.

The long journey from the single-celled fertilized ovum (zygote) to the mature human organism containing 200 trillion cells of many different types is accomplished by two processes, cell duplication and cell differentiation. Cell duplication is the process by which the cells increase in number by precisely duplicating all of the genetic information they contain, and undergoing a division of this material. A dividing cell produces two new cells, each of which receives exactly the same genetic information that was present in the original cell. Cell differentiation, on the other hand, is the process in which some cells in the body acquire specialized functions. This permits some of them to become liver cells, for example, while others become muscle cells. This differentiation into specialized cell-type occurs, not by varying the amount of genetic information in different cells, but by turning some genes on and other genes off in the specialized cells. The process of development into a mature, functioning organism is dependent on the sequential activation and inactivation of genetic information in a delicately controlled way. This process can be disrupted, not only by various intrinsic abnormalities in the program of development (gene defects), but also by certain hostile factors in the environment in which the human embryo develops (e.g., viral infections or maternal exposure to drugs or radiation).

Types of Genetic Disease

In order to understand the nature of genetic defects, it is necessary to distinguish five different types of genetic disease: (1) autosomal recessive, (2) X-linked, (3) autosomal dominant, (4) multifactorial traits, and (5) chromosomal imbalances. As described below, these five types are distinguished from one another by the precise manner by which the inherited trait is transmitted from parent(s) to child.

1. Many genetic disorders result directly from alterations in the genes. These alterations result either in the failure of the normal product of that gene to be produced or else in the failure of the abnormal product that is produced to function properly. If the defective gene codes for an enzyme and there is a normal gene for that product on the other member of the chromosome pair, the normal process controlled by the enzyme will usually occur. But if the information is abnormal in both chromosomes, meaning that both parents carry the abnormal gene, the process will be abnormal or will not occur at all since the required enzyme is lacking. Most enzyme deficiency diseases are produced in this way. The two normal-appearing parents are both carriers for the mutant gene, each of them possessing one normal and one abnormal gene. They produce an offspring who inherits the defective gene from each of them. The two parents on the average have a 1/4 risk of producing an affected offspring with each pregnancy and a 1/2 risk of producing normal-appearing carriers. Examples of autosomal recessive defects are phenylketonuria (PKU) Case #1, pp. 31-32), Tay-Sachs disease (Case #2, pp. 32-34), cystic fibrosis (Case #3, pp. 34-36, and sickle-cell anemia.

2. Some genetic diseases result from abnormal genes on the X

chromosome. Since females have two X chromosomes, they are usually normal in appearance despite the absence of proper information on one of the chromosomes. But their sons who inherit their abnormal X chromosome have no compensating normal information and can be severely affected by the defective gene. A carrier female will usually have a 1/2 chance of producing an affected son or a 1/2 chance of producing a carrier daughter. Examples of X-linked defects are Duchenne's muscular dystrophy (Case #4, pp. 36-38, hemophilia, and some forms of color blindness.

3. Some genetic abnormalities result from alterations in a single gene of a gene pair. The process by which an abnormality occurs even in the presence of a normal gene is for most diseases not well understood. Autosomal dominant defects will occur in about 1/2 of the offspring of affected individuals, even though the children who inherit the defective chromosome possess the normal chromosomal information from the normal parent. Examples of this type of genetic defect are Huntington's Disease (Case #5, pp. 38-42), neurofibromatosis (Case #6, pp. 42-44), and Marfan's syndrome (Case #7, pp. 44-45).

4. The first three types of defects are said to be "simply inherited" single-gene diseases because they arise from the inheritance of a defect in a single gene or pair of genes. There are other defects that are said to be due to "multifactorial inheritance," in which inheritance clearly plays some role and defective genes predispose individuals to a condition, but other factors appear necessary for the occurrence of the disease. For example, there is growing evidence for the role of inheritance in such common disorders as coronary heart disease, diabetes mellitus, hypertension, schizophrenia, susceptibility to certain infections and allergies, and possibly sensitivity to environmental agents that cause cancer. The inheritance of these conditions is difficult to decipher, but even before the mechanism underlying these disorders has been understood, it is often clear that inheritance plays some role, since the risk of contracting a disease is greater in families with a history of the disorder than in those without such a history. The chance of occurrence in relatives of an affected person can be calculated from experience (empiric risk figures). This is one area in genetics that has lately received much increased attention. The risk of giving birth to a child with a neural tube defect (Case #8, pp. 45-47), is a good example of such multifactorial inheritance.

5. Other defects result from errors in the packaging of the genetic material. No single gene is defective, but large numbers of genes have become scrambled, lost, or misplaced. An entire chromosome may be missing (monosomy), or there may be three homologous chromosomes rather than a pair (trisomy). Pieces from one chromosome or the entire chromosome itself may have gotten attached to a nonhomologous chromosome belonging to another pair (translocation). Such chromosomal excess, deficiency, or rearrangement produces a gross imbalance of genetic material and disrupts the delicate process of cell differentiation. A number of defects may result, especially malformations in the development of the nervous system. In a few cases these chromosomal-imbalance disorders are inherited from one of the parents who is a carrier (Case #9, pp. 47-49). In the vast majority of cases they arise when a defective germ cell (the sperm or the ovum) is produced or when the cell is subjected to some change, as when the ovum suffers partial decay owing to the advanced age of the woman (Case #10, pp. 49-50). The resulting abnormalities of differentiation are usually so severe that the embryo is arrested in its development and a spontaneous abortion occurs. Down's syndrome (Cases ##10 and 11, pp. 48-50, 50), is one of the most common examples of a defect involving an improper packaging of the genetic material.

It should be evident from this discussion that genetic disorders are almost infinitely varied. They may be mild (nearsightedness) or severe (blindness). They may involve one organ system or many. They may be manifest at birth or have a late onset. Some are treatable whereas others presently are not. Some genetic disorders produce disability regardless of the environmental conditions whereas others produce a significant disease only under a special set of circumstances. A rare but clear example is the inherited deficiency in an enzyme called cholinesterase. The absence of this enzyme has no known consequences except when affected individuals are exposed to certain muscle relaxants during anesthesia. These individuals may die under these circumstances because of an inability to degrade a muscle relaxant that most of us would degrade very rapidly. Finally, the autosomal-dominant defects in particular may manifest what is called "incomplete penetration": the individual is diagnosed as having defective genes and yet there are no manifest clinical symptoms. Thus, the severity of the expression of certain diseases, or whether there are indeed any symptoms at all, may depend on environmental factors or on factors that are at present entirely unknown.

From the early part of this century the patterns of inheritance of the autosomal and X-linked varieties were recognized, but it is only within the last twenty years that we have gained sufficient understanding of the makeup of the human chromosome to recognize the true extent of the human problem posed by genetic disease. There are at present (1978) approximately twenty-eight hundred diseases that are known or strongly suspected to be inherited as single-gene defects (see McKusick, 1978). Each one of these defects is individually rare, but their aggregate is substantial. It has been estimated that between 1/100 and 1/50 of all newborn children are affected by single-gene disorders; and some believe that this estimate is too low, for many genetic defects only become apparent many years after birth (Polani, 1973). Of the children born affected by single-gene defects, approximately 1/2 suffer from autosomal-dominant defects, 2/5 from autosomal-recessive defects, and 1/10 from X-linked defects.

Early chromosome studies provided evidence that trisomy and monosomy were responsible for a large number of congenital malformation syndromes (Lejeune et al, 1959). Examples of these diseases are trisomy 21 or Down's syndrome (1/600 live births), monosomy X or Turner's syndrome (1/3000 live female births), XXY or Klinefelter's syndrome (1/600 live male births), and the birth defect syndromes associated with trisomy 13 (1/5000 live births) and trisomy 18 (1/7000 live births). Subsequently, extra or missing pieces of chromosomes were identified as causes of birth defects and mental retardation. In a small minority of parents of these children, chromosomal abnormalities were found that enormously increased their risk of producing further children with chromosomal imbalance (Hamerton, 1971). Newborn surveys have shown that 1/200 liveborn children have a recognizable chromosomal aberration (Jacobs et al, 1974).

Human embryos that had spontaneously aborted early in pregnancy have been studied and found to possess a very high (3/5) incidence of chromosomal abnormalities (Rowley et al, 1963). These studies led to the conclusion that chromosomal packaging errors occur with very high frequency in human conceptuses, possibly 1/10 or even 1/5. Most instances of these abnormalities thus appear to result in early spontaneous abortions. Only in the minority of pregnancies is there produced a child capable of extrauterine viability. Comparisons of frequency in the newborn period and frequency in spontaneous abortions indicate that even the more commonly recognized imbalances in the newborn population (Down's syndrome and Klinefelter's syndrome) occur much more frequently in human conceptuses but the majority abort spontaneously.

Little at present is known about many of the multifactorial traits. Disabilities that for some time have been recognized as multifactorial, such as the risk of giving birth to a child with a neural tube defect (Case #8, pp. 45-47), may be only a very small part of the problem. Indeed, if the suspicion is verified that there are genetic dispositions to coronary heart disease, diabetes, hypertension, schizophrenia, and particular forms of cancer, then the role of multi-factorial inheritance may come to be seen as the single most important problem in all of genetic medicine.

In spite of the fact that genetic medicine is rapidly increasing in importance, it would be a mistake to conclude that we are today experiencing a genetic disease epidemic. Genetic diseases probably occur no more frequently today than they did at the turn of the century. One explanation for the increased importance of genetic medicine can be provided by noting the advances in the pure science of genetics, but such an explanation would be only partial. The growth in the importance of medical genetics has been equally dependent upon dramatic advances in other areas of medicine. The drastic reduction in the frequency and morbidity of diseases attributed to infection, parasitic infestation, and malnutrition has changed the nature of the common causes of disability. Infantile diarrhea, tuberculosis, poliomyelitis, and rheumatic fever were enormously important causes of disability and mortality in the early years of this century. In each case, the fruits of medical research provided means of prevention or successful treatment which dramatically reduced the importance of these once-significant medical burdens. As the mortality and morbidity from these diseases has fallen, the relative importance of diseases atttributed to genetic factors has increased. It now becomes clear that these disorders presently account for a significant proportion of the burden of disease.

Approximately twenty thousand children are born each year with major chromosomal or biochemical disturbances (Lubs and Ruddle,

1970). These disorders are second only to cancer as causes for mortality in children under five. Recent surveys of major children's hospitals in developed countries indicate that between twenty-five and thirty percent of the admissions have been for genetic diseases, congenital malformations, or mental retardation (Clow *et al,* 1973; Day and Holmes, 1973); and one author suggests that genetic factors may be responsible for as much as fifty percent of all pediatric bed occupancy (Rosenberg, 1974).

Antenatal Diagnosis

The growing recognition of the importance of genetic disease has been coupled with the development of techniques for diagnosing them and with a growing public awareness of the availability of these techniques. Diagnosis is of two major types. Prior to the conception of a child, prospective parents may undergo tests to determine whether they are carriers of genetic defects and to assess the probability of their conceiving an affected infant. After conception but prior to birth, the fetus itself may be tested *in utero* to determine whether it is affected.

The testing of normal-appearing adults to determine whether they are at risk for producing a defective child can take a number of forms, depending on the nature of the suspected defect. Most tests use blood samples, employing techniques of chromosomal analysis referred to above, or else involve a search for abnormal levels of various enzymes. In the case of certain metabolic disorders, analyses of urine specimens can be run. For some disorders of the nervous system muscle biopsies may be performed. X-rays may be employed for other disorders.

In this section, attention will be focused on an outline of the current status of antenatal diagnosis as well as prospects for the future. Much of this material has been drawn from a report of a Consensus Development Conference sponsored by the National Institute of Child Health and Human Development (NICHD, 1979). The remainder of the section will touch on the elements to consider for a value assessment of these technologies.

Current Status of Major Antenatal Diagnostic Technologies

Antenatal diagnosis is today rather crude but is rapidly growing in sophistication. There are eight general categories of diagnostic techniques, seven of which involve methods that monitor the condition of the fetus directly, whereas the last comprises indirect methods of monitoring the fetus through the mother:

Radiography — X-ray studies are done to determine skeletal problems such as anencephaly, hydrocephaly, as well as dwarfism and other bony abnormalities. Soft-tissue radiography demands that radio-opaque dyes be introduced into the amniotic fluid or directly into the fetus. Such procedures are not considered good medical practice at the present time, since they carry with them a considerable amount of risk for the unborn.

Electrocardiography — This technique may be considered to include any device, even the ear, used to sense heart beat, heart rate, etc. The common method of diagnosing death *in utero* has traditionally been loss of heart beat. EKG capability is utilized to diagnose more serious heart problems suspected from a stethoscopic examination.

Sonography — This procedure has replaced radiography as a means of visualizing the fetus. It grew out of submarine-detection technology and employs sound waves to locate the position of the fetus. The method probably causes no harm to the mother or the fetus and is non-invasive. Although sonography fails to give the bony detail that X-rays provide, it does give a better picture of soft tissue and sufficient detail to diagnose most skeletal abnormalities. Radiography is now used to confirm problems discovered by sonography. The past decade has seen a great increase in the use of this procedure which practice has shown to be relatively harmless for both mother and child. Currently there are two principal uses of this technology.

1. Sonography is seen as an accepted procedure to be used in conjunction with mid-trimester (i.e., second trimester, when the fetus is 3 to 6 months old) amniocentesis, and with fetoscopy or placental aspiration to ascertain the exact location of the fetus. It is strongly recommended for these uses.
2. Sonography is also used as a means to detect certain structural abnormalities in the skeleton of the fetus and in other organs. Inasmuch as this application is considered to be research, it should be used only by those who have had the necessary training and experience (NICHD, 1979, p. I-6 to 7)

Fetoscopy — This technology is an application of fiber optics and permits direct visualization of the fetus and makes possible the obtaining of minute samples of fetal blood. A thin tube is introduced into the amnion and a light-carrying fiber and reflector are inserted.

13

Developmental abnormalities may thus be seen, and, it is hoped, direct physical manipulation, injection, or even surgery, may one day become possible. To some degree the fetoscopy does endanger the fetus since the tube inserted is rather wide in diameter and may cause trauma.

Because this technique — now approved by the Ethics Advisory Board * — is still in its developmental stages, it is not recommended except by persons who have had the requisite experience and training (see *Federal Register,* 1979; Monteleone and Moraczewski, 1980). At present the limitations of instruments used in fetoscopy do not permit full view of the fetal surface anatomy. Accuracy to date for the diagnosis of possible hemoglobinopathies (blood disorders such as sickle-cell anemia and beta thalassemia) has been about 98 percent. Fetal risks are greater than amniocentesis with the current figures being about 3 to 5 percent miscarriages resulting from the procedure. There is danger, too, of maternal sensitization to fetal antigens as a result of fetoscopy (NICHD, 1979, p. I-8 to 9).

Alpha fetoprotein (AFP) — By measuring the amount of a specific fetal protein (AFP) in the amniotic fluid or in the blood serum of pregnant women (at 14-20 weeks) it is possible to diagnose the presence (or absence) of a major structural defect in the formation of the brain and spinal cord of the fetus (neural tube defects [NTD] such as anencephaly and spina bifida). At present, the accuracy of this test, however, is not fully satisfactory. The use of this procedure is considered appropriate at this time for pregnant women who are known to be at risk for fetal neural tube defects. However, it is considered premature at this time to employ this technology for the screening of unselected pregnant women (NICHD, 1979, p. I-9 to 10). A British study which attempts to weigh the "likely human consequences of a national maternal serum A.F.P. screening programs" for England and Wales, concludes that to prevent the birth (by screening and abortion) of 523 anencephalic children and 555 spina bifida children would "cost" 120 dead or harmed normal infants (Chamberlain, 1978).

Biopsies — It is possible to perform biopsies on fetal tissues, either from membranes, the placenta, or the fetus itself. Biopsies of the membranes or the placenta, although rarely called for, are

---

*This board is advisory to the Secretary of the Department of Health, Education and Welfare.

procedures that are reasonably easy to perform given the information provided by sonography.

Amniocentesis — This is one of the more common procedures used today in prenatal diagnosis. Sonography is used to locate the placenta and the pockets of amniotic fluid. A needle is then introduced trans-abdominally into the amniotic fluid avoiding the placenta and the fetus. The amniotic fluid is a mixture of chemical compounds primarily produced by the fetal metabolism. Cells of fetal origin from the fetus itself or from the amnion are found in the fluid by about the fifteenth week of development. Since 1968 to the present, about 40,000 amniocenteses were performed of which approximately 15,000 were done in 1978. In more than 95% of the cases the results were negative, that is, the fetus was found to be free of the genetic disease for which the procedure was done. At the present time, analysis of the fluid and/or cells obtained for amniocentesis can be useful for the detection of most chromosomal abnormalities, for the diagnosis of almost 75 serious inborn metabolic disorders, and for the identification of neural tube defects in the fetus. When used by experienced persons, these techniques have had an accuracy of about 99% in establishing the presence or absence of most of the above mentioned disorders. In most areas amniocentesis is regarded as acceptable medical practice for certain pregnancies at increased risk for certain genetic diseases or congenital disorders (NICHD, 1979, p. I-4 to 6).

Indirect Methods — Such procedures include the examination of cells or compounds of fetal origin which have crossed the placental barrier and are found in the mother's circulation, excreta, or tissue, such as fetal lymphocytes in the mother's blood and estriol excretions in the mother's urine (Omenn, 1978). Maternal reaction to the fetus or transplacental fetal material can also be indicative of fetal health.

Future Prospects for the Major Antenatal Diagnostic Technologies

In general, the consensus of the experts is that there will be in the future an increased utilization of these technologies. Just as amniocentesis is now recognized as an accepted method for the detection of certain defects, the experts anticipate that sonography, alpha fetoprotein measurements, and perhaps fetoscopy in the near future will achieve the status of established and accepted procedures (NICHD, 1979, p. I-13).

In addition, the consensus conference of experts made a series of recommendations for future research (NICHD, 1979, pp. I-21 to 25).

1. Need for Additional Assessments of Safety and Efficacy
   a. As amniocentesis services expand outside the university and research laboratory settings, further safety and efficacy studies should be initiated in these new settings.
   b. Since as many as 10,000 midtrimester amniocenteses in Rh negative women can be envisioned each year in the U.S., a controlled prospective study should be initiated to evaluate the efficacy and safety of the administration of Rh immune globulin at 16 to 20 weeks of pregnancy.
   c. Data should be collected on the outcome of pregnancies in which ultrasonography is performed. Both control and exposed populations should be grouped by procedure (to estimate exposure) and stage of gestation.
   d. Ongoing assessment of risks from fetoscopy must continue along with careful assessment of diagnostic methods. Follow-up of children after birth is also indicated.
   e. From both the amniotic fluid and maternal serum AFP* data currently being developed, periodic and comprehensive assessment should be conducted to determine:
      (1) Frequencies of false negatives and positives,
      (2) Whether the prevalence of neural tube defects in this country, and the factors mentioned above in (a), warrant continuance of serum AFP screening or of amniotic fluid AFP determination in pregnancies having amniocentesis for other indications and
      (3) The effect of routine maternal serum AFP screening on the prevalence of NTDs,** on the costs, and on emotional stresses it may create (either to reassure unduly or to cause undue concern).

2. Need for Further Technological Development
   a. Research directed to delineating the pathogenic mechanisms and basic etiologies of hereditary diseases and congenital defects should be regarded with highest priority. Such investigations could broaden our understanding of the causation of such conditions and, in turn, lead to more primary and more generally applicable forms of prevention of such disorders.
   b. Similarly, research should be directed to the development of methods or technologies for the administration of effective

---

*Alpha fetoprotein; see page 14.
**Neural tube defects; see pp. 45-47.

treatment regimens (either in prenatal or postnatal life) for hereditary diseases or congenital defects.

   c. Further research to improve and broaden the applications of existing diagnostic technologies should be conducted, particularly in automated karyotyping, increasing the number of detectable disorders, developing new methodologies for antenatal diagnosis, reducing the time interval from amniocentesis to diagnosis, gene mapping, cell sorting, and carrier identification.

   d. Continued development of high resolution echo sonographic equipment and related technology should be encouraged.

   e. Other uses of fetoscopy/placental aspiration for fetal diagnosis and for possible means for fetal therapy should be supported.

3. Need for Assessment of Impact (Medical and Nonmedical)

   a. Studies are needed to ascertain the natural history and impact on families of the birth of children with hereditary diseases or congenital defects, to provide a measure against which the impact of antenatal diagnostic technologies could be compared.

   b. Studies are needed to determine the current level of knowledge, attitudes and behavioral practices among consumers and physicians regarding amniocentesis and its utility in the prenatal detection of hereditary disease and congenital defects. Similar assessments of public and professional perceptions of social and ethical issues related to the prediction and prevention of hereditary disease should be made.

   c. An assessment of the reduction of birth incidence of selected disorders and of the economic impact of wide-spread utilization of these technologies would be useful.

   d. As genetic counseling provides a critical component of the technology, an evaluation of the relationship between current counseling approaches and the level of information communicated, as well as the degree of "informed consent" achieved, would be valuable. Exploration of various educational modalities is strongly recommended to establish an optimal content and means for delivery of relevant information to consumers and health care providers.

The preceding section has reviewed briefly the current status and future prospects for some of the principal technologies used in the antenatal diagnoses of genetic diseases. The subsequent section will deal with several general considerations, mostly of non-technical nature, which must also enter into a value assessment of these technologies.

Elements for a Value Assessment of These Technologies

Major advances in diagnostic techniques have increased the number of conditions which can be diagnosed antenatally or for which there are reliable tests for carrier status. As we have seen, great effort is being directed toward the improvement of the old and the development of new diagnostic procedures. As a consequence, the mass media have made increasing numbers of prospective parents aware of the possibility and value of antenatal diagnosis. For example, it is becoming generally recognized that women over thirty-five have an increased risk of giving birth to an affected child (see Case #10, p. 49). The experience in particular with amniocentesis has provided evidence that the procedure is safer than had been originally anticipated and yet — it must be stressed — not entirely without risks.

Amniocentesis carries a risk because the abdominal wall of the mother is pierced and the needle penetrates the uterine wall, the fetal membranes, and enters the amnion. Infection may occur at as high a rate as that found with venipuncture. The reported empirical risk figures indicate that detectable harm may occur in between 1/100 and 1/500 amniocentesis procedures (Milunsky and Atkins, 1974). In one large-scale study of approximately one thousand amniocenteses, there was a 3.5 percent occurrence of miscarriage after the procedure, compared with 3.2 occurrence in a control group, and there was no significant difference in birth defects (other than the one for which the amniocentesis was performed) between the control population and the patients who had had amniocentesis (NICHD, 1976). Additional studies (Simpson *et al,* 1976); Golbus *et al,* 1979) have tended to support the relative safety of amniocentesis. However, a British Study (MRC Working Party, 1978) concludes more cautiously while an editorial in *Lancet* (1978) raises some pointed questions:

> There is at present a considerable demand for amniocentesis but is this an informed demand? Is it possible that, faced with the human-cost/human-benefit figures revealed by the MRC Report, prospective parents would be less enthusiastic?

The first amniocenteses were performed prior to the widespread introduction of sonography; and because the position of the fetus could not be determined accurately, there was an appreciable risk that the needle would puncture the fetus. Most authorities believe that the use of sonography should lower this risk significantly (Frigoletto and Griscom, 1974).

The fact that certain of these diagnostic procedures carry with them some risk of harm raises important moral questions. The relevant principle in matters of this kind is the Principle of Double Effect, which under certain conditions allows the taking of risks if the seriousness of the harm and the probability that it will occur are balanced by a proportionately significant benefit.* The required conditions, or presuppositions, are that the action itself under consideration is not morally evil, that the intention is good, and that the proportionately good effect is not obtained by means of evil effect. Granted these conditions being verified, this principle, presumably, would justify the risks run by the mother: if she is a competent adult and reasonably informed of the risks to herself of the diagnostic procedures, she might quite legitimately decide that the psychological benefit to herself of knowing the condition of her baby is sufficiently great to warrant her running those risks. But the issue becomes problematic when considerations of the risk to the unborn child are introduced. The difficulty arises not because the fetus cannot consent to the diagnostic procedure but because there is usually no proportionate benefit in prospect *for the fetus*. Parents are able legitimately to consent to risky operations for their children because of the prospective benefit for the children themselves. In contrast, the procedures of antenatal diagnosis usually appear to offer no hope of benefit for the unborn. It is this fact that poses a problem concerning the moral justifiability of many of the antenatal diagnostic procedures (Powledge and Fletcher, 1979).

There are, indeed, several conditions in which antenatal diagnosis can be of considerable benefit to the fetus. For example, the development of the fetus of a diabetic mother can be monitored in order that the child may be delivered prior to term, after it has become viable but before damage has occurred. Rh incompatibility provides a similar example. A few genetic conditions, such as PKU and galactosemia, may be treated by restricting the diet of the child. But in these cases treatment does not begin until after birth, and it would seem morally preferable, because less dangerous, to test the child after

---

*This phrase should not be confused with what has been termed "the principle of proportion" (see Ashley and O'Rourke, 1978, pp. 189-192 for a clear discussion; McCormick, 1973; Curran, 1977). This principle denies that the act itself can be morally evil apart from any consideration of intention or circumstance, and then proceeds to weigh the total values against the disvalues of that action.

birth rather than *in utero*. It is to be hoped that new therapy or therapies will be developed in the future, but it remains nonetheless true that for the vast majority of diseases the level of diagnostic ability today is far beyond the level of our ability to treat. Of course, if one prefers to see the women or the couple as the sole patient in the prenatal diagnostic situation, then all genetic defects detectable *in utero* allow of "treatment" in the form of an abortion.

Most of the early work in developing antenatal diagnosis occurred when there were still rather restrictive abortion laws in most of the states. Under these conditions it was assumed that amniocentesis, for example, would be justifiable in relatively few pregnancies. In 1973 the Supreme Court decisions of *Roe v. Wade* and *Doe v. Bolton* changed the legal situation and thus altered the attitudes of many toward antenatal diagnosis. These rulings made a *decision* of abortion prior to the third trimester a private matter between the woman and her physician, and her decision to abort a right guaranteed by the Fourteenth Amendment. Because so few genetic defects are treatable in any ordinary sense of that term, the widespread awareness and employment of prenatal diagnostic procedures simply cannot be understood without adverting to the legality and social acceptability of abortion for reasons of genetic defect (selective abortion).

Application to Genetic Screening and Sex Selection

Genetic Screening Programs — With the increasing safety (sometimes overstated) and efficacy of these technologies there is associated a growing advocacy of resorting to massive genetic screening programs designed to detect all individuals significantly at risk for producing a child with a genetic defect. Having declared amniocentesis to be a safe and accurate diagnostic procedure, a study sponsored by the National Institute of Child Health and Human Development (NICHD) suggested that sound medical practice would dictate that all pregnant women above the age of thirty-five should be offered amniocentesis. The study concludes: "Yet a survey by Milunksy indicates that only 4.1 percent of the pregnant women more than thirty-five years old in Massachusetts actually had amniocentesis performed in 1974. Hopefully, the results of this study will stimulate increased use of the procedure, for only if it is used can its potential be realized" (NICHD, 1976).

However, as we have already noted (p. 15), amniocentesis does carry with it some not insignificant risks. Furthermore, the procedures of aborting a child identified as having a genetic defect, or of urging contraception and contraceptive sterilization as a means of reducing the number of genetically defective persons in our population, are not acceptable means to many persons and are opposed to official Church teaching. The morally acceptable use of amniocentesis, consequently, remains limited.

As this juncture an important distinction must be made which pertains to the relationship between genetic screening and genetic counseling.

The testing of Askenazi Jews for Tay-Sachs carrier status has shown that large-scale screening programs for that condition are feasible. Another disease that has received a great deal of attention in this area is sickle-cell anemia. Approximately 1/12 of the black population are carriers for this autosomal recessive trait, and carrier couples can be advised of their risk of giving birth to an affected child.

These programs are expensive to develop and implement, and yet their proponents maintain that they are cost-effective, that they save more money than they cost. Even though genetic disease afflicts a small proportion of the population, the cost of care for these individuals is quite high. At least two programs for screening all newborns for inherited metabolic disorders, such as PKU and galactosemia, have been shown not only to alleviate the suffering of affected individuals but also to save families and the state sufficient money by removing the need for institutional care of the affected children to more than justify the expense of the program (Massachusetts Department of Public Health, 1974). But because most of the disorders for which tests are already developed or in prospect cannot at present be treated, the only way in which such mass screening programs can be cost-effective is by the prevention of the conception or birth of affected children by the use of contraception, sterilization, or abortion. Amniocentesis may have come to be seen as closely connected with abortion for the reason that amniocentesis is cost-effective only when the options of contraception and contraceptive sterilization have not been foreclosed. Yet it should be recalled that the improved methods of natural family planning are morally acceptable and effective means of conception control for couples who are at high risk for conceiving a child with a genetic disease.

A model of a national screening and counseling program has been proposed by a group of medical geneticists advising the National

Foundation/March of Dimes (National Research Council, 1975). Although genetic disorders as a group are becoming increasingly significant, the individual rarity of each one of them and the specialized laboratory services required for many genetic diagnoses make it impossible to provide a complete array of genetic services in all communities. Instead, medical service areas or regions need to be defined and services planned and developed on the principle of a network of interrelated resources and facilities of varying degrees of professional and technical capability. Such a system, accordingly, would be composed of three tiers of service: primary care in physicians' offices, clinics, or other health facilities (Level I); secondary resources for diagnosis and evaluation in community hospitals or other appropriate facilities (Level II); and a medical genetics center, most often a university-affiliated teaching hospital with a full range of diagnostic, counseling, and treatment services (Level III).

Level I care, provided by the private physician, requires nothing but that the physician have some understanding of genetics to be able to participate in delivery of services (diagnosis and counseling). The Level II units would be satellite clinics affiliated with a tertiary center. The estimated case loads of these facilities would be roughly 250 new families per year. Directing the clinical activities of such a unit would occupy about fifty percent of the effort of a physician with specialty training in medical genetics. The Level III or tertiary units would be the medical genetics centers, each of which on the average would have three affiliated Level II units. Each tertiary unit would see from five hundred to a thousand new families a year, roughly half of whom would have been referred from Level II facilities for specialized laboratory studies. It is hoped by proponents that by the implementation of such a network of primary, secondary, and tertiary centers, the general population will receive the benefits of recent developments in genetic medicine, thus improving the general health of the population and reducing some of the costs of medical care.

In spite of all the advances and the plans for extensive screening programs, the great majority of defects being tested for *in utero* are at present untreatable (Milunsky, 1975). The most common cases in which there is therapeutic value for the fetus in antenatal diagnosis are situations in which it is useful to monitor the child's viability so that he might be delivered as early as possible. These are not unimportant uses, but the vast majority of women undergoing amniocentesis and other forms of antenatal diagnosis today are not concerned about conditions for which such diagnosis can be said to be of therapeutic benefit for the fetus. For example, the estimation has been made that ninety-five percent of all antenatal tests would be done for Down's syndrome alone if all pregnant women over the age of thirty-five were tested (Milunsky and Atkins, 1974). We have already noted that for some couples there is considerable benefit in relieving their anxiety and that this relief can be expected also to have beneficial effects on the unborn. But it seems undeniable that the majority of women who undergo antenatal diagnosis are at least contemplating abortion in the event that the tests for a defect are positive. Indeed, one observer has suggested that prenatal diagnosis should not even be undertaken unless the family is already committed to an abortion if one is deemed "appropriate" (Littlefield, 1971). This attitude is another reason why amniocentesis appears to be such a tainted procedure to those who are opposed to abortion: the major explanation for most women's wanting to know whether their child is affected seems to be that they plan to abort the child if it is shown to be "defective." This is also why groups who support amniocentesis are concerned to argue that amniocentesis, paradoxical as it may sound, is really a life-saving procedure. As will be seen from the cases discussed in Chapter 2, many women would abort the child unless they can be assured that the child is unaffected. Even in very high-risk situations, such as couples who are both carriers of recessive defects, 3/4 of the amniocenteses can be expected to provide reassurance that the fetus is unaffected. This fraction approaches one for other disorders. In the very large group of pregnant women over age thirty-five, 49/50 of the tests can be expected to reveal a chromosomally normal infant.

Sex Selection — Although antenatal diagnosis has been accepted as an unqualified good by a large segment of the community, there remains at least one area in which there is considerable debate — even by those who accept other aspects of antenatal diagnosis — about the moral legitimacy of the procedure. This is the area of sex determination. There are reported cases of pregnant women seeking amniocentesis to determine the sex of the child in order that a child of the undesired sex may be aborted. A couple with two daughters, for example, might decide that they wish to have only one more child and that a boy. Amniocentesis followed by abortion in the event of a "positive" diagnosis (i.e., a girl) would be a possible "solution." Until now very few women have employed the technology for this purpose because diagnosis and abortion have been rather expensive and risky procedures. But the increasing safety of amniocentesis and the development of new and safer techniques of abortion, coupled with the growing costs of raising children and the increasing concern for population control, may together lead to more frequent resort to antenatal diagnosis for the purpose of giving birth to a child of the desired sex. Clearly, however, such procedure for sex selection is unacceptable since a child of the unwanted sex suffers the ultimate rejection — abortion. Few counselors at this time believe that this constitutes a legitimate use of their medical expertise. Most are unwilling to become involved in antenatal sex determination where no medical condition justifies the procedures, but experience of the recent past indicates how rapidly attitudes can change. Indeed, there are signs that a change of attitude is taking place. Recently, one ethicist has stated that he would not oppose abortion as a means of sex selection (Fletcher, John, 1979).

Summary

With this brief reflection on genetic screening and sex selection, Chapter 1 of this study comes to a close. In this chapter we have provided an overview of genetic defects: their nature and diagnosis. The next chapter we consider the nature of genetic counseling and exemplify some of the problems by citing eleven case histories.

Chapter 2

Genetic Medicine
in the
Clinical Setting

Introduction

The previous chapter reviewed briefly some basic facts of genetics, outlined the 5 types of genetic diseases, discussed eight general categories of antenatal diagnostic techniques, and noted some of the associated moral concerns. Now in this chapter, attention will be focused on the nature of genetic counseling. Of necessity, the distinction between directive and non-directive counseling will be reviewed as well as a few of the moral and legal issues which arise for the genetic counselor in this matter. Finally, since genetic counseling is concerned about persons, couples or families who are facing an actual or potential genetic disease, this chapter includes a selection of eleven case histories which represent the range and variety of problems which can confront families or individuals.

The Nature of Genetic Counseling

Genetic counseling may be characterized as a process of communication which attempts to deal with the human problems associated with the occurrence, or risk of occurrence, of a genetic disorder in an individual or family (Sly, 1973). This process involves an attempt by one or more appropriately trained persons to help an individual, couple, or family:

1. To comprehend the medical facts, such as the risk of occurrence or reoccurrence of a disorder, the possibilities for diagnosis, the probable course of the disorder, and the available therapies
2. To appreciate the ways in which hereditary and environmental factors contribute to the disorder, and the extent to which specified relatives are at risk for being affected or for producing an affected child
3. To understand the options for dealing with a positive diagnosis, such as methods of contraception or sterilization, abortion, institutionalization, adoption agencies and other social services
4. To choose the course of action that seems appropriate to the clients in view of their own values and goals and to act in accordance with that decision
5. To make the best possible adjustment to the disorder in an affected member of the family or to the risk of a recurrence of the disorder.

Such a characterization embodies the prevailing and deeply held opinion among genetic counselors that their service is educational only and essentially *nondirective*. In order to understand the nature and rationale for this method of counseling, it is important to contrast it with so-called directive counseling. This latter form of counseling proceeds on the basis of the counselor's own formulation of the problem as well as on the counselor's considered opinion about the course of action to follow. The emphasis in the counseling session is on the intellectual resources of the client, for the relationship between the counselor and client seems to be primarily that of teacher to pupil.

In nondirective or client-centered counseling (Sorensen, 1973) the role of the counselor is considerably different. A major initial task is to see the problem from the client's point of view, to appreciate the situation in terms of the client's own history and system of values. Using professional expertise, the counselor attempts to present the relevant information, but does so in ways which assist the client in coming to a more adequate understanding of the problem without doing violence to the client's own values. The counselor assists the client in articulating these values and in understanding how the various possible courses of action relate to them. The counselor may not share all of these values and may personally prefer that a particular course of action be undertaken that is different from the one chosen by the client; but the role of the counselor is not that of a moral judge. The main professional concern of the counselor is to make certain that the full significance of the medical and scientific facts is understood by the client to the extent of the client's ability to grasp them and that the actual decision is made by the client personally in a manner consistent with the client's own values.

> The basic assumptions underlying nondirective counseling can be summarized as a profound belief in man's capacity for growth and self-determination, a recognition of man's ability to understand and to experience the issues in his life that are causing him pain and discomfort, and a faith in man's potential to achieve insights that will lead to positive solutions and outcomes (Kaback, 1958).

Most individuals or couples who come for counseling do so voluntarily and are active in the process. Almost all are attempting to act responsibly and not selfishly. They recognize that the decisions they make will have a profound influence not only on their own lives but on the lives of others.

Many observers have noted the seemingly inherent inequality of status in the doctor-patient relationship: the patient is ignorant, the doctor wise; the patient is suffering, the doctor healthy; the patient is abnormal, the doctor normal; the patient is frightened, the doctor calm. The exploitation of such an inequality of status by thrusting the stronger person's values on the weaker is both unprofessional and unethical. Thus, it is inappropriate for the counselor to withhold or distort relevant information and use a superior technical expertise and professionial status in order to influence the decisions of the client, to undermine the client's moral autonomy, and to "sandpaper" the client's basic human right to make personal decisions. Genetic counselors, therefore, should present to their clients all of the relevant information solely as an educational matter, in order that the clients may decide freely and for themselves.

There can be no doubt that this description of nondirective counseling represents an ideal difficult to achieve in practice. It has been said, for example, that the very ways in which the counselor conveys the information, the tone of voice, facial expressions, etc., betray attitudes and values. All of this may be incontestably true, but the ideal of nondirective counseling remains nonetheless an ideal. The counselor may inevitably influence clients in particular ways, but the intent would still be to allow clients to make their own decisions, and respect for the clients' autonomy would still be sincere.

This ideal, as valid as it may be, presents a serious personal moral problem for the genetic counselor who opposes selective abortion. Presenting abortion as one of the possible alternatives, as though it were morally indifferent or morally on a par with carrying the child to term, seems to do violence to such a counselor's conscience. It might be said that the counselor's task is simply to state the facts and to keep personal opinions out of sight. But such a way of stating the matter subtly prejudices the issue, for if the counselor is correct then the fact that selective abortion is morally wrong is as much a fact about selective abortion as the fact that it is legally available. Certainly the moral status of abortion is as important and relevant a matter in deciding among options as its legal status. Again, it may be argued that the individual or couple come to the counselor for the sake of counselor's professional and technical expertise; the counselor's personal moral stance regarding abortion is not why they sought that particular counselor. This point may or may not be true, for many clients will be seeking moral as well as professional guidance from the counselor. But even when it is true in a particular case, this is of little help to the genetic counselor who legitimately questions whether professional ethics can finally absolve one from responsibility in the matter.

The legal availability of abortion also creates problems of a nonmoral nature for the genetic counselor. Failure to inform the pregnant woman of the possibility of elective abortion may subject the counselor to civil liability under the law of torts (Milunsky and Annas, 1976). If an affected child is born as the result of such a failure, then the application of ordinary malpractice standards to the counselor may lead to a civil suit charging that the counselor is liable for damages. Such a suit may take one of two forms: "wrongful life," in which the action is brought by the child's guardians on behalf of the child; or "wrongful birth," in which the action is brought by the parents on their own behalf. In the first type of case the plaintiff (child) argues that his nonexistence is preferable to his existence with defects, that it would have been better for him never to have been born, so that his existence is a wrong done him through the willful negligence of the counselor. In a wrongful birth case the parents sue for damages, arguing that they would never have been subjected to the emotional and financial strains of caring for a defective child had they been informed of the reasonableness and legal availability of abortion. These and subsequent legal issues are examined at some length in the Appendix.

These legal difficulties are by no means restricted to the genetic counselor. Many obstetricians and general practitioners have in the past been reluctant to discuss antenatal diagnosis with their patients, either because the physicians were not well informed about the procedures or because they feared that a positive diagnosis of genetic defect might lead the women to choose an abortion. This failure to inform is also difficult to defend legally. Several cases have already reached the courts involving older women who had given birth to children with chromosomal abnormalities without being informed by their obstetricians of their increased risk of having a defective child (see: *Karlson v. Guennot,* 1977; *Howard v. Lecher,* 1977).

The significance of these legal issues extends far beyond the sphere of legality and its impact on individual counselors and obstetricians, for they raise profound moral and social questions concerning the responsibility to care for defective children and to support parents who must face the burden of an affected child. The legal issue of "wrongful life" raises the question of how we are to assess the value of an individual's life. If we judge that it would have been better for a person never to have been born, then we are basing our judgment on assessments of the quality of that person's life, perhaps suggesting that some individuals' lives are more valuable than the lives of others.

These are complex and far-reaching questions, but they are not the ones of immediate concern to the genetic counselor who must help a particular individual, couple, or family deal with an overwhelming problem which often has come upon them seemingly out of the blue. In what follows we shall be examining individual case histories to provide a further explanation of the nature of genetic diseases and an appreciation of the medical, moral and legal problems posed by genetic disease from the standpoints of those most directly involved.

Case Histories

Eleven case histories are presented in this section. They were chosen to exemplify different types of genetic defects as well as to illustrate the variety of ethical issues which can arise in genetic counseling. The first group [phenylketonuria (Case #1, Tay-Sachs

(Case #2) and cystic fibrosis (Case #3)] are autosomal *recessive* diseases. Both parents must be carriers in order for their child to manifest any of these diseases. The second type of genetic disease, exemplified by muscular dystrophy (Case #4), exhibits the X-linked recessive condition. In this situation, the disease is transmitted through a carrier mother. Half of her male children will manifest the disease, while half of the female will be carriers. The remaining male and female offspring will be normal. The next group [Huntington's Disease (Case #5), neurofibromatosis (Case #6), and Marfan's Syndrome (Case #7)] are autosomal *dominant* diseases. They are distinguished from the recessive diseases because only *one parent* need possess the defective gene. Some diseases have a multifactorial condition; those involving neural tube defects (Case #8), as in anencephaly and spina bifida, represent this group. Several defective genes from each parent, with the possible involvement of an environmental factor, cause this condition to manifest. Some cases involve multiple birth defects and mental retardation which can be inherited from a carrier parent. These diseases are due to some chromosome imbalance (Case #9) which can be detected in the parents' white blood cells. Finally, two forms of Down's syndrome (mongolism) are documented. One represents Down's syndrome resulting from advanced maternal age at time of conception (Case #10) while the other is associated (relatively independently of age) with a previous child's having had the condition (Case #11).

Each of these case histories contains some elements unique to the disorder and some elements that are general. Nevertheless, it should be recognized that every situation is to some extent unique in that it represents a problem for a particular family in particular circumstances. To that extent no two counseling situations are exactly comparable, even when the disorder for which the two families seek counseling is identical in medical terms.

Although there are many different reasons for seeking counseling, most persons at this time come for counseling after the birth of an affected child. These are usually concerned, responsible people who are either struggling with the tragedy of having lost a child or else trying to meet the challenge of giving the special love and care an affected child needs. They have lived through the experience and know the kind of suffering genetic disease involves.

Case #1. Phenylketonuria

Phenylketonuria (PKU) is a rare inborn error of metabolism which occurs in about 1/10,000 births among descendants of northern Europeans (Knox, 1972). PKU is an inherited deficiency of a liver enzyme that normally converts phenylalanine into tyrosine. Since PKU is an autosomal recessive defect, parents who produce an affected offspring are both carriers of the trait. They appear normal, although each carries one normal and one PKU gene. They have reduced levels of the enzyme but at a level sufficient to metabolize normal amounts of phenylalanine in their diet. Children who inherit one PKU gene from each parent have too low a level of the relevant active enzyme and accumulate excess levels of phenylalanine in the body when placed on a normal diet. Severe consequences result if PKU is untreated. Mental retardation (I.Q. between twenty and fifty), growth disturbance, and eczema are nearly certain consequences if PKU is not treated. Dramatic improvement in the prognosis is possible if careful attention is paid to restricting phenylalanine in the diet. This diet must be followed at least until the child begins school, after which time the diet may be normalized. Frequent checks of serum phenylalanine will be required in the growing child to determine whether the restriction is sufficient but not too severe, for a too stringent restriction is also deleterious and may affect growth and I.Q.

Mr. and Mrs. L. were referred for counseling and management because their newborn girl was discovered to have a positive urine test for phenylketonuria. The child had done well over the first month of life. An artificial diet restricting phenylalanine intake was instituted as soon as the diagnosis was made. The girl was their second child. Their three-year-old son was normal, and had had a negative urine test for PKU. The couple, in their mid-twenties, were concerned about the prognosis for their daughter, the likelihood of the same problem in subsequent pregnancies, and the significance of this diagnosis for their normal son. Thus, Mr. and Mrs. L. must plan on living within access to a professional experienced in dietary management of PKU. The risk for Mr. and Mrs. L. is 1/4 for each subsequent pregnancy that they will produce another child affected by PKU.

Their normal child is unaffected, and will not produce affected offspring unless he is a carrier (the odds are 2/3 that he is) and he marries a carrier (the odds are about 1/50 that a non-relative would be a carrier). Thus the risks in his offspring are low ($1/300 = 2/3 \times 1/50 \times 1/4$).

The risk for their affected daughter producing offspring with congenital defects in quite high (Howell and Stevenson, 1971). Offspring of mothers with PKU have a 1/4 chance of congenital anomalies, a near certainty of intrauterine growth retardation, and about a 9/10 chance of mental retardation. This is owing to the mother's continually high level of phenylalanine affecting the growing fetus, and not to any genetic condition of the fetus itself. Although dietary management in pregnancy may modify this risk somewhat, the few available studies are not promising. It is thus likely that their daughter will have a strong reason to avoid pregnancy, even if her chances for producing children with PKU itself are relatively low.

There are presently only cumbersome and questionably reliable methods of identifying carriers with this trait. At present there are no methods of identifying affected offspring *in utero*. Mr. and Mrs. L. will have to weigh the relative importance of a further child against the burden of management of the PKU child in deciding whether to risk the 1/4 chance of a PKU infant in a subsequent pregnancy.

This is an example of a reasonably well-understood, inherited condition for which there is a favorable, although costly and somewhat inconvenient, treatment which allows the affected child to escape most of the serious consequences of the genetic disease. It is unique in that an affected female has additional problems in adulthood because her condition, even if successfully treated, makes the birth of normal offspring unlikely.

Case #2. Tay-Sachs Disease

Tay-Sachs disease is an autosomal recessive disease due to an inherited deficiency of an enzyme involved in breakdown of a complex lipid (Sloan and Frederickson, 1972). Affected infants are produced by carriers of the trait, each of whom has one normal, and one Tay-Sachs gene. Statistically, 1/4 of the offspring of carrier couples inherit the deleterious gene from each parent, and suffer from the enzyme deficiency. The disease results from a progressive storage of undigested lipid in many tissues, but particularly in the brain. The clinical course is quite typical and inevitably fatal.

Mr. and Mrs. K. respectively were fifty-six and fifty-eight years of age. The first of two daughters was born in 1942 and was thought to be completely normal until eight months of age when she failed to sit up and was considered retarded. At one year of age, abnormal physical and neurological findings suggested Tay-Sachs disease. The child regressed slowly but steadily from that point and died at three-and-one-half years. During this three-year period, the initially normal-appearing infant developed gradual loss of motor function, weakness, inability to feed, blindness, frequent epileptiform seizures, and, finally, a completely vegetative state. The family suffered immensely as they watched the progressive deterioration. It was difficult for them to accept this condition as an inherited disorder. The shame they felt from carrying a defective gene that produced this tragedy caused the father to forbid his wife to divulge the diagnosis to anyone. The only reason for bringing it up at this late date was that their other daughter, now in her mid-twenties, who had never been told of her sister's diagnosis, was married and expecting her first child. Having learned that carrier detection was possible and that amniocentesis early in pregnancy could identify an affected infant, the mother felt compelled to divulge her secret to her daughter and son-in-law and to refer them for counseling.

The frequency of carriers of Tay-Sachs is much higher in descendants of Eastern European Jews (Askenazi) than in other populations. Between 1/25 and 1/30 of the Askenazi population are carriers of this gene. Thus, 1/900 marriages in this population involve couples who are both carriers. Of the live-born children in this community, 1/3600 are expected to be affected. Since Mr. and Mrs. K. produced an affected child, they are certainly carriers. Their non-affected daughter has a 2/3 chance of being a carrier. Her husband, also an Askenazi Jew, has a 1/30 chance of being a carrier. Prior to any testing, therefore, the couple may be assigned a 1/180 (2/3 x 1/30 x 1/4) risk of producing an affected child.

Carrier testing can be done on the husband using a simple blood serum sample. Carrier detection on his wife requires a more complicated test on white blood cells because pregnancy (and birth control pills) make the serum test unreliable. The daughter was identified as a carrier, the husband as a non-carrier. Thus, although half of their offspring would (on the average) be carriers, inheriting the deleterious gene from their mother, none would be affected with the disease.

The parents had decided that if they were both identified as carriers, they would probably have requested amniocentesis to determine whether the fetus was affected. Although this young expectant mother felt she would probably have considered abortion had she required amniocentesis and an affected child been identified, she never had to face this decision. She will not have to consider this option in any subsequent pregnancy with the same father.

This case illustrates an example of a relatively rare inherited recessive disorder that occurs at higher frequency in a defined population, for which a reliable carrier detection test has been developed, and which can be diagnosed *in utero* on cells cultured from the amniotic fluid. These three particular properties of Tay-Sachs disease have made it attractive as a model for a disease prevention and eradication program using mass screening of a population at risk to identify carrier couples and offering selective abortion of affected fetuses identified in pregnancies of couples known to be carriers, either because they have been identified through the screening program itself or because they have previously produced an affected child.

Because Tay-Sachs disease is at present untreatable, it is clear that a program of antenatal diagnosis for the fetuses of all carrier couples can in no way be therapeutic, at least for the fetus. It is true that an individual woman might choose to undergo amniocentesis without having made a firm decision favoring abortion in the event of a positive diagnosis. She might, indeed, have decided irrevocably against an abortion but wishes to have her anxieties allayed, knowing that the chance of a favorable diagnosis is 3/4. Nevertheless, such a woman does not seem to be typical of women undergoing antenatal diagnoses for untreatable diseases, and it is unrealistic to believe that screening programs involving antenatal diagnosis for untreatable conditions would have received their existing widespread attention and support were abortion not anticipated for many or most cases where a defect is indicated. One observer who has done extensive studies of the context in which genetic counseling occurs has concluded that "the structure of the situation calls for a readiness to be committed to abortion as a means of managing a positive diagnosis" (Fletcher, 1972).

Case #3. Cystic Fibrosis
Cystic fibrosis is one of the most common recessively inherited traits in the white population (Vaughan and McKay, 1975; Bowman and Mangos, 1976). Carrier frequency may be as high as 1/20. No

certain reliable carrier test is available, although several are in the experimental stage. The affected infant inherits one abnormal gene from each parent. Cystic fibrosis is a disease which produces severe disability and leads to an early death. Although prognosis is improving with early diagnosis and better treatment, 1/2 of affected infants die by age ten, 4/5 by age twenty, and few survive beyond age thirty.

The basic enzyme defect is not understood. Most of the serious consequences of the disease result from abnormally thick mucous secretions from glands. Pancreatic insufficiency, excessive loss of electrolytes in sweat, and pulmonary insufficiency are prominent clinical manifestations. There is considerable variation in severity and rate of progression of the disease. The chief factor affecting a patient's outlook is the rapidity of development of respiratory involvement. Those who survive to age fifteen without serious pulmonary incapacity have a good chance of surviving to adulthood. Affected males are usually sterile, whereas affected females can be fertile if they survive to adulthood.

Mr. and Mrs. J. had two children, twenty-five and seven months old. Their second child had been found to have cystic fibrosis. Diagnosis was made at the age of five months, when he was referred to the counselor because of pneumonia which failed to clear after nearly two months of antibiotic therapy. There was no evidence of psychomotor retardation, but growth delay was evident.

Mr. and Mrs. J. realized that they were at high risk of producing another affected child. The economic and emotional burden of caring for their child affected with this disease seemed to them a strong deterrent to contemplating further children. They inquired about the possibility of diagnosis of this disease *in utero* and were told that this was not then possible. They were extremely concerned about the possibility of an accidental pregnancy because of previous lack of success with one of the Natural Family Planning methods.* Mrs. J. had been unable to use oral contraceptive agents because of severe headaches which seemed related to their use. The pregnancy that produced the affected child was unplanned, occurring shortly after oral contraceptive agents had been discontinued. Although initially they were hoping to avoid pregnancy only temporarily, they now were anxious to have no more children because of their genetic risk.

*During the period of adjustment, after a couple have used oral contraceptives, N.F.P. methods cannot be used reliably.

This case is illustrative of two important features characteristic of many counseling sessions. The first of these is that many couples come already burdened by the anguish and financial costs of caring for an affected child, and all of the information presented and alternatives discussed must be presented in a manner that takes into account this experience. The second point to note is how contraceptive options can be extremely limited and how sterilization can seem to be the option of choice in the minds of some persons.

Case #4. Muscular Dystrophy

Muscular dystrophy is an example of an X-linked recessive disorder, where females who are known to be carriers have a 1/4 chance with each pregnancy of producing an affected male whose only X chromosome bears the mutant gene (Vaughan and McKay, 1975). Unfortunately, carrier detection tests for X-linked muscular dystrophy are imperfect and as many as 1/4 of the carriers may be missed. This disorder is typical of X-linked defects for which there is presently no way of distinguishing affected males *in utero*. Amniocentesis for this situation can identify only the sex of the infant. Female infants are expected to be clinically normal, though half of them will be carriers like their mothers. Half of the males will be normal and half of them affected. Many expectant mothers have amniocentesis with the expectation that they will abort males, especially if they had a vivid experience of watching a brother deteriorate with the disease. Many carrier mothers today would choose to abort any pregnancy if a procedure to determine the sex of the child were not available.

Mrs. A. was a twenty-year-old woman who was nine weeks pregnant when she was referred to the counselor because of suspected carrier status for muscular dystrophy. She was one of five siblings. Her mother's fifth pregnancy ended with toxemia and convulsions and produced a male child, then aged ten, who had muscular dystrophy. Her mother was hypertensive, epileptic, and severely debilitated following this pregnancy. The brother experienced muscle weakness at age six and lost the ability to climb stairs over the next year. Duchenne-type muscular dystrophy was diagnosed and he became bedridden within three years. Each of his four sisters were examined for serum enzyme levels, which are elevated in about 3/4 of the carriers of Duchenne's muscular dystrophy, at the time of diagnosis. Two of them, including the client, were diagnosed as possible carriers.

Mrs. A. was extremely depressed. She was unable to sleep or concentrate and was subject to crying spells without reason. She had married a man who had a three-year-old child from a previous marriage, the ceremony having taken place only five months before. The child had some form of debilitating muscular disease. She felt she had made a poor adjustment to her marriage and to her sick stepson. Her experience with her mother's pregnancy, which she had observed when she was ten, left her terrified of becoming pregnant. Her difficulty adjusting to her marriage and her seriously ill stepson added to her desire to avoid pregnancy. She feared that a second child, even if normal, would seriously strain her marriage. Her risk of producing a dystrophic child who might suffer the fate of her brother added to her fear. She had been unable to use oral contraceptives because they produced nausea and they seemed to accentuate her depressive feelings. She was using a vaginal foam contraceptive when she became pregnant.

Now that she was pregnant, she wished to determine whether her carrier status could be confirmed. If she were a carrier, she felt she would elect to have amniocentesis and abort any male fetus. She already undertood that if she were a carrier, 1/2 of her male offspring would be affected. She felt anxious to preserve the pregnancy if carrier status could be ruled out or if she could determine that she was carrying a female child.

Several serum determinations were done, and none of these was elevated. On the basis of this reassuring though not definitive information, she chose not to have amniocentesis and to carry the child to term. Later in the pregnancy (twenty-four weeks) she had a severe depressive reaction and strongly regretted having passed up the opportunity to determine the sex of the infant and abort if the child were male. She felt she had made a serious mistake by assuming any risk of delivering an affected child. Mrs. A. delivered a male infant and suffered intense anxiety while still in the hospital. She was lost to follow-up very shortly. Several rapid changes of address made it impossible to learn what happened to her or to the child. The changes of address led the counselor to suspect that her marriage was breaking up.

One of the significant moral questions associated with Duchenne's muscular dystrophy arises from two facts: the disease is sex-linked and there is no method currently available which detects affected fetuses. Thus, what functions as a "positive" diagnosis in this type of disease is the determination that the fetus is male. Furthermore, the willingness to abort in the event of a "positive" diagnosis means a willingness to run a risk of 1/2 of aborting an unaffected male child. Nor would the moral problems be resolved were there a reliable test for detecting affected fetuses, for a fundamental moral question would still remain about what may be called the "substitution mentality." According to this way of viewing the matter, fetuses are interchangeable: if a fetus is found to be defective, then it is aborted and the cycle of diagnosis and abortion continues until an unaffected fetus is diagnosed. In this way the technique of antenatal diagnosis permits a couple to have a normal and healthy child. Of course, it does not make it any more likely that the couple will conceive an unaffected child. Nor can anything be done to heal the affected infant. The same result could be achieved by simply giving birth to all children until a normal child is produced, but the emotional and financial strains of caring for one or more defective children might make it humanly impossible to wait until a healthy child is conceived. Antenatal diagnosis allows the couple to minimize the burden of bearing defective children by aborting them before they have caused undue hardship for the parents. What is important about the mentality of substitution is that this cycle of diagnosis and abortion is not seen as resulting in a significant net loss, except for the emotional, financial, and medical burden placed upon the couple. The fact that a number of affected fetus' lives may be lost is not an important consideration for the substitution mentality: all that matters is fulfilling the couple's desires for the birth of a normal child.

Case #5. Huntington's Disease

Huntington's Disease is inherited as a dominant condition, so that having a single gene for Huntington's Disease will usually result in the disease (Goetz and Weiner, 1979). The condition is passed on through each generation with every child who has one affected parent having a 1/2 chance of inheriting the disease. Currently some 20,000 persons in the United States have the disease. The actual diagnosis depends on the onset of symptoms which usually do not occur until about age thirty-five. The uncontrolled muscular movements associated with Huntington's Disease progress through neurological degeneration including dementia to death over a ten- to twenty-year span. Suicide occurred in one study in 4.8 percent of affected men and

6.4 percent of affected women. There is, at present, no proven method of discovering those who will be affected. There does exist a drug which brings on Huntington-like symptoms for a brief period in half of the offspring of affected individuals, but the safety and accuracy of this test are still in question (Klawans *et al,* 1972).

Mr. and Mrs. B., aged thirty-five and thirty-two, were referred for genetic counseling subsequent to the birth of a Down's syndrome child. After taking the mother's medical and family history, which was essentially negative, the father's medical and pedigree history was started. He had just discovered that his mother had died of Huntington's Disease but he still did not know about its inheritance. It became necessary then to discuss the disease with the couple. The emphasis shifted from the risk of having another Down's syndrome child (comparatively remote) to the risk of the father's having been affected with Huntington's Disease — about 1/2.

Those who learn about this disease and their risk of being affected generally have already experienced the demise of a parent who suffered from it. The very unpleasant and often pitiful course of Huntington's Disease hanging over their heads as highly probable causes great mental anguish. Mr. B. was referred to a neurologist for evaluation and follow-up and he has since sought intensive psychiatric care. His brothers were referred to a genetic counselor in their area of the country.

A person above the age of thirty who discovers the possibility of having the disease will almost always decide against further procreation. Younger couples are more likely to take the risk. There have been cases where the presence in the family of the disease and the risk involved were kept secret from a spouse.

This case may be used to raise a number of moral and legal problems associated with the clinical setting. The first concerns the moral responsibility of the counselor to provide the patient with information judged by the counselor to be of harm to his client. Mr. B. sought counseling originally because he feared the birth of a child affected by Down's syndrome. Clearly, Mr. B. was concerned lest he conceive a child affected by any genetic defect, although he was aware only of the risk of Down's syndrome. In this case the counselor's revealing the unsuspected risk of Huntington's Disease is obviously related to the purpose of the interview. But let us alter the particulars of this case slightly and suppose that the risk of giving birth to a child with Down's syndrome was quite high, so high that Mr. and Mrs. B. decided to forego the birth of any future children and Mr. B. sought sterilization. In this modified case, the question arises concerning the counselor's obligation to disclose information which would not affect the outcome of the counseling process but which would place a tremendous emotional burden on the couple. We may question, then, whether the counselor has the responsibility of disclosing all the information obtained in the counseling process or whether the counselor may in some circumstances withhold important information which could not benefit the client.

A second moral issue arises from a point mentioned in passing: it sometimes happens that a client refuses to permit information obtained in the counseling process to be conveyed to others, even though that information would be vital to them. The client, for example, may not wish his spouse to be apprised of his affected or carrier status. Or he may not wish his siblings or other members of his family to be told that they, as relatives of a person with a genetic defect or with a carrier status, are at risk for being similarly affected. The client's sense of shame or fear of the repercussions of disclosure would have to be most profound to lead him to take such a drastic step as refusing to permit those most concerned to be informed on this vital matter; nonetheless, such refusals do occur. On the one hand, the counselor is committed by a primary duty to the welfare of the client and by the requirement of confidentiality never to disclose information gained within the privileged setting of the doctor-patient relationship against the wishes or interests of the client. On the other hand, there is the consideration that considerable harm might be avoided were the relatives informed of the fact that they are at risk of transmitting a genetic defect. The counselor's dilemma becomes more acute if the client withholds information not because of understandable human weaknesses such as fear or shame but because of motives of malice and the desire to hurt. This latter possibility may be extremely rare, but it does serve to raise questions about the assumption that information ought never to be disclosed contrary to the wishes of the client.

The two moral problems of full disclosure and confidentiality involve legal questions as well. There is the question of the civil liability of the counselor should information be withheld that is judged potentially harmful to the client. Also, if the counselor possesses information that would be important to others, but the client refuses to permit disclosure, the counselor may be caught in a legal bind: if the information is not given them, the counselor may be subject to a legal suit brought by them, whereas if the information is given, the counselor may be subject to a suit brought by the client for violation of confidentiality. These legal issues are examined in detail in the Appendix.

All genetic diseases raise the issue of the moral responsibility on the part of known or suspected carriers not to run the risk of giving birth to defective children. One may question whether all couples possess a God-given or natural right to bear children. There may be some defects such that it would be morally wrong to risk giving birth to affected children. The uncertainty is compounded by three considerations. The first of these is that risks vary greatly depending on the type of the defect and the family history and may range from less than 1/10,000 to 1/2. Second, the severity of defect may vary considerably with the disease. Someone might hold that a 1/4 risk of giving birth to a child with PKU is not too high, whereas it would be too high if the disease were Tay-Sachs. Third, even for a single disease the range in severity may be considerable and the prognosis in a particular case may be highly uncertain. Thus, probabilities must be compounded by further probabilities, imponderables balanced against other imponderables.

Huntington's Disease presents special problems concerning the responsibility not to procreate. Younger couples appear more willing than older couples to run the risk of transmitting the defect, but one may wonder whether this greater willingness is supported by any morally relevant distinction. A *prima facie* case can be made for saying that if it is wrong for a person over thirty to contemplate having a child even though he knows that he is at risk for Huntington's Disease and for passing on the defect, it likewise must be wrong for a person at any age who is similarly uncertain. We may be able to understand why an older individual would likely be less willing to run the risk, since he is approaching the age at which symptoms may begin and the disease looms larger in his mind; but it is difficult to see how this psychological difference could ground a moral difference. The general lesson to be drawn from this is that it appears inadequate to justify the decision to procreate simply on the ground that the couple are willing to take the risk. *They* may be willing to run the risk for themselves; the question is whether it is permissible for them to run the risk for another.

This notion of running a risk for the child is also a problematic one and involves the difficulty of making quality-of-life judgments for another. Presumably, to say that for the sake of the unconceived child a couple ought not to risk conception and birth is to imply that nonexistence is preferable to existence with that particular defect. But the justification for such an implied assertion is not at all obvious, particularly in the case of Huntington's Disease and others like it which allow for an extended period of normal or near-normal functioning.

Case #6. Neurofibromatosis

Neurofibromatosis is another dominant disease inherited by half of the children of an affected individual (Vaughan and McKay, 1975). The disease can be detected usually in the first ten years of life by the presence of several coffee-colored spots on the body. These spots increase in size and number, usually on unexposed areas. Cutaneous tumors are common and usually benign, although in about 1/10 cases the tumors become malignant (Fienman and Yakowac, 1970). Tumors follow nerve trunks and often the central nervous system is involved. Skeletal changes also may occur. The disease is slowly progressive, but most affected individuals have a normal life span and normal activities, with much of the discomfort being cosmetic.

On two separate occasions a thirty-year-old man with neurofibromatosis, including cutaneous tumors, skeletal involvement, and darkening of the skin had brought women (both of them nurses) to counseling. On each of the occasions he was considering marriage, but he was reluctant to have a child who would have to live with his deformities.

The disease, and its inheritance, were explained to each of the women, first with the young man present and then by herself so that she could feel free to ask questions. Neither woman was put off by the physical problem, for they saw him as a lovable person. Nevertheless, the first was disturbed by the possibility of their children being affected, and the second was troubled by his reluctance to father any children.

This case illustrates the psychological and emotional problems that may result from any genetic disease, even ones that are most benign. The stigma placed by our society on any individual who is less than normal or perfect is one of the most serious burdens of those affected by genetic diseases.

All of this raises serious questions about the long-term social consequences of a widespread appeal to selective abortion. There are many who fear that such a social policy bespeaks and lends support to an attitude of intolerance towards any defective. A not uncommon willingness to abort can be noted in the following situations when:

1. The chance is 1/2 that the fetus is unaffected (muscular dystrophy — Case #4, pp. 36-38)
2. The defect is at least partially treatable (PKU — Case #1, pp. 31-32)
3. The defect is known to be of a type that either is not particularly grave or allows for a number of years of normal or near-normal life (neurofibromatosis — Case #6, pp. 42-44, Huntington's Disease — Case #5, pp. 38-42)
4. The "affected" individual may never have any manifestations of his genetic "disease" at all (incomplete penetration) because of the complex interplay between his genetic endowment and his environment or because of the complexities in the redundant or self-correcting genetic material (neural tube defect — Case #8, pp. 45-47)
5. It is not known how severe the manifestations of the defect will be (Down's syndrome Case #10, pp. 49-50).

It must also be recognized that there is always some risk — which varies with the type of defect — of a false positive, that is, of an infant falsely diagnosed as affected. Furthermore, there are cases in which it is not clear whether the genetic abnormality truly represents merely a *defect* on the molecular level or *disease.* An excellent case in point is that of the XYY male, or "super male" (Hook and Henly, 1977; Philip *et al,* 1976). Since the individual possessed a double dose of the Y chromosome and since it seemed natural to assume that a male's greater aggressiveness is inherited, it was concluded that XYY males were likely to be aggressive and anti-social. The myth that Richard Speck, the Chicago nurse-murderer, was an XYY male may never be laid to rest. In fact, XYY males are at no discernible risk for becoming psychopaths (Gerald, 1976); but there remains the tendency to suppose that because someone is abnormal (i.e., statistically unusual) he must therefore be defective.

All of these features tend to express and reinforce an attitude of intolerance toward someone who is in any way abnormal or unusual. This attitude is reinforced by increasing concern for population limitation. "Prenatal diagnosis is seen as a means of quality control in a quantity-limited system" (Lebacqz, 1973). The notion here is that if the size of families must be limited, then parents should be entitled to have normal children rather than abnormal ones. If the felt pressures of what is considered to be excessive population continue to grow, anything less than complete normalcy may come to be seen as intolerable.

Case #7. Marfan's Syndrome

Marfan's syndrome is an autosomal dominant disorder of connective tissues and manifests itself by tall stature, extra long digits, progressive involvement of heart valves and major blood vessels, and impaired vision which may progress to blindness. The disease also is associated with a shortened expected life span. Because of his stature and the history of early deaths in his family, it is suspected that Abraham Lincoln was affected by this disease. The prevalence of this condition is estimated at 4 to 6 per 100,000 people (Pyeritz and McKusick, 1979). .

A young couple (ages twenty-six and twenty-eight) came for counseling because the wife had been diagnosed as having Marfan's syndrome. They wished to find out if they had an increased risk of their offspring's having heart defects or blindness. They already had one healthy child and wanted more children. They were also concerned about the stress of a pregnancy on the wife's already weak heart.

Discussion centered around the 1/2 risk of having an affected child, the severity of the disease, the problems the husband would face if his wife should die and leave him with small children. The life span for a person in her condition is about forty years. The stress of a pregnancy on her heart was a very real problem and they were told that any pregnancy would constitute a grave risk for her. The couple had also been seriously upset by the recent loss of the wife's brother at age fifteen. He, too, had Marfan's syndrome. The husband was worried about the complications that oral contraceptives might produce with an underlying disease like Marfan's. All other means of birth control were discussed in case the couple should decide not to have more children. They were also concerned about their little boy who appeared normal at age three but who still might have the gene without manifesting any symptoms of the disease; and they were worried about who would take care of him if the mother died. There were no living grandparents.

This case illustrates the many problems involved for a family with a high risk of a severe disease. The whole family is affected and the stability of the family unit is involved. The 1/2 risk of Marfan's disease in future children, the continuous medical care of such children, the danger in the wife's becoming pregnant, the danger in using certain forms of birth control, and the fear of a motherless home are all problems illustrated by this case.

Case #8. Neural Tube Defects (NTD)

The risk of giving birth to a child with a neural tube defect (anencephaly or spina bifida) is an example of the presence of a multifactorial trait (Smith, 1976). The tendency to give birth to children with such defects runs in families and thus appears related to heredity, but the precise mechanism by which the defect is produced is as yet unknown. Neural tube defect is sometimes due to non-genetic causes, but the two etiologies can seldom be told apart. As a multifactorial trait, pattern of inheritance is said to be polygenic, depending on many genes and not just on one gene or one gene pair. The pattern of inheritance, then, is not like that of any of the diseases already discussed but is more like the patterns represented in the inheritance of height or intelligence. In the case of neural tube defect one can postulate several genes donated by each parent which together achieve a threshold effect and the defect then becomes possible. Environmental factors may play a role in raising or lowering this threshold.

At implantation in the uterine wall, the undifferentiated ball of cells becomes organized. The cells become layered and head and tail ends are designated. By ten days after implantation and seventeen days after fertilization the nervous system begins to form. A sheet of cells, the neural plate, is produced. In the midline, from head to tail, a groove appears in the neural plate which has become thickened. The crests of the groove grow upward and fold together to form a hollow tube, the neural tube, beginning in the center of the embryo and extending toward both extremities. Through this tube will eventually flow the spinal fluid. The tube normally closes within a week, about twenty-four days after fertilization. Failure to close at the head end can lead to anencephaly (literally, "no head"). The affected individuals die *in utero,* or soon after birth. Anencephaly occurs in about 1/1000 live births, but in some geographic locations it is much higher in frequency (Alter, 1962). If the neural tube fails to close at the tail end, a condition referred to as spina bifida (literally, "split spine") occurs. The child born has multiple problems. Within one or two days of birth, neurosurgery is ordinarily performed to avoid death. A child who has been saved in this way generally has normal intelligence. A shunt often must be placed in order to drain spinal fluid from the hollow area of the brain and avoid hydrocephalus (fluid in the cranial cavity) which would otherwise occur in almost all cases. The opening in the back is closed to avoid infection. The size of the opening and the level at which it occurs varies, but children have complete or partial paralysis from the point of lesion down. Thus, bowel and bladder control can be lost and the ability to walk may be either lost or greatly impaired. Continuing neurosurgical and urological care is necessary.

Mr. and Mrs. A. were referred to a spina bifida clinic for genetic counseling. One child, a girl aged four, was being cared for at the clinic for the continuing problems of repaired spina bifida. The pertinent family history consisted of three pregnancies. One resulted in the girl with spina bifida, one was a normal child, and one was an anencephalic child who died at birth. The remaining history was non-contributory in a medical sense but showed a very anxious mother who was overly "helpful." By her interruptions and addenda she displayed her discomfort at any idea that the conditions of the two affected children in her family might have some relationship. The father was a quiet and accepting type of person.

The embryology of spina bifida was explained as well as how anencephaly and an open spine were similar kinds of events. For the first time Mrs. A. was able to acknowledge the relatedness of her two abnormal pregnancies. The theory of inheritance of this condition was explained and the risk of recurrence given. In the counseling session, emphasis was placed on the mutual contribution of causative genes by both parents. The risk of recurrence has been established empirically by collecting data on families with one or two affected children and determining how often a second or third affected child is born in a subsequent pregnancy. For this family the risk of neural tube defect in another pregnancy was 1/10. Some time was spent explaining probability and what such a figure means.

Mrs. A. looked on the present difficulty as merely an accident of nature which she and her husband were handling with all the love and care they could muster from a strong religious and moral background. They were delaying further pregnancies because of the problems associated with their present child. She concluded that any risk-taking might be impractical.

In the event of a subsequent pregnancy a method which can predict whether a particular fetus has an open neural tube defect or not is available. This test consists of performing an amniocentesis and examining the amniotic fluid for increased levels of alphafetoprotein. This test will detect approximately 9/10 of the children with a neural tube defect. It is most accurate in finding those who will be severely affected and least effective is discovering the less severe cases. In a sense, the less severe cases present the greatest problems because they survive and need continuing care and attention, whereas the more severely affected children do not survive. Since neural tube defect is not currently treatable *in utero,* the major reason for undergoing amniocentesis is to abort a child found defective.

The couple was encouraged to look at the risk involved in amniocentesis and the effect of having another child with the condition. The risk might be considered acceptable by the couple, depending on the effect another such child would have on the present family. The A.'s were warned of the need to come to a common, explicit decision.

The A.'s were subsequently seen on their regular visits to the spina bifida clinic or when the affected child was hospitalized for treatment (about once a year). A call was received about two years after the counseling visit announcing with great anxiety a pregnancy. Mrs. A. was distraught. She and her husband had obviously decided that taking the risk of having a child was too high, given the care, expense, and time needed to handle their present family. Nevertheless, the pregnancy existed and she wanted to talk about possible abortion. After much discussion the pregnancy was carried through with anxiety, and a normal girl was delivered. The A.'s decided that the wife would not become pregnant again.

Case #9. Translocation Chromosomal Defects

It is possible to inherit translocation chromosome defects through a carrier parent (Riccardi, 1977). Whether one of the parents is a carrier can be determined by a chromosomal analysis using the parents' blood. These carriers are usually detected after the birth of an

6522

affected child. Many chromosomal disorders manifest themselves by multiple birth defects and severe mental retardation in the child. When a parent is a carrier, the recurrence risk is usually very high.

A four-week-old female infant was seen who had multiple congenital anomalies, including severe mental and motor retardation. She expired at age one year. The child was the first offspring of a twenty-three-year-old father and a twenty-year-old mother. Chromosomal analysis on the blood of the child revealed an extra part of a chromosome. The mother's chromosomal constitution was normal, but the father's cells contained an abnormal arrangement of some of his chromosomes. The recurrence risk of spontaneous abortion or multiple congenital anomalies and mental retardation, probably incompatible with sustained life, was about 1/2. This couple wanted children very badly but they wanted to know their risk of recurrence before deciding on future children. They also wanted to know if the father's siblings were carriers and wanted them to have the chromosome analysis.

Their high risk for this severe disorder was discussed. The couple was concerned about the high risk and about the means of birth control to use if they decided not to have more children. They bore a large financial burden from their first child, with multiple hospitalizations necessitating frequent round trips of two hundred miles from their home. The emotional trauma of producing babies who would expire in the first year of life was overwhelming for them. The father stated that he felt very badly that he caused his baby's problems. A discussion was undertaken concerning the financial and emotional aspects of having a severely retarded child with multiple physical defects and of the strength of their desire to have children. It included the procedure of amniocentesis, its morbidity, i.e., its risks (see pp. 15, 18-19) false positive and false negative results, and the problems the couple would face if the results showed a chromosomal abnormality in the fetus. Adoption agencies, the requirements for adoption, family acceptance of an adopted child, and the shortage of newborns available for adoption were topics also discussed. They consulted the wife's obstetrician about the methods of birth control available. The siblings of the father were checked for carrier status and all were normal. After taking all of these factors into consideration, the couple decided not to have more children at that time but to consider pregnancy and amniocentesis at a later date.

This and the previous case illustrate the high risk a couple can have for children who are spontaneously aborted or born with multiple birth defects and severe mental and physical retardation, with ensuing death within the first year of life. They also show the tremendous sense of guilt a carrier parent may bear.

Case #10. Down's Syndrome (Advanced Maternal Age)

Advanced maternal age is an important factor in the incidence of chromosome abnormalities. The incidence of Down's syndrome in the population as a whole is 1/500, but after the age of thirty-five the risk of a woman's producing an affected child increases significantly owing apparently to chromosomal decay in her ova.

Mrs. M. was a pregnant woman forty-two years old. She had been married for seventeen years with no prior children or pregnancies. She had had an ovary removed because of a cyst fifteen years before. She was told at that time that it was very unlikely that she would ever become pregnant. She and her husband had thus not used any birth control method for the past fifteen years. Her last menstrual period started four months before she was seen. At ten weeks following her last period, she had begun to note some slight increase in breast size, a slight weight gain, and she became suspicious that she might be pregnant. She had a pregnancy test that was positive. She had heard about an increased risk for an older mother of having a child with a chromosome anomaly and about amniocentesis from a friend. There was no prior history of a chromosome anomaly, but she did have a first cousin who had a child with spina bifida.

The counseling content involved discussion of the nature of the procedure of amniocentesis and the use of sonography for localization of the placenta. Mrs. M. was interested in amniocentesis because at her age the incidence of a chromosome problem is approximately 1/40. The amniocentesis procedure was explained to her as relatively safe (but see discussion, pp. 15, 18-19).

It was emphasized that no one could guarantee a normal child and that the risk of a significant abnormality at birth is between 1/100 and 1/50 for any parents, and many authorities would place the overall risk as somewhat higher (Marten *et al*, 1964). She was informed of the possibility of alpha fetoprotein and chromosome tests on the amniotic fluid. It was explained to her that a cousin's having a child with spina bifida did not significantly increase the risk of having an affected child.

On the basis of this counseling, Mrs. M. elected to have

sonography and amniocentesis. She said that she was uncertain what she would do if the results were abnormal, though she suspected she would choose to abort. The results were available within four weeks and showed normal chromosomes and no increased level of alpha fetoprotein. Mrs. M. specifically requested that she not be told the sex of the infant. Her only concern was ruling out the possibilities of a chromosomally abnormal infant owing to her advanced maternal age or of a child with spina bifida.

Mrs. M. was elated by the normal results of the amniocentesis studies and looked forward to the birth of her first child, who was delivered and did well. The case illustrates the concerns of an older parent and the strong possibility that many parents would abort a high risk pregnancy if amniocentesis were not available to reassure them that the fetus was indeed normal.

Case #11. Down's Syndrome (Previous History)

A young couple, aged twenty-four and twenty-seven, had one child three years old with Down's syndrome and came for counseling. The father did not wish to have children if there were any increased risks and stated that he had a very difficult time accepting their first child and that it "turned his house upside down." The mother was also concerned about an increased risk. This couple had a 1/100 risk of future Down's syndrome children because of the birth of a previously affected child. A chromosomal analysis of this child revealed an extra chromosome and chromosomal analyses on both parents were normal.

Some of the factors that are important to consider when deciding to have children were discussed: the strength of the marriage, the risk for affected offspring, the emotional need for children, the psychological makeup of the couple, the stability of the entire family unit, the financial aspects of the disease in question, and the moral and religious beliefs of the parents. The family decided not to take the risk and to have a sterilization procedure performed on the wife.

This case is illustrative of the tremendous fear, hostility, and stress that some families experience with the presence of a mentally retarded child in the home (Smith and Wilson, 1973). These feelings, often not expressed or admitted by the family, need to be sensitively handled by the counselor.

Summary

The genetic counselor, as well as the counselee, who has moral objections to abortion, to contraceptive sterilization, and to contraception, will find the problems associated with genetic disease additionally difficult to manage. The eleven cited cases reveal to some extent the pain, the anger, the frustration, and the resentment frequently experienced by persons who are closely and personally associated with a genetic disease.

With the presentation of the eleven specific genetic disease cases, Part I of this study comes to a close. The next two chapters, which together comprise Part II of this study, will examine the social, philosophical and theological context in which the moral issues surrounding genetic disease and counseling are seen today.

PART II

The Social, Philosophical and Theological Context

Chapter 3

The Meaning of the Human: Cultural and Philosophical Perspectives

After briefly presenting in Part I an overview of fundamental genetics, genetic diseases and of the major techniques available for antenatal diagnosis, we considered the nature of genetic counseling and illustrated some of the anguishing personal and moral problems which can arise in genetic disease by citing eleven case studies. At this point we must now (in Part II) consider the cultural context in which the associated moral issues are raised, understood and resolved.

So that the presentation in the following chapter of the Church's understanding of the human can be better appreciated, in this chapter we shall be examining briefly four separate but related issues: (1) the impact of scientific developments on human self-image; (2) the radical shift in modes of understanding which has occurred within this century; (3) the three alternative understandings of humanity that are vying for acceptance within our contemporary culture; and, (4) the social ramifications of these three alternatives.

Science and Human Self-image

On December 7, 1965, the Fathers of the Second Vatican Council issued an unequivocal proclamation of the values that must guide all human beings in their dealings with one another. The "Pastoral Constitution on the Church in the Modern World" (Vatican II, 1965b) represents a reflection on the meaning of human existence as interpreted by the saving message of the gospel of Jesus Christ. Thus, the Constitution addresses not only Catholics and others committed to the service of Christ but "the whole human family seen in the context of everything which envelops it" (#2)*. The following brief summary presents the Constitution's view of the impact on human self-understanding arising from the rapid and profound changes which have taken place during this century.

Human beings today, perhaps as at no other time in their history, find themselves perplexed about the situation that confronts them. They are uncertain about the meaning of current trends, their own place in the universe, the significance of individual and group activity, and the nature and destiny of the human race. They have entered a new age of history in which profound and far-reaching changes occur with increasing rapidity, so that old and cherished values seem no longer appropriate while few new and untested values have arisen to take their place. These changes have not been produced by the blind forces of nature but are the result of human intelligence and activity; yet these changes recoil upon their source, modifying desires and ways of thinking in a manner that would have been inconceivable as little as fifty years ago. Human power has increased dramatically, power not only over the nonhuman world but power over humans as well, and yet that increase has not always benefitted them. They recognize the harm human intelligence has done in the past, and now humans are perplexed about how to guide a course for the future (see ##3, 4).

Nowhere have the changes been more significant or had a deeper impact than in the field of scientific knowledge. In the first place, the models of reasoning in the mathematical and natural sciences — mathematical deduction and experimental reasoning — have created new standards of thought that have impressed themselves on scientists and on the wider nonscientific community. In the second place, the growth of the pure sciences has led to a bewildering variety of technological advances that are capable of reshaping the face of the earth and humanity. No longer at the mercy of natural events, humans are now able to control and modify these events, directing them for their purposes. Human beings have become aware of recently undreamt possibilities for controlling their own future and that of the world. Nature is no longer seen as static, as a given to be obeyed.

---

*In this and subsequent references in this chapter the number in parentheses refers to the paragraph number of *The Pastoral Constitution on the Church in the Modern World.*

Rather, in place of this old conception, nature is seen as dynamic, as evolving, and humans recognize themselves as able to direct that process as they will. Advances in the natural sciences of chemistry, biology, physiology, and psychology, and in the social sciences of sociology, history, and economics provide humans with a greater understanding of themselves and with the technical means of modifying themselves and their non-human environment (see #5).

These developments provide the grounds for great hopes, and yet they raise doubts and fears as well. "Man is growing conscious that the forces he has unleashed are in his own hands and that it is up to him to control them or be enslaved by them" (#9). But the question faces humans: upon what basis should decisions be made? What values should guide their choices? Tremendous endeavors have been undertaken on the part of individuals and of whole societies, but humans wonder about the meaning and value of all this enterprise. Human beings recognize the need for wisdom to guide them into an uncertain future opened up by their increased powers of control (see ##33, 15).

Contemporary Modes of Understanding

The past fifty years have seen a radical shift in the modes of human understanding. This change in some respects can be viewed as a shift from what might be called classical to modern or post-modern culture (Lonergan, 1967). The classical worldview attempted to understand reality within the categories of universality, necessity, certainty, and the changeless, whereas the contemporary worldview approaches the problem of knowing with an entirely different set of categories, emphasizing change and development, probability, and a plurality of methods for understanding the world in which humans live. These changes have also produced an irreversible alteration in human self-awareness, and any attempt to provide an understanding of the human must be appreciative of this shift in self-consciousness. The changes that have been most significant in producing an altered mode of awareness may be looked at under eight aspects.

The *first* shift is one from a concern with certitude and certainty of results to a concern for probability. In contemporary culture, there is a search for genuine understanding rather than a need for absolute certitude. There is wide dissatisfaction with a "proof" method, and a move toward as complete an understanding as possible of all the data at hand in terms of their mutual intelligible relationships. In short, the age of certitude has ended with the advent of the age of probable understanding.

The *second* shift marks a move from the classical insistence on the changeless and immobile to the contemporary interest in change, movement, and development. This shift is evident in such areas as the developments in mathematics, evolutionary theory, genetic psychology, and the interests of various human sciences and philosophies in the dynamic and changing nature of humanity. There is also a greater appreciation of historical development which has permeated all areas of science and philosophy.

Thirdly, whereas classical culture was concerned with the "necessity" of things as expressed in Aristotelian metaphysics, contemporary culture wants to know the intelligibility of things by giving meaning to facts that are known empirically. And in the *fourth* place, there has been a shift from an exclusive concern with the universal to a dominant concern for concrete and particular facts and their meaning as these facts develop and unfold.

The *fifth* shift from classical to modern culture is from a concern for formal objects to an interest in a field. "A formal object is the subject under which [*ratio sub qua*] any theoretician considers and attains the object of his study. A field, on the other hand, can be defined as a region of the concrete universe which the particular science in question aims to master by the skilled use of those certain basic operations and methods peculiar to his speciality" (Tracy, 1970). In classical culture it was sufficient to consider something solely in the "objective" order, whereas contemporary culture insists on examining a particular area both in terms of objectivity (what it is) and subjectivity (how a particular science views the object). This demands that the contemporary thinker be much more sophisticated in his approach to any issue or problem, for there are a whole range of methods or theories for any given set of issues.

The *sixth* shift relates to the process of inquiry into a particular issue. The classical process involved a movement from particulars to universal definitions, axioms, and principles, followed by a logical movement from the universal principles to practical conclusions about particular matters. The contemporary thinker, on the other hand, moves in a more circular manner. In this movement, the scientist "moves from carefully controlled data through insight to hypothesis to verification via experiment and, finally and secondarily, to logical deductions from the hypotheses" (Tracy, 1970). The method in contemporary culture is inductive as contrasted with the logical, deductive approach of classical culture.

The *seventh* shift is from the classical interest in the essence of things, i.e., the search for the one, ultimate and intrinsic ground of reality, to a concern for pluralism and perspectivism. Whereas the classical mind wanted to know the one true reality of things, the contemporary thinker acknowledges that reality is too broad, too rich, and too deep to be penetrated and captured in one "essence." The contemporary mind does not look for the one explanation of reality but for a cluster of approaches. Furthermore, modern culture tries to understand the historical nature of any one approach to reality, and recognizes that meanings can change with history.

The *final* shift is understood as a movement from the classical concern for the permanence of achievements to a contemporary effort at collaboration and an openness to further development and change.

Classical culture, in brief, was normative, stable and based on the eternal truths and unchanging laws. Its concern was the unchanging essences of things. Once the essence was grasped, the changes that happened in concrete daily life were accidental and of no lasting value. Since it was universal, classical culture was normative for all persons at all times. Contemporary culture, on the other hand, does not pretend to be normative. It is empirical and therefore embraces more than classical culture. Contemporary culture recognizes that all peoples have a genuine culture, and it respects diversity and plurality. No one thought pattern is believed to hold a monopoly on true insights into reality. Contemporary culture is therefore on the move; it possesses a dynamic, developmental, and historical consciousness. Because it is not out to perpetuate the wisdom of the past, contemporary culture sees persons collectively and holds them responsible for the world in which they live.

Because of these changes, "pluralism" becomes a respectable term in every field. In the midst of this painful process of change, we are struck with the breakdown of common meaning. For many persons today the Judeao-Christian worldview, as one example, no longer is the sacred canopy for the search for truth. This perspective is now only one among many possible interpretations. In this context of cultural change the exploration of the realities and implications of modern medicine takes place. The changing worldview of the historical, natural, and empirical sciences has stamped our lives; and we no longer live within a framework of homogeneous Christian culture and value systems.

Three Philosophical Approaches to the Human

This section, in part following an analysis by Callahan (1970), examines three proposed answers to the question: what is it to be a human being or human person? This question may be rephrased in a number of ways: when (or how) does a human organism, genetically distinct from either parent, become a human being or person with the rights possessed by mature human beings? What are the criteria, the necessary and sufficient conditions, for an individual's possessing the quality of humanhood or human personhood? Each of three alternative answers to this question is examined below. The first answer holds the position that in order to be a person one must be accepted as such by one's parents or society. Personhood is a status conferred or bestowed upon a member of the human species by the society of human persons. This school of thought will be called the *social school* approach. The second alternative proposes that full humanhood is a state into which a human organism develops or grows at some time after the point of conception. This position will be referred to as the *developmental school* of thought or approach. The third alternative approach will be called the *genetic school* or approach. According to this position, a human being or person begins to exist from the time of fertilization-conception and ceases to live only when the human body is no longer alive, when it ceases to function as a living unity. These considerations will be followed by a brief look at the social implications of these three approaches.

A preliminary elucidation is vital at the outset of this discussion in order to distinguish between two senses of the word *human*. The first of these may be called the *genetic* or *scientific* sense. According to this sense of the word, to be a human is to be a member of the species *Homo sapiens*. Whether or not an organism is a member of this species is a question to be determined by science, in particular, the science of genetics. In Chapter 1 it was noted that the human genetic component normally consists of twenty-three pairs of chromosomes in each somatic cell. These pairs are, in their totality, unique to the human species, and serve to mark it off sharply from all other species.

Genetically defective individuals do not possess a normal set of human chromosomes, but so distinctive are these chromosomal pairs in human cells that the geneticist has no difficulty generally in deciding whether or not the cells in question come from an individual who genetically is a human being. For example, a female with a monosomy X condition (Turner's syndrome) has only forty-five chromosomes, and a male with an XYY set of sex chromosomes has forty-seven; but these individuals are seen, nonetheless, by the geneticist as definitely human, although defective in some respect. One may take the following as a practical guide to the meaning of *human* in this sense: whatever is of true human parentage, whether born or unborn, is human.

Some have falsely concluded from the above that the geneticist is able to demonstrate conclusively that the (human) fetus is a human being worthy of respect. They would argue as follows: "The geneticist can show that the (human) fetus is of the human species, therefore the human fetus is worthy of the respect due to a human being." But to believe in this way would be to commit a fallacy, since the inference is based on an equivocation of the word *human.* In the premise ["the geneticist can show that the (human) fetus is human"], the word "human" is being used in the genetic or scientific sense, whereas in the conclusion ("the human fetus is therefore a human worthy of respect") the word "human" is being used in what may be called its *normative, ethical,* or *moral* sense. In this sense of the word, to say that the individual is human is to say that he is a human person possessing human rights. From the fact that the term *human* applies in the scientific sense it does not follow necessarily that it applies in the normative sense. From the fact that a being is genetically human, it does not follow (without further argumentation) that it is a human person with moral rights. It is important to recognize this distinction because although the genetic school holds that all genetically human beings are also moral persons, the developmental and social schools deny that this relation holds. The latter two approaches maintain that there are some genetically human individuals who are not moral persons and so lack fundamental human (i.e., moral) rights. Although a formidable case can be presented for the position of the genetic approach, it is important that that approach not be seen to base its case on any equivocal use of terms. For the sake of terminological precision, *human organism* in this chapter will be used in the genetic or scientific sense, whereas *human being* will be employed in an exclusively moral sense. The question, then, may be restated as follows: are all human organisms human beings? If not, when (or how) does the human organism become a human being?

To define what is morally or *normatively* human is no easy task. The various attempts arise from the desire to do justice to our experience of what it means to be a person. It is vital that a society possess an appreciation of what it means to be a person, to be a member of the human community. Such an appreciation is necessary for any understanding of the realtionships holding between human beings and the world and among the various members of the human community. A common appreciation of what it means to be a person must be possessed by the community as a whole, for such an understanding welds a collection of human individuals into a community. Indeed, without a shared appreciation of the meaning of human personhood, the collection of individuals cannot truly be said to be a community at all. Only insofar as they share a common set of values grounded upon a shared sense of what it means to be a person, can they possess a life together and hold shared aspirations and commitments. A society may continue to function within, and even encourage, a certain degree of pluralism: a completely monolithic society is neither inevitable nor desirable. Nevertheless, there are limits to the possibility of such pluralism. Widespread and sharp disagreement about who is a member of the human family means that those individuals who hold such divergent views must, in a real sense, remain strangers, alien to one another.

The Social Approach

The social school of thought emphasizes the communal nature of human personality: to be a truly human being is to belong to the human community, to be accepted by it and relate to others on a personal level. Aristotle provided perhaps the best expression of this way of thinking when he wrote, by way of hyperbole, in the *Politics* that outside of the *polis* (society) there are beasts (subhumans) and gods (superhumans) but no men (Bk. 1, Ch. 2, 1253a). We are educated, brought up, and trained in being human. The human being cannot begin *to exercise* his truly human characteristics until he has developed the human skills of language, social interaction, and rational thought. Paraphrasing Aristotle one might contend that outside of the community there are human organisms but no human beings. Moral humanity is the result of a process of humanization, of civilization, of growth into personhood under the tutorship of the adult community. The human being possesses rights that other organisms do not possess only because — according to the social school — the person acquires distinctive modes of operation and consciousness, and acquires these only within the human community. The phrase of John Donne that "no man is an island" may have become trite, but it remains nonetheless perfectly true; a human organism raised in isolation on a desert island, if such there could be, would never *become* a human being (although the individual may already be one). Studies of feral children who have been raised by animals in the wild tend to support this school of thought, for the children, who were not exposed to human companionship during a crucial period in their lives, appear incapable of acquiring full human *functioning* after they have been reintroduced into human society.

If in order to possess human rights a human organism must be a human being and *if* one becomes a human being only after acceptance into the human community, then clearly it cannot be an injustice to a human organism to exclude it from the human community. To call it injustice would be to imply that the human organism has rights, and this would mean that the organism was a human being prior to its acceptance by the community, a position contrary to the social school of thought.

In Chapter 1 a question is raised concerning the use of antenatal diagnosis to detect the sex of the unborn with a view toward abortion if the child were of the wrong sex. It is pointed out (p. 24) that most genetic counselors would find this an improper use of their technology and probably would refuse to perform the amniocentesis procedure. This issue raises an important question for adherents of the social school of thought; how could they justify interfering with the decision of the parents in this matter if the unborn itself has no rights? What can be wrong about killing a human organism for any reasons if it has no rights?

The phrasing of the question in this way carries with it the implicit assumption that it is the parents who are to decide whether the child is to live or die, but there is nothing within the logic of the social approach that requires this assumption. In fact, its logic seems to lead in a quite different direction, for it need not be only within the *family* that the human organisms may become human beings. It is only outside of the *polis* that there are no humans. Human organisms become human beings in orphanages and on the streets where human beings roam. There is nothing within the social approach that requires human beings becoming such within the nuclear family of husband and wife. This process of becoming a human being may perhaps be best carried on within the context of the family, but this context is not necessary as "socialists" from Plato to the present day have recognized. One might appeal to parental rights, arguing that it is the right of the woman or the couple to decide; but rights frequently come into conflict with other rights and must be balanced against one another. One could appeal, for example, to the right of the community not to be burdened by the consequences of the couple's irresponsible decisions and to be concerned about the social implications of parental choices. Thus, contained within the social school of thought is an implicit feature tending to justify an arbitrary community decision about the unborn's right to life. Whether this tendency can be overridden by other factors is a debatable issue. What is clear is that from this perspective the rights of the unborn cannot be invoked to protect it.

The Developmental Approach

In a way that is not at all dissimilar to the social school of thought, the developmental school asks the question: what is it about the human organism that makes it uniquely valuable? It is not simply that the organism exists, nor that it is alive, for we do not value inanimate objects or animals of other species in the way that we value human beings. What, then, is special about human beings that makes us value them in the way we do? As with the social school, the answer must be given in terms of the functions of which the human being alone is capable. The possible answers to this question obviously admit of a great deal of variety, but an influential article by the Anglican priest and ethicist, Joseph Fletcher, may serve as a general indication of the kinds of answers given by the developmental approach. The article is entitled "Indicators of Humanhood: A Tentative Profile of Man." It is clear that Fletcher is concerned with *human* in the normative sense: "we need to explicate humanness or humaneness, what it means to be a truly human being" (Fletcher, Joseph 1972). The operative word here is *truly,* for the use of the word implies that Fletcher does not believe that all human organisms are human beings in the important (i.e., normative) sense. Fletcher lists fifteen characteristics that we

64

value about human beings, characteristics that make human beings special:

1. Human intelligence, at least intelligence above some minimal level — below IQ 40, one is questionably a person, while below 20, one is not a person
2. Self-awareness or self-consciousness
3. Self-control
4. A sense of time, or time consciousness
5. A sense of the future
6. A sense of the past
7. The capability of relating to others
8. Concern for others
9. Communication
10. Able to control one's own existence
11. Curiosity
12. The ability to change
13. A balance of rationality and feeling
14. Idiosyncrasy; "To be a person is to have an identity, to be recognizable and callable by name "
15. Neo-cortical function; "In a way, this is the cardinal indicator, the one all the others are hinged upon."

The indicators by no means exhaust the possible answers. Other indicators that come to mind are the ability to laugh, the ability to blush with shame or embarrassment, the consciousness that one will die, and the affirmation of one's existence in the face of the absurdity of the universe. Nevertheless, Fletcher has noted that neo-cortical function (Characteristic #15) seems to be in some way fundamental as the necessary condition for the possession of the other valuable traits that make human beings special. Thus, there seems some basis for the thesis that human personhood really begins with the presence of neo-cortical function. Nonetheless, that argument fails to take into account that what is significant is not the *actual* capacity here and now to exercise the unique powers of a human being, but rather the *radical* capacity to exercise those powers. Infra human beings such as cats, dogs, or chimpanzees do not have that radical capacity whereas a human fetus or newborn does. (See McCarthy and Moraczewski, 1976, pp. 22-24).

It should not be inferred from these considerations that there is any unanimity among adherents of the developmental school about the key and indispensible condition for humanhood. Whereas all might accept Fletcher's list as reasonably inclusive, there are sharp differences among the adherents about what is most important. Thus, Michael Tooley (1973) emphasizes Characteristic #2 as the most important condition, for it is this condition that distinguishes human beings from individuals of other species. Tooley maintains that *person* is a moral term: to call an individual a person means, in effect, that the individual has a serious moral right to life. All, and only, *persons* possess a moral right to life. Tooley continues on to say that an individual has a right to something implies that he is capable of desiring that thing, and this implies that he is capable of possessing a concept of that thing. Thus, being persons implies that the individuals are conscious of themselves, for only in this way can they desire that they continue to exist. Tooley and others, then, hold to the primary of self-awareness.

G. R. Grice (1967) argues that there is a complex connection between having a right and being the kind of individual with whom it would be in the interests of mature men and women to make contracts. Although Grice in his argument is not concerned to analyze the concept of humanhood, it is not difficult to see how someone who agreed both with Grice on this point and with Tooley's contention that being a person entails having a serious right to life could conclude that before children are capable of entering into contracts they are not persons. The argumentation would read: since one can have rights only when one is capable of entering into contracts, and since one can be a person only if one has rights, then a person must be an individual capable of entering into contracts. This kind of reasoning may appear far-fetched to some, but it would not appear unreasonable to one who holds to the importance of self-direction (Characteristic #3) and independence (Characteristic #10) as features of the human being that are uniquely valued.

This discussion could be extended almost *ad infinitum,* listing all the possible positions, arguments, and implications of the many strands of the developmental school of thought (Atkinson, 1977). But this cursory examination is sufficient if it makes a point clear: one of the most serious difficulties facing any developmentalist is that of convincing fellow developmentalists that the proposed criterion is *the* unique characteristic or set of characteristics that makes human beings valued by others. For a time it might have appeared that a *modus vivendi* could be worked out among the developmentalists on the basis of the 1973 *Roe* and *Doe* decisions: an individual becomes a person at viability or when born. Nevertheless, this basis for a practical consensus is in the process of breaking apart, if in fact it ever existed, by those who are concerned to justify terminating a human life at either end of the continuum of postnatal existence.

At the one end, there is a considerable agitation for what is called "pediatric euthanasia" which encompasses what used to be called infanticide, the killing of infants judged to be incapable of meaningful life. Thus, F. Raymond Marks and Lisa Salkovitz (1976) suggest a "delayed personhood policy" that would permit the killing of newborn human organisms who, from the standpoint of "good medicine," are judged incapable of leading a satisfactory existence. Indeed, Marks and Salkovitz suggest "we could perhaps define a category of babies [i.e., postnatal human organisms] who should be *killed* independent of the wishes of any of the actors" (italics in original). At the other end of the continuum, we find Fletcher saying in connection with Characteristic #15 that "what is definitive in determining death [i.e., the death of a human being as opposed to the death of a human organism] is the loss of cerebration, not just of any or all brain function. Personal reality depends on cerebration and to be dead 'humanly' speaking is to be ex-cerebral, no matter how long the *body* remains alive" (Fletcher, Joseph 1972; italics in original).

The developmental and social schools of thought may not differ greatly in their implications for social policy, but it is nonetheless useful to keep the two schools of thought distinct. Both schools hold that *some* human organisms are not human beings and so possess no rights. Yet, there is this difference in theory: a member of the developmental school, by definition, must hold that there is some point or some period of time at which a human organism becomes a human being, regardless of whether he is in fact accepted into the community. The organism's achieving that state may in fact depend on the community's acceptance, but once that state is achieved, the community's acceptance becomes irrelevant. It is important that this distinction be kept in mind. Later in this chapter an argument will be presented to the effect that the logics inherent in either the social or developmental approaches contain no bases for opposing the killing of any human entity regardless of its condition, but that the justification for this assertion is different for the two positions.

The Genetic Approach

The members of the genetic school maintain, in contradistinction to those of the social and developmental schools, that a human organism does not *become* a human being, that if it were not a human being from the very beginning it could never become one for there is no point at which, and no agency through which, such a change could take place.*

The basic problem with the genetic school is to answer the question: how can the one-celled zygote be anything other than a *potential* person or human being? From what we know about what makes human beings unique and especially valuable, to many it *seems* unreasonable to maintain that a human being is actually present as the one-celled zygote scarcely visible to the naked eye. We may value the zygote, such individuals would say, just as we value hoped-for grandchildren or future generations; but the hoped-for grandchild and the generations to be born in the twenty-first century are not *now* the *subjects* of rights; *they* do not yet exist to possess or act as bearers of rights. Nor should the fetus be understood as a bearer of rights. It may be valued, but from this perspective no person yet exists who is capable of possessing those rights. One physician-ethicist notes (Engelhart, 1973):

> Even the more concrete potentiality of the fetus is not yet the potentiality of anyone — there is not yet a "who" present whose potentiality it is. There is not yet a "who" to have personal rights. Rather, the fetus' value is in terms of its promise of, or potentiality for becoming a person. But the fetus is not yet valuable to itself but to others for whom it has value; the fetus is not yet a person to whom things have value. That is, the value of the fetus is implicit in the fetus, and for others, but not for itself. The fetus does not yet have value in and for itself. (p. 23)

The genetic approach would not have any difficulty in arguing its position if it valued merely biological life or merely the biological life of the human species, or what we have called simply the human organism. But the genetic approach to the "human being" goes beyond that claim. Furthermore, the genetic approach explicitly recognizes that only in relation to one another do persons find their

---

*An earlier publication of the Pope John Center (McCarthy and Moraczewski, 1976) contains a detailed presentation of the genetic approach. This present section includes only a few excerpts from the argument as presented in Chapter III and the appendix of that publication.

true value and meaning. Only within the community of persons are individuals capable of developing their capacities of relating to one another in *mutual* understanding, love, and respect. Accordingly, McCarthy and Moraczewski (1976) note:

> Seen in this light, *personhood is correlative to community*, even a community composed of just two individuals. However, it seems that a larger number of individuals are required to provide those variations of personal interaction necessary for a full development of the person. That is, the community exists in virtue of the persons; but the persons themselves can achieve full expression of personhood only in and through the life of the community. (p. 24)

If the activities of human beings we value become possible only after a great deal of physiological development and social growth, then the problem faced by the genetic school consists in showing how the undeveloped human organism *in utero* can be capable of *any* valuable and distinctively human activity. The basis for the answer as given by the earlier study (McCarthy and Moraczewski, 1976) is as follows:

> Obviously most of these fetal activities are possible only after some degree of fetal development. But the *capacity* to respond thus, and the capacity to be a human infant, child, adolescent, adult is already programmed in the zygote, primarily coded in the 23 pairs of chromosomes. The fetus from its inception shows a gradual growth and differentiation without any significant discontinuities until the death of the individual. Thus the human fetus shows itself as an organism with an inner dynamism which, apart from accident or defect, naturally leads it to full adulthood in a smooth progression. Gradually, characteristics are manifested, which in their later developed state, will distinguish the fetus as an *adult* person. (p. 26)

Therefore, in regard to an individual person, one must ask: When did *this* person begin, and, when did his or her biography end? At what point in time did this person emerge as a distinct individual having his or her life process to live out? If this moment is later than conception, then there should be some empirical evidence of an actual time, a threshold at which this human person begins to exist. Efforts to pinpoint such an exact time (implantation, viability, birth, socialization), as will be argued below, do not stand up under examination. It is very difficult to conceive how an individual human organism already in existence and already in the process of individual development, can at a subsequent point of time become a person. As the eminent Methodist theologian Albert Outler has said, "Personhood is not a *part* of the human organism, nor is it inserted into a process of organic development at some magic moment. It *is* the human organism oriented towards its transcendental matrix, in which it lives and moves and has its being." [Outler, 1973]

On the other hand, if one decides that human personhood begins at conception, this requires the acceptance of the idea of a person who is a single, minute cell. At first glance, it seems preposterous to believe that the almost infinitely complex system which constitutes a human personality could be present in such a tiny bit of protoplasm, yet this is what is implied. As the Jesuit theologian Joseph Mangan has said, "It would be incorrect to refer to the human body as being only virtually or potentially present in the zygote. The human body is *actually* present, the *adult* human body is potentially present." [Mangan, 1970] Paul Ramsey also says, "In a remarkable way, modern genetics also teaches there are 'formal causes,' immanent principles, or constitutive elements long before there is any shape or motion or discernible size." [Ramsey, 1968]

Yet, this seemingly incredible assertion becomes more plausible by fully rejecting the Cartesian dualism of "body" and "mind." If the human person is actually a body-mind unity, then there is nothing unreasonable in believing that as the human body develops out of a single cell as a continuous organism, so human personhood develops out of a single cell as a continuous, unique individuality. As Emmanuel Mounier, a leader in personalist thinking, has said, "I am a person from my elementary existence upward, and my embodied existence, far from depersonalizing me, is a factor essential to my personal status." [Mounier, 1975] Or as philosopher Louis Dupré says: "Although personhood is essentially a dynamic entity not fully realized even at life's peak, it must neverthelesss be minimally present already at life's humble beginnings." [Dupré, 1973] (p. 27-28)

The preceding material provides an answer to the question posed in introducing it: what activity of the undeveloped human organism *in utero* could conceivably be uniquely valuable and distinctively human? The answer from the foregoing should be clear: it is the self-directed activity (i.e., an activity carried on from within the organism itself, ordered to its own completion, and based on the distinctive genetic component present from the time of fertilization) of growth through the various stages of human development into an adult member of the human species. It is true that the sperm and ovum are distinctively human products and uniquely valuable, but they are essentially incomplete and normally require each other for continuation, growth and development. It is also true that many individuals are conceived in such a defective manner that they are incapable of growth to full maturity. Nonetheless, if they are indeed self-directed and self-organized on the basis of their genetic information, and if that chromosomal component contains all but a very small part of the normal human complement of chromosomes (monosomy X and XYY individuals, for example, are still humans), then these organisms would be human beings as well.

Ashley (1976) argues that the human being begins when the process of fertilization has been successfully completed. This process is a delicate one and often is only partially successful. Thus, there are many growths, such as teratomas, that result from incomplete or defective fertilizations. These probably would not be human beings. The position of the genetic school is this: an organism capable of self-directed and self-initiated activity with a normal or near-normal set of human chromosomes is a human being worthy of respect and protection.

Social Ramifications of the Three Approaches

This section first examines the question: is there any individual who is indisputably and irrevocably a human person on the basis of the social or developmental schools of thought? The answer is negative: there is *nothing within the logic of either approach* that forecloses having one's neighbor or oneself declared a nonperson and thus outside the pale of the human community. Both approaches hold that there exists a "magic circle" within, but not coextensive with, the species *Homo sapiens*. There is no basis in either approach for demonstrating that any given member of the wider class *must* be placed within the "magic circle." This point is easily misunderstood, for it is tempting to confuse a point about logic with an observation about psychology. The thesis being argued for here does not imply that adherents of the two schools must or are likely to run out and declare their aged grandparents to be nonpersons. If that were indeed the implication of the logical thesis, then it would be shown to be manifestly false. Rather, the position being argued is that a refusal to consider aged and senile humans as nonpersons by adherents of either school represents a conviction on their part that cannot be rationally justified within their own theory.

71

More will be said about the implications of this at the conclusion of the section.

A question must be asked of the social approach: if a human organism receives its moral humanity by reception into the society, then can that status be taken away from it by that same society? Is the society's acceptance revocable? The crucial difficulty for the social school is that the logic of the position provides no basis for the contention that society's acceptance must be irrevocable. If a human organism becomes a human being by acceptance into the community, then its expulsion from the community eliminates the moral humanity of the individual and returns it to the status of a merely human *organism.* If adherents of the social school believe that this last thesis is false, then they have unwittingly abandoned the social school and become an adherent of the developmental school. They are claiming that there comes a stage in the development of the human organism at which acceptance by the community becomes irrelevant. It may be, in fact, the case that an organism can attain this stage only after having first been accepted by the community, but if the acceptance is irrevocable once the organism has reached that stage, then it is the development to that stage that is the key and no longer social acceptance. For example, if one were to contend in the manner of Michael Tooley that once the acceptance by the society of a human organism permitted that organism to become conscious of itself so that it now acquires the basic human right to life, then it is upon that developmental fact that everything rests and not upon social attitudes. Thoroughly consistent adherents of the social approach cannot hold to anything but a conceivably revocable social acceptance. If they maintain otherwise they have been infected by implicitly developmental ways of thinking.

The foregoing provides reason for believing that there are few consistent representatives of the social school. Social acceptance is vital in this school for an organism's obtaining a particular stage, and before the stage is reached the organism possesses no human rights and is not a human being and may be killed if the parents (or society) choose to do so. But if after that stage there can be no revocation of social acceptance as a human being, it is because the human organism *has developed into* a human being.

If this is how the case stands with the social school, then the question must be put to the developmental school: can an argument be made for the irrevocability of the status of human being? Again, the answer must be in the negative. Any conclusion to the effect that the status of moral humanity is irrevocable must, from within a consistently developmental framework, be based on the prior argument that the human organism has developed into a human being, and the developmental framework provides no basis for such an argument.

The situation may be seen by considering the following argument scheme:

1. Quality Q is what is basic, unique, or essential to human beings
2. Therefore, once an organism has attained quality Q it has become a human being with moral rights
3. Therefore, even if acceptance by the society is necessary for the organism's attaining quality Q, once that quality has been attained the acceptance cannot be revoked (without violating that human being's rights).

On the assumption that human beings possess irrevocable rights, this argument scheme is formally valid. That is, if one accepts statement (1), then conclusion (2) and conclusion (3) logically follow. But the problem, of course, depends on the truth of statement (1), on whatever quality Q is held to make statement (1) obviously true. But there is nothing within the logic of the developmental school that can justify calling any single quality or set of qualities that magic quality Q. What is held to make statement (1) an obvious truth does not depend on argument but on a conviction unsupported by any feature of the developmental position itself. Any conceivable quality could in theory be proposed as the magic quality Q that serves to delineate the magic circle. The practical issue depends on what quality will be able to win a consensus among developmentalists, and we have seen that developmentalists themselves are sharply divided on this point. It does appear inconceivable that adult, effective, and independent human organisms, who are not members of racial or social minorities, would ever submit to the choice of a quality Q which would put them outside of the magic circle. But with that exception, the only thing precluding the upgrading of Fletcher's 20/40 IQ condition to 60/80 IQ would be the powerful members' "sense of humanity," a notoriously fluctuating standard.

The argument presented here does not pretend to show that

either the social or the developmental school of thought must lead to widespread dehumanization. Rather, the contention is simply that they provide neither a protection against it nor a reason for thinking that it will not occur. Adherents of either approach believe that such a fear is absurd and groundless, but they should admit that their opposition to what they would consider to be the dehumanization of the weak and infirm is for them a conviction without any foundation within their own system. People do not easily give up their convictions, and it would be unreasonable to expect or fear that the present adherents of the two approaches will give up their biases. But the argument is not concerned with the present but with the future, and concerning the future adherents of the two schools, the present adherents are not at liberty to make definitive pronouncements: the future adherents will have to speak for themselves.

Summary

The success of science and its impact on human self-image are no doubt far reaching. With the discovery of the universe's vastness, its unimaginably great age (more than 15 billion years old, or half that age if recent recalculations are validated), with a deeper understanding of life's origins and evolutionary development, with the psychoanalytic and psychological probings of human's inner life, with the challenge of computers and artificial "intelligence," human beings have, on one scale of values at least, been gradually but inexorably displaced from the center of things.

Another displacement caused by the scientific view of reality comes with the notion of change and truth. Reality as interpreted and proclaimed by science is in constant flux. Truth is arrived at step-wise by a series of approximations; new data require us to reformulate or change our conclusions. Consequently, our assertions are always provisional — including this one. At least, that is the view of many scientific spokesmen. Yet to say that truth is arrived at by a series of approximations is to admit that *there is* a truth which is being approached. Most scientific advances do not totally *contradict* the "truth" of a previous validly arrived at conclusion. Rather, they refine it and state it in increasingly more precise terms.

Intertwined with the change in human self-image resulting from scientific advances and a scientific interpretation of reality, has been the shift from a classical to contemporary culture. This is a shift from a culture which was normative, stable, and based on immutable truths and universally applicable moral laws, to the contemporary Western culture which is pluralistic in values, dynamic and developmental with regards to truth, and relativistic with regards to moral laws.

In light of such a change, the social and developmental schools' position on the human can be more readily understood. The social school of thought makes an individual's humanity dependent on the community defining it to be such by accepting that individual within its fold. In that spirit the Supreme Court's 1973 decision excluded certain human individuals from the human community. The developmental school is willing to grant that at some point in the individual's development it *becomes* a human being with rights. However, there is no agreement at present among the position's adherents as to when that "magic moment" is reached.

With the unborn human individual's personal status in flux according to the social and developmental schools, the genetically defective child — before birth at least — is vulnerable to destruction at the will of the parents or society. Only the genetic approach to the human being or person which identifies the beginning of human personhood with the time of fertilization can provide a stable and principled basis for protecting the unborn child afflicted with a genetic disease.

Building on the above discussion, the next chapter will provide additional reasons for a Christian to treat the unborn children from the time of their conception with the full respect due to human persons.

Chapter 4

The Meaning of the Human: Biblical, Magisterial, Personalistic Perspectives

Introduction

Each of the three philosophical schools of thought examined in the previous chapter have numerous adherents in contemporary American society. Each one of the approaches tells us something about what is important and uniquely valuable about human beings. It is the belief of the Christian that what is supremely important is not what humans think of themselves but what God thinks of them.

What is man that you should be mindful of him,
or the son of man that you should care for him?
You have made him little less than the angels,
and crowned him with glory and honor (Ps. 8:5-6).

The Christian sees humans as creatures of God, so that it becomes impossible adequately to understand human beings without turning to their origin, to their Creator.

For the Catholic Christian, the nature of the divine understanding of the human person is revealed in two closely related sources, the inspired word of God contained in the Old and New Testaments, and the Spirit-guided reflection on the message of Christ contained in the official teachings of the Church. The three philosophical schools of thought considered in the previous chapter present alternative answers to the question as to when a human being with moral significance comes into existence. Preference was given to the genetic school because only it provided a solid and principled basis for treating all human beings with respect on grounds of their inherent dignity rather than as developmental quality or an extrinsic attribution.

In this chapter the light of divine Revelation will be used in reflecting on the meaning of the human. The first section of this chapter accordingly examines briefly what answer the sacred scriptures provide to this question. (See McCarthy and Moraczewski, 1976, pp. 42-49, for a complementary analysis.) A second section summarizes the contemporary understanding of the Magisterium as to the meaning of the human, while the final section briefly considers the viewpoint of contemporary Christian personalism.

Selected Biblical Teachings Regarding the Human

To be Human is to be Known by God

The book of the prophet Jeremiah tells of a number of actions Jeremiah was commanded by the Lord to perform. These actions were taken by Jeremiah to be "enacted words," signs of what the Lord was about to do with the people of Judah. A relevant example of these commanded, symbolic actions was for Jeremiah to buy a linen loincloth, wear it for a while, and then take it off and hide it in the cleft of a rock. After some days Jeremiah was commanded to return to the place and fetch the loincloth. Jeremiah did as he was commanded, and upon retrieving the loincloth he found that it had rotted and was good for nothing.

> Then the message came to me from the LORD: Thus says the LORD: So also I will allow the pride of Judah to rot, the great pride of Jerusalem. This wicked people who refuse to obey my words, who walk in the stubbornness of their hearts, and follow strange gods to serve and adore them, shall be like this loincloth which is good for nothing. For, as close as the loincloth clings to a man's loins, so had I made the whole house of Israel and the whole house of Judah cling to me, says the LORD; to be my people, my renown, my praise, my beauty. But they did not listen (Jer. 13:8-11).

The meaning of a person's or a community's life is the plan God has for that life. What is striking about the revelation that came to Jeremiah is the profound intimacy with God into which the community of Israel was called. God was calling the people of Israel not to be his slaves but "to be my people, my renown, my praise, my beauty," to enter with him into a union so intimate that the only

78

imagery approaching adequacy is sexual. Such sexual imagery is to be found elsewhere in the Old Testament, especially in the writings of prophets Isaiah, Ezekiel, Amos, Hosea and in the Song of Songs. With Hosea commenced the tradition of presenting the relationship of Yahweh and Israel as that of husband and wife:

> On that day, says the LORD,
> She shall call me "My husband,"
>   and never again "My baal."
> I will espouse you to me forever:
>   I will espouse you in right and in
>   justice,
>   in love and in mercy;
> I will espouse you in fidelity,
>   and you shall know the LORD (Hos. 2:18, 21, 22).

The word for "know" in the Hebrew is *yādá,* a word which, like the English, can have sexual connotations: "Now Adam knew *(yādá)* Eve his wife, and she conceived and bore Cain" (Gen. 4:1).

The theme of knowing the Lord and being known by him is carried over into the New Testament, an example of which is Matthew's account of the closing days of Jesus' ministry. In the parable of the wise and foolish virgins, the foolish virgins have gone to buy oil for their lamps when the bridegroom enters and the door is shut:

> Later the other bridesmaids came back. "Master, master!" they cried. "Open the door for us." But he answered, "I tell you, I do not know you" (Mt. 25:11-12).

While it is important to know the Lord, for the believing Jew or Christian it is even more important to be known by him.

The vital question then becomes: who is known by the Lord? The teaching of the Old Testament on this point is clear: the being in the womb is capable of being known by God and of entering into an intimate relation with God through the unilateral action of God's providential love.

> The word of the LORD came to me thus:
> Before I formed you in the womb I knew you,
>   before you were born I dedicated you,
>   a prophet to the nations I appointed you (Jer. 1:4-5).

> Truly you have formed my inmost being;
>   you knit me in my mother's womb.
> I give you thanks that I am fearfully,

> wonderfully made;
>   wonderful are your works.
> My soul also you knew full well;
>   nor was my frame unknown to you
> when I was made in secret,
>   when I was fashioned in the depths of the earth.
> Your eyes have seen my actions;
>   in your book they are all written;
>   my days were limited before one of them existed
>   (Ps. 139:13-16).

The teaching of the Bible, then, is twofold: (1) that the most important thing that can be said about human beings is that they are capable of knowing, and being known by their Creator, that is, capable of entering into an intimate relationship of love with their God, and (2) that this capability is, in some sense, already present in the womb. A newborn child is brought into the circle of the family and enters into a relationship of love with each parent even before the infant is capable of responding to that love and loving in return. Indeed, it is the fact of being loved already that permits and fosters the child's growth into a mature and loving person. "I say that we are wound/With mercy round and round/ As if with air," wrote Gerard Manley Hopkins (1948).

The clear teaching of the bible is that the unborn child is as "visible" to God as is the adult, "For you darkness itself is not dark, and night shines as the day" (Ps. 139:12). The Old and New Testaments are not concerned to answer or even to ask philosophical questions about the precise instant of ensoulment since such implied dualism is not part of biblical anthropology. But we may infer from what they teach that there is something fundamentally wrong with any approach to the human that grounds the transcendent worth of human beings in social acceptance, human perfection, intellectual capability, or mature independence. A right approach will base the worth of human beings on a reality intrinsic to them, on a given which ultimately comes from God.

Suffering and on Being Human

The meaning of human existence is given by saying that human beings are capable of loving and being loved by God, that the human world is infected by sin, and that through Christ's death and resurrection humanity has been redeemed and receives the power to overcome sin in this world. It is in the light of these truths that suffering takes on meanings; as a result of sin, and as a means of redemption, Christ is the "Man of Sorrows," so that any complete understanding of the human must embody an appreciation of the New Testament's message of the life, suffering, death, and resurrection of Jesus Christ. Indeed, these are part of any total Christian definition of the human. But to understand properly that New Testament message we need to see how the Old Testament perceived suffering.

A concise summary of Old Testament reflections on suffering is conveniently provided by a scriptural writer (Cleary, 1974). Suffering as seen by the Old Testament writers can be grouped under eight headings. They interpret suffering to be:

1. Mysterious — Without God's revelation suffering is utterly meaningless to mere mortals (see the Book of Job)
2. Illusory or transitory — It is only for the moment because the Lord will come to save (see, e.g., Psalms, 41, 57, 107)
3. Retributive — Humans choose their own destiny for ultimately blessing comes to the good and punishment to the evil (see Deuteronomy, 30: 19ff).
4. Disciplinary and educational — Suffering can lead a person to God and to practice virtues such as humility and compassion (see Proverbs, 3:11ff)
5. Probationary and evidential — Patiently enduring suffering reveals one to be a true disciple of God (see Psalm 73)
6. Revelational — Suffering can reveal something of God's nature insofar as it is the absence of some good or order (see Hosea, 1-3)
7. Sacrificial — Suffering can be a means of reconciliation with God (Isaiah, 40-55)
8. Eschatological — Accepted in faith, suffering contributes to the coming of the eschaton when God brings forth final deliverance (see Daniel, Isaiah, 4-27)

These insights of the Old Testament are reinforced and clarified by the teachings and life of Jesus. Various books of the New Testament speak of suffering in numerous passages. On one occasion Jesus designates the power of Satan as a source of some suffering (Lk. 13:10-17; similarly Paul in 2 Cor. 12:7; see also Acts 10:38). Suffering can be, but need not be a medicinal punishment for sins. According to Lk. 13:1-6, when Jesus encounters special cases of misfortune he sees them on the one hand as punishment that is deserved and on the other as a warning to others. But according to Jn. 9:1, we should not inquire about the cause of the suffering of the man born blind, but rather its purpose. It is an opportunity for the works of God to be made manifest. The Jewish idea that sickness can be the result of sin and so punishment finds expression in one passage of Paul (1 Cor. 11:30-32). But both Jesus (Lk. 16:19-31) and the New Testament in general deny altogether the prevailing doctrine of the Pharisees that all suffering is retribution for sin.

In order to understand the attitude of Jesus and of the New Testament writers towards suffering, we must take as our starting point the Old Testament reflection on suffering and the reality of Jesus' own suffering and what he has to say about it. His messianic work consisted of suffering in manifold forms. Jesus has neither home (Mt. 8:20; Lk. 9:57), nor family (Mk. 3:31-5), and as he journeys through villages and towns of Galilee the works he there performs are exhausting. Yet he encounters a complete absence of understanding on the part of people and bitter hostility from their leaders. The result is widespread rejection and death on the cross. He has not only predicted this, but even emphasized that it is in accord with the will of God (Mk. 8:31, 9:31, 10:33, 14:21; Lk. 13:24f.). He is the suffering servant of God, who must lay down his life on behalf of the many (Mk. 10:45; Lk. 22:17). It is through suffering that he must enter into his glory (Lk. 24:26). And just as suffering belongs to Jesus' own fate, so it belongs to the life of his disciples. To be a disciple is to follow him in his suffering. It is to carry the cross after Jesus (Mk. 8:34ff; Mt. 10:38; Lk. 14:27). It is to tear oneself away from the most cherished human ties (Mt. 8:19-22; Lk 9:57-62). Being a disciple implies a renunciation of life's enjoyments, of worldly esteem and repute (Mt. 10:43f). It entails slander and hatred and persecution and even death as its consequences (Mk. 13:1-13), and for this reason demands self-denial to the point of laying down one's life (Mk. 8:34; Mt. 10:39; Lk. 17:33; Jn. 12:24f). Blessed is the disciple whom the Lord finds worthy to follow him even to a martyr's death (Jn. 11:28f.)! Only persons who lose their lives for Jesus' sake will save them (Mk. 8:35). Jesus has come to bring division upon the earth, to introduce discord even into families (Lk. 12:49, Mt. 10:34-36), and this because he compels humans to decide whether they are for him or against him.

The reason for this manifold suffering consists primarily in the condition of fallen human nature for which the gospel is a scandal and a folly, and which therefore hates and persecutes Jesus' disciples even as it hated and persecuted Jesus himself. But this persecution and suffering, although in no way willed by God, is nevertheless included by him within his divine plan. It is precisely for this reason that the cross which the disciples must carry after Jesus is also the mark of election, and therefore reason for joy. Jesus pronounces those blessed who suffer slanders, calumnies, and persecutions for his sake (Mt. 5:11f; Lk. 6:22f.).

The passion of Jesus represents a special problem not confined merely to early Christian apologetics, for in it the element of the divine is wholly hidden under weakness and deepest degradation. Here suffering becomes the problem of Christology. What took place on Good Friday was not only a stumbling block to Jews and a folly to Gentiles (1 Cor. 1:23), but has appeared to his disciples also as incomprehensible and shocking. (See Mk. 8:31-3.) In order to overcome this shock to faith, Paul views the passion in connection with the resurrection (1 Cor. 15:3f), and then, connecting it further with Jesus' own words concerning the fact that his suffering is in accord with the will of God, goes on to explain it in the light of Old Testament prophecies. For the Jews who demand signs (proofs of divine power), and for the Greeks who seek wisdom, the preaching of Jesus crucified is indeed folly; but for those who are called it is precisely in him that the power and wisdom of God stand revealed (1 Cor. 1:22-4). While his human adversaries thought that they had vanquished Christ, in reality it was God who had "delivered him up" (Acts 2:23, 3:13-18, 4:10, 5:30f., 13:27-30; Rom. 4:25, 8:32) and thereby made atonement for the world through him (2 Cor. 5:19).

The words of Jesus concerning the necessity of suffering are echoed throughout the life of the faithful. The Jewish idea is also present that suffering is a means of divine chastisement or discipline (Heb. 12:4-11; Rev. 3:19), that it is a test by which the believer must prove himself (Rom. 5:3f.; 1 Pet. 1:7), and for this reason the Christians should rejoice over their suffering. The many sufferings which the Christians encounter are endured "for the sake of the name of Jesus" (Acts 5:41), and in imitation of his example (Heb. 12:1f., 1 Pet. 2:20f.). Suffering falls especially upon preachers of the gospel (Acts 9:16). God has "set them in the world as the last of all, like gladiators sentenced to death" so that they have become a spectacle for the world, for men, and for angels (1 Cor. 4:9ff.). But Paul not only suffers *like* Christ, in accordance with his example (1 Pet. 2:20f.), and *for* him, that is for the sake of Christ (2 Cor. 4:11); he also suffers *with* him (Rom. 6:3ff.). His sufferings proceed from the fact that he "exists in Christ." In what he has to endure day by day he continually bears the death of Jesus in his own body (2 Cor. 4:10). Because in baptism, as Paul says in Rom. 6:2f., he has died with Christ and risen to a new life, he can and must also "become like Christ in his death" (Phil. 3:10). In suffering he takes the cross of Christ upon himself (Gal. 6:14), experiences what it is to have a share in the sufferings of Christ (Phil. 3:10). Therefore, he can call his sufferings "the sufferings of Christ" (2 Cor. 1-5, Phil. 3:10, Col. 1:24) and the marks of the wounds which have been inflicted upon him in the exercise of his apostolic ministry, the marks of the wounds of Jesus (Gal. 6:17).

Suffering brings Christians to an awareness of their own weakness and guards them against the presumption of relying on their own strength instead of the strength of God (2 Cor. 1:9, 12:7). But Paul also knows that he does not suffer as an isolated individual for himself alone. The sufferings which come upon him are for the benefit of the Church, not only because they cannot be thought of apart from his work as an apostle (2 Cor. 11:23-9) and because he, having been consoled by God in his sufferings, can also console others (2 Cor. 1:4-7), but also because they contribute directly to the salvation of the Church, the formation of the body of Christ (Col. 1:24). If death is at work in Paul, this is in order that life may be at work in others (2 Cor. 4:12-16), and because it has this significance for him he has overcome suffering inwardly. So far as he is concerned, suffering no longer represents any problem of theodicy, nor is there any element of harsh compulsion in it. Rather it is a grace (Phil. 1:20; see also 1 Pet. 2:20), so that he can say: "I rejoice in my sufferings" (Col. 1:24). This does not mean that he is in any sense merely a Stoic who meets the afflictions that come upon him with the strength of some unassailable human calmness. On the contrary, he is acutely aware of the reality of suffering and experiences it for what it really is; but the strength which preserves him from breaking under the burden of his sufferings is the strength of Christ who lives in him.

For Paul, as for the New Testament writers in general (Acts 14:22; 1 Pet. 4:13; Heb. 2:10; 2 Tim. 2:11f.), the sufferings of the present moment are surpassed by the future glory, "provided we suffer with him in order that we may also be glorified with him" (Rom. 8:17). Viewed in the light of the glory that is to come, Paul's present sufferings seem to him "not worthy of mention" (Rom. 8:18), "For this slight momentary affliction is preparing us for an eternal weight of glory beyond all comparison. Because we look not to the things that are seen, but to the things that are unseen. For the things that are seen are transient, but the things that are unseen are external" (Cor. 4:17). The glory to be revealed in us is at present only dimly discerned. The Christian does not fully understand what purposes God has in permitting sufferings to occur, but he waits in hope, confident in the faith that God at last is good enough, powerful enough, and wise enough to bring greater good out of evil, "that in everything God works for good with those who love him, who are called according to his purpose" (Rom. 8:28).

The Contemporary Magisterial Teachings Concerning the Human

The concept of what it means to be a human person has received much attention in the official Church teachings in the recent past, and perhaps it has nowhere been given a more precise formulation than that developed by Vatican II in its document, *Pastoral Constitution on the Church in the Modern World* (Vatican II, 1965b), previously referred to in Chapter 5. The Council did not attempt to restate a definition of human life in the static philosophical terms of body-soul entity; rather, the Council presented a mosaic of the characteristics of human nature formulated in a dynamic understanding of personhood and history. The Council speaks of the fundamental unity of the person. By stressing the inseparable unity of the person, the Council strives to avoid any dualism. Body and spirit exist as one, constituting, sustaining, influencing and penetrating one another. To be a person, then, is to be an incarnated spirit. Though there exists a profound unity of body and spirit, the person is completely identified with the body. Consequently, there is an ambiguity in the midst of unity, for human beings possess a certain interiority which is the specific dimension of human life separating persons from others (see Vatican II, 1965b, #14)*. This interiority is specified, first of all, as intellect which seeks the truth and is perfected by wisdom (#15); secondly, as

---

*All subsequent references in this chapter to this document will cite only the paragraph number.

85

conscience which directs an individual toward the good (see #16); and thirdly, as freedom which makes self-direction possible (see #17). It is the aspect of interiority that sets human life apart from other material realities, and thus there is a tension between the bodily and the spiritual aspects of the person. In reflecting on this, one author (Christian, 1975, p. 246) has said:

> For, while man is his body, he shares his material bodiliness with all creatures whereas his interiority is his alone. His ability to know in self-consciousness and in rational reflection, his ability to discover values, his ability to choose one value over another, his capacity to direct himself into his own future, his ability to love others even more than he loves himself, all of these are what make man the unique creature he is, and, while these abilities and capacities do not exist in man in a disembodied way and even depend on the body for their operation, yet neither can they be reduced to the materiality which man shares with other created beings.

In the *Church in the Modern World,* the Fathers of the Vatican Council were especially concerned with emphasizing a number of basic values. These may be grouped under three major headings:

1. The dignity of the human being made in the image of God
2. The progress of human society as part of God's plan
3. The primacy of moral values

Accordingly, the relevant magisterial teaching will be discussed under these three topics.

The Dignity of Human Being Made in the Image of God

The first of the basic values centers around the sublime dignity of the human person as created in the image and likeness of God and raised to an undreamt-of status through the Incarnation of Christ (see ##26, 12, 22).

The human person stands above all other things in the created universe; a person's rights and duties are inviolable; all organizations, institutions, and social conditions ought ultimately to work for the person's good. "He ought, therefore, to have ready access to all that is necessary for living a genuinely human life: for example, food, clothing, housing, the right freely to choose his state of life and set up a family, the right to education, work, to his good name, to respect, to proper knowledge, the right to act according to the dictates of conscience and to safeguard his privacy, and rightful freedom even in matters of religion" (#26).

The source of the person's dignity comes to humans from Someone outside of themselves. "For sacred Scripture teaches that man was created 'to the image of God,' as able to know and love his creator, and as set by him over all earthly creatures that he might rule them, and make use of them, while glorifying God" (#12). Furthermore, God did not create human beings as solitary creatures but, rather, made them for one another. "God created man in his image; in the divine image he created him; male and female he created them" (Gen. 1:27). From the very beginning God created the partnership of man and woman as the first form of community between persons. "For by his innermost nature man is a social being and if he does not enter into relations with others he can neither live nor develop his gifts" (#12).

The human person is aware that he or she is more than simply a body among other bodies. "Man is not deceived when he regards himself as superior to bodily things and as more than just a speck of nature or a nameless unit in the city of man" (#14). Humans recognize that they possess immortal life as a gift. God has created human beings with a destiny transcending the limits of their earthly life, for God has created them to be with him forever. "Let all be convinced that human life and its transmission are realities whose meaning is not limited by the horizons of this life only: their true evaluation and full meaning can only be understood in reference to man's eternal destiny" (#51). Faced with the reality of death, humans are able to affirm that death does not mean the complete loss of personality. The faithful man or woman is able to have confidence that death will be at last swallowed up by the divine life that knows no death, suffering, or decay. This confidence of the Christian is based on faith in Christ who by his death and rising again has freed us from the tyranny of death. "Faith, therefore, with its solidly based teaching, provides every thoughtful man with an answer to his anxious queries about his future lot. At the same time it makes him able to be united in Christ with his loved ones who have already died, and gives hope that they have found true life in God" (#18). Thus it is the mystery of the Incarnate God that the mystery of the human person becomes clear. "For Adam, the first man, was a type of him who was to come, Christ the Lord. Christ the new Adam, in the very revelation of the mystery of the Father and of his love, fully reveals man to himself and brings to light his most high calling" (#22). Human nature, united with Christ, has been raised to a dignity beyond compare. His life provides us with meaning for our own. "By suffering for us he not only gave us an example so that we might follow in his footsteps, but he also opened a way. If we follow this path, life and death are made holy and acquire a new meaning" (#18).

The Progress of Human Society as Part of God's Plan

The second group of values taught by the Vatican Council clusters around the truth that since the world was created good and humankind must be of great importance (see ##34, 39). Individual and collective activity to improve the circumstances of the world is in accordance with the plan of God. Humans were created to rule the world and all it contains with justice and holiness, to acknowledge God as the creator, and to relate themselves and the totality of creation to the creator so that the name of God might be praised through all the earth. Thus, even daily tasks are elevated and made part of the divine plan. In their service to their community, human beings may see themselves as carrying on the work of the creator, "their personal contribution to the fulfillment in history of the divine plan" (#34). The conquests achieved through human intelligence and effort are by no means opposed to God's power. "Christians ought to be convinced that the achievements of the human race are a sign of God's greatness and the fulfillment of his mysterious design" (#34). Earthly progress, therefore, should be of vital concern to the members of the Kingdom of God, for such progress can be a means of producing a better human society. Growth in knowledge not only serves to improve the human condition but it also produces a corresponding growth and improvement in human beings themselves, deepening their faculties and increasing their self-awareness. Thus, the gradual discovery and exploitation of the laws of matter and society are good. "By the very nature of creation, material being is endowed with its own stability, truth and excellence, its own order and laws. These men must respect as he recognizes the methods proper to every science and technique" (#36). There should be no fear, then, that the advances of scientific understanding and control are in any way contrary to the faith, providing that they are carried out in accordance with sound moral principles.

This last point is eloquently explored by Pope John Paul II in his initial encyclical, *Redeemer of Man:*

The development of technology and the development of contemporary civilization, which is marked by the ascendancy of technology, demand a proportional development of morals and ethics. For the present, this last development seems unfortunately to be always left behind. Accordingly, in spite of the marvel of this progress, in which it is difficult not to see also authentic signs of man's greatness, signs that in their creative seeds were revealed to us in the pages of the Book of Genesis, as early as where it describes man's creation, this progress cannot fail to give rise to disquiet on many counts. The first reason for disquiet concerns the essential and fundamental question: Does this progress, which has man for its author and promoter, make human life on earth "more human" in every aspect of that life? Does it make it more "worthy of man"? There can be no doubt that in various aspects it does. But the question keeps coming back with regard to what is most essential — whether in the context of this progress man, as man, is becoming truly better, that is to say more mature spiritually, more aware of the dignity of his humanity, more responsible, more open to others, especially the neediest and the weakest, and readier to give and to aid all (John Paul II, 1979, #15).

The Primacy of Moral Values

Clearly, then, advances in science and technology point to the need to affirm a third set of values, moral values in a world infected by sin (see ##13, 15, 16). Sacred Scripture teaches that although God created man and woman in a state of freedom and justice, they misused his freedom, rebelled against God, and attempted to attain his goals in opposition to the will of the creator. This teaching is confirmed by experience. By refusing to recognize the obedience owed to God, men and women have also upset the proper relationship with other humans and with nature. "Man therefore is divided in himself. As a result, the whole life of man, both individual and social, shows itself to be a struggle, and a dramatic one, between good and evil, between light and darkness. Man finds that he is unable of himself to overcome the assaults of evil successfully, so that everyone feels as though bound by chains" (#13). Thus, although material progress and increasing scientific knowledge and control are most desirable, they must be achieved in a way that acknowledges the human person's proper relation to the creator. But as knowledge increases, so do temptations to misuse that knowledge. "The great advantages of human progress are fraught with grave temptations: the hierarchy of values has been disordered, good and evil intermingle, and every man and every group is interested only in its own affairs, not in those of others" (#37). The attempt by man to set himself up in opposition to God and thus to assure man's dignity is a "way leading to the extinction of human dignity, not its preservation" (#41).

Human beings are implicitly aware of these fundamental values. By their intellect they have been able to make great strides in the empirical sciences, in technology, and in the liberal arts. But humans have also always sought for and found truths of a higher order. The human mind is not confined to the knowledge of those things that can be apprehended through the senses. "The intellectual nature of man finds at last its perfection, as it should, in wisdom, which gently draws the human mind to look for and love what is true and good. Filled with wisdom man is led through visible realities to those which cannot be seen" (#15).

> For man finds within his heart a moral law inscribed by God. His dignity lies in observing this law, and by it he will be judged. His conscience is man's most secret core, and his sanctuary. There he is alone with God whose voice echoes in his depths. By conscience, in a wonderful way, that law is made known which is fulfilled in the love of God and neighbor. Through loyalty to conscience Christians are joined to other men in the search for truth and for the right solution to so many moral problems which arise both in the life of individuals and from social relationships (#16).

It is only in freedom that man can turn himself towards what is good. Freedom is highly valued in our day, and rightly so, but human freedom correctly understood does not mean the license to do anything man wishes.

But that which is truly freedom is an exceptional sign of the image of God in the human person.

> For God willed that man should be left in the hand of his own counsel so that he might be of his own accord seek his creator and freely obtain his full and blessed perfection by cleaving to him. Man's dignity therefore requires him to act out of conscious and free choice, as moved and drawn in a personal way from within, and not by blind impulses in himself or by mere external constraint. Man gains such dignity when, ridding himself of all slavery to the passions, he presses forward to his goal by freely choosing what is good, and, by his diligence and skill, effectively secures for himself the means suited to this end (#17).

The emphasis placed on the human person means that everyone must look upon one's neighbor as another self, and this requires attending to the means required for that neighbor's living in a dignified way. Special responsibilities extend to the weak and defenseless: the more dependent they are on others, the more weighty are the obligations to them. "I assure you, as often you did it for one of my least brothers, you did it for me" (Mt. 25:40). Abortion, euthanasia, and willful suicide are "criminal: they poison civilization; and they debase the perpetrators more than the victims and militate against the honor of the creator" (#27). "God, the Lord of life, has entrusted to men the noble mission of safeguarding life, and men must carry it out in a manner worthy of themselves. Life must be protected from the moment of conception: abortion and infanticide are abominable crimes" (#51).

Earlier noted it was that the Council recognizes the truth that man finds himself unable to overcome evil, that everyone feels as though bound by chains. But the document continues: "But the Lord himself came to free and strengthen man, renewing him inwardly, and casting out the 'prince of this world' (Jn. 12:31), who hold him in the bondage of sin" (#13). All of human history has been a story of struggle with evil. It is with God's grace and at much cost to themselves that they are able to achieve their own inner integrity. The Church listens to the words of the apostle Paul, "Do not conform yourselves to this age but be transformed by the renewal of your mind, so that you may judge what is God's will, what is good, pleasing, and perfect" (Rom. 12:2). This renewal is made possible only because human activities are purified and perfected by the cross and resurrection of Christ. "Redeemed by Christ and made a new creature by the Holy Spirit, man can, indeed he must, love the things of God's creation" (#37). Christ revealed that God is love, and that the fundamental law of human perfection and the basis for transforming the world resides in Christ's commandment of love for one another (see #38).

These points might be summarized by saying that human life implies a person created by God, in the image of God, for God. It implies the capacity for self-awareness and self-transcendence; it implies a capacity and responsibility to interact with the world and with others; it implies the capacity for and responsibility to know the truth and to seek the good in freedom; it implies that individuals live in a state of tension between good and evil, between success and failure, and between the desire for growth and expansion and the fear of limitation and termination; and finally it implies the possibility of sharing fully in the life of Christ, "the New Man."

Christian Personalism

In the opening section of this chapter, we saw that the feature that best characterizes human existence is that the human being is capable of both knowing the Lord and being known by him. This concept is elaborated upon in recent studies of the theme of Christian personalism. While the central importance of the human person was long recognized by Christian thought, the prevalent scholastic analysis had proceeded on the basis that human nature could be objectively and adequately known by a study of human behavior. Many contemporary theologians, variously influenced by a perspective of existencial philosophy, look to man's subjective life for a deeper understanding of human personhood.

Thus, beginning simply from the standpoint of human experience, contemporary personalism suggests that the phrase that best characterizes human existence is openness to the world (Scheler, 1961). Unlike animals, human beings are not limited to particular environments but are ever open to new experiments and possibilities. Humanity compares itself with the animal world and discovers that human nature is not equipped with an innate instinctual system or specific pattern of behavior. Rather, humanity has the capacity for conscious activity, the ability to create cultures and the creative power and imagination to raise itself up in freedom. These creative powers, however, should not be seen as the only distinctive feature of human beings.

Human life is characterized by openness that goes beyond the world of nature in creating cultures. This is humanity's destiny, but not its lasting goal. Cultures are constantly replaced because human beings are not fully satisfied with their own creations. There is a driving force in human life which moves us beyond our achievements toward a seemingly undefined goal. There is an inner impulse which moves humanity beyond every stage that has already been attained. This dynamic thrust implies a dependence on something. Just as animals are driven by instinctual impulses to acquire food because they are dependent on food for survival, so we can say that the drive or thrust in human life must also be dependent on something. Because human life is characterized by a need that is not satisfied, humanity appears to be dependent on something outside itself, indicating an infinite dependence that presupposes "a corresponding, infinite, never-ending, other-worldly being" (Pannenburg, 1970). We give meaning to the expression "openness to the world" by stating that the infinite being upon which we depend is God.

We may also speak of this dynamic character of human life as self-transcendence. There is a continual movement beyond the self which is not a mere option for an individual to accept or to refuse. Rather it is a central part of what it means to be human. As Scheler (1974) says:

"Man" in this new sense is the intention and gesture of "transcendence" itself; he is the being that prays and seeks God. We do not say "man prays", but rather "he is the prayer of life transcending itself." We do not say "he seeks God" but rather "he is the living seeker of God.". . . God is the sea and men are the rivers, and from their original gushing forth from their origin the rivers are aware of the sea toward which they are flowing.

As a self-transcending being, the human person is not only spiritual but exists as a unity, as an incarnate spirit. The body is essential to personal existence in relation with the world, with others, and with God. The body is essential to the person because it is through the flesh that an individual relates to the world as one who controls and gives direction to created realities. Outside of the body, or separated from one's flesh, there is a loss of one's identity as a master of the world. The body is also a means of personal disclosure through which an individual reveals the self to others. Inasmuch as the person is identified with gestures, physical appearances, countenance, details of speech, etc., an individual is said not only to have a body but *to be* one's body. The flesh is also the means by which the world is revealed to the person. Only insofar as the person, in bodilyness, is vulnerable, sensitive, and susceptible, can the word disclose itself in its diversity and splendor. Professor Louis Janssens (1970) has said:

The exercise of our intentionality — our relationship with the world, with others, with God — is deeply affected by our bodily condition. The body is a necessary medium for all our relationships; as such, it makes them possible, but imposes limits on them. It is necessary, for instance, if another person is to become aware of my love, that I incarnate this love in objective elements — signs, gifts, favors, etc. — and the medium of this incarnation is my body, and through it the realities of the world. For a community to render worship to God there must be the mediation of the body and of external realities, so that the members of the community might participate.

Every person shares in the qualities of openness to the world, transcendence of self, and "bodilyness." This gives every human being a certain equality; but we must also say that every human person is unique and original. This originality is revealed especially in a relationship of love. The one who loves actually perceives more value and originality than others who do not love. The person who loves is concerned with the dynamic growth of the unique and original other who is encountered in relationship. As individuals called and loved by God, human persons are addressed in their uniqueness and in the totality of their beings — actual and potential. Each person is called to become what he or she is (Janssens, 1970).

Each person has particular tendencies, potentialities, talents, and characteristics that are developed according to the uniqueness of the individual. These develop into a unique personality, an irreplaceable human being. Every human being exists in a life-long situation which is unique, which cannot be repeated, and for which there is no substitute. As Abraham Heschel (1965) says:

> Being human is a novelty — not a mere repetition or extension of the past, but an anticipation of things to come. Being human is a surprise, not a foregone conclusion. A person has a capacity to create events. Every person is a disclosure, an example of exclusiveness.

Being human means that an individual exists in historical reality. As a person, an individual is related to other human beings in time and in community. But these relationships are in a constant process of change. By nature, humanity is historical, each person living in an interconnected series of events. This series of events is made up of individual concrete decisions and experiences, as well as those things that happen to a given person or group. Each life history is unique and open to the future, particularly as an openness to God. Yet this life history is not isolated from others, but completely interwoven with the history of other individuals and the community. The community also has its own historical movement which marks the individuality of a people, nation, or culture (see Pannenburg, 1970 and Janssens, 1970).

This dynamic view of the human person cannot be ignored in the moral evaluation of human actions. However, Christian theologians cannot accept an absolute autonomy of the human person in the creation of value or establishing the goodness or evil of human actions. They recognize a moral order to which all human persons belong by reason of their creatureliness. From this order flow general principles of justice and morality which bind human persons with moral obligation in the exercise of their gift of freedom. Hence each person must attempt to find the right human action in the individual and unique situation of every free choice. The individual circumstances and the motive of action can never be ignored because they enter into the concrete reality of that action.

Christian theology insists upon the reality of sin and guilt. It teaches that human persons can and do perform wrong actions knowingly and willingly. Hence the subjective decisions in individual human situations, while truly creative and truly independent, are made in the context of principles and values which persons accept or reject. Catholic moral theology has studied and articulated these principles and values throughout its long history. One such principle, the inviolability of innocent human life, has stimulated the long and historic concern of the Church for the evil of direct induced abortion. Another principle, the inviolability of the procreative potential of conjugal intercourse, has stimulated the long and historic concern of the Church for the evils of direct contraception and sterilization.

In the serious efforts to re-examine the historic moral teaching of the Church which began with the Second Vatican Council the universal and exceptionless binding force of prohibitive moral principles such as the two just mentioned has been challenged. The question has been asked, cannot mitigating circumstances and good intentions sometimes provide exceptions to these moral prohibitions?

A terminology has developed which characterizes violations of these principles as ontic evil or premoral evil. The reason for such terms is that this newer theological analysis admits the possibility that these actions may not be morally evil in certain limited situations. To some degree this approach flows from the dynamism of the Christian personalism just reviewed. In this approach human persons may in some sense rise above the ontic evil in specific situations of responsible decision making. This approach goes beyond the past concessions of Catholic moral theology which traditionally held that objective evil may not always be subjectively culpable, or that a material sin may not be a formal sin.

Rather, in this approach, on the basis of the circumstances and intention of the human person, the actions of contraception or abortion may not, as physical actions, deserve the appellation of "moral evil." The ontic or premoral evil may be overcome by the strength of the particular values the person achieves in the action. Hence in this approach no human action should be called "intrinsically evil" and the term "moral evil" can only be applied to actions in which proportionate values do not overcome the ontic evil inherent in the action.

substitute *omit* [This approach developed in the late 1960s, as some Catholic] lead to total relativism and subjectivism in morality. If the approach is used within the context of a wise and prudent consensus of responsible moralists concerning which values might overcome ontic evil, it may offer only a few exceptions, as, for example, by offering very limited exceptions to the universal evil of abortion.

This approach developed in the late 1960s as some Catholic moralists sought to mitigate the rigid binding force of universal negative prohibitions, often called moral absolutes, as presented in the Catholic tradition of natural moral law. The application of their methodology to justifying the use of contraception for the sake of conjugal love and spontaneity found wide sympathy and support. Major authors who have developed this methodology include Peter Knauer (1967), Josef Fuchs (1963, 1971), Bruno Schüller (1973), Charles E. Curran, (1968, 1969, 1974, 1975, 1978a, 1978b), and Richard McCormick (1972, 1973a, 1973b, 1974, 1976, 1977, 1978, 1979). Timothy E. O'Connell (1976), used it in his textbook on fundamental Catholic moral theology and Philip S. Keane (1977) used it in his book on Catholic sexual morality — or so it would seem.

On the other hand, some Catholic moralists have strongly criticized this methodology as reducing the teleology of the Catholic understanding of natural moral law to a form of consequentialist calculus. Major authors who have raised this criticism include Germain Grisez (1964, 1970a, 1970b, 1974, 1978, 1979), William E. May (1975, 1977, 1979), John Connery (1973, 1977, 1978, 1979), Benedict Ashley (1976, 1978), and Kevin O'Rourke (1976, 1978).

96

Authors on both sides of this dispute respect the mystery of human personhood and the creativeness of human moral choices. Those in the new approach, sometimes called proportionalism, appeal to the autonomy of the person in making a responsible moral judgment even though directly willing ontic evil. Those who reject the new approach argue that human persons are not morally free to choose ontic evil. They maintain that while human persons might readily judge that justifying circumstances and good intentions outweigh ontic evil, such judgments do not change the nature of the ontic evil and the act which embraces it.

The authentic magisterial teaching of the Church has not embraced the new approach just described. Church teaching continues to condemn without qualification the actions of abortion, contraception, and sterilization. The "Declaration on Abortion" in 1974 said, for example, "it is objectively a grave sin to dare to risk murder" (#13). The U.S. Bishops' Pastoral on Moral Values in 1976 reiterated the core teaching of *Humanae Vitae,* "the wrongness of such an act [contraception] lies in the rejection of this value [procreation]" (NCCB, 1976, p. 18)

This firm magisterial teaching need not be interpreted as a rejection of personalism. The Second Vatican Council's treatment of marriage (Vatican II, 1965b, ##47-52) and the encyclical, *Humanae Vitae,* both incorporate a new and attractive version of personalism in their approaches to marriage and human sexuality. The magisterial teaching continues, though, to insist upon the nature of the human person and the nature of human sexual activity as normative for individual and personal moral judgements. Hence, even the serious problems raised by genetic defects cannot be resolved, according to magisterial teaching, by resort to abortion, contraception, or sterilization.

Summary

This consideration of Christian Personalism concludes Part II. Chapter 3 presented, briefly, an overview of the changes — largely due to the impact of science — that have taken place in the human self-image. Three different ways of defining the constitutive characteristics of humanness were next considered. The concluding chapter essayed a view of the human derived from insights provided by Sacred Scripture and the teachings of the Magisterium.

The next chapter begins Part III — the response Christian individuals and institutions ought to make in the face of genetic disease. This response is predicated on the view of the human as sketched in Chapter 4 and is ultimately only intelligible in light of that faith the Christian has espoused. Differing responses to the moral and social issues raised by genetic diseases will be better appreciated from the perspective of the various views of the human as outlined in Chapter 3.

PART III

---

*Christian Concerns
and Responses
to Genetic Disease*

Chapter 5

Moral and Social Issues
Arising in Genetic Medicine

Introduction

The preceding two parts have been, in a sense, background discussion for Part III. The first part provided an overview of genetic medicine while the second presented the social, philosophical and theological context in which the moral issues associated with genetic medicine arise and are to be evaluated. Accordingly, Part III begins with this chapter which lays out a number of moral problems facing the individuals and institutions as a result of genetic disease.

Abortion is most frequently *the* moral problem within genetic medicine because many counselors recommend it to a woman-patient who has been diagnosed to be carrying a child with a serious genetic defect. However, abortion is only one among many issues, and we shall also briefly consider some of the others. After an examination of the arguments for and against abortion, this chapter will point up some of the moral concerns associated with genetic screening and will conclude with the particular problems presented to the parents, the counselor, and society as a whole.

Abortion

Pro-abortion Arguments

The reasons for an abortion may range from relatively trivial to most grave. Among the most serious and weighty reasons given to justify abortion are those relating to the possibility or actuality of some abnormality in the unborn child's genetic component. Concerned parties have claimed that for such reasons abortion is not only justified but perhaps even obligatory. Their arguments put forth five predominant types of considerations:

1. There are the considerations that relate to the affected child himself. The argument here is that the sufferings attendant on genetic abnormality are so great as to make the life of an affected child not worth living. It is true, as the case histories mentioned in Chapter 2 show, that the sufferings associated with severe genetic abnormality are some of the gravest ills known. We have seen that so great is the suffering of some afflicted individuals that to some observers it appears plausible to argue that life under these conditions constitutes a wrong done the individual, a tort for which a civil suit is possible. It is said that an individual has a right to a sound physical and mental constitution, and thus that the failure to prevent the birth of a child known to be defective is a violation of that child's rights.

2. There are the welfare and the rights of a parent to be considered. These include: the severe financial and emotional strains of caring for a seriously defective child with the consequent threat to the stability of the marriage; the right of the parents to have healthy and normal children; and the right of the woman to exercise control over her own reproductive system guaranteed by the Fourteenth Amendment's concepts of personal liberty and restriction on state action. We have seen that this concern for the parents' right to healthy children becomes particularly important when there is an increasing emphasis on limiting family size owing to a greater awareness of the problem of overpopulation. If the size of the family is to be limited and the parents are to be entitled to a small number of children, then, the argument runs, they have a right to normal ones.

3. There are considerations relating to the welfare of the siblings. They are likely to be deprived of proper parental care owing to the financial and emotional burdens placed upon their parents in caring for the defective child. There is a further argument that the welfare of the normal child who would not be born if no abortion were performed ought to be taken into

consideration. If a defective child is not aborted, the child's parents may refuse to have any more children either because of fear that later children would also be defective or because the difficulty with the care of the affected child precludes the giving of proper care to any subsequent child even if it is normal. On the other hand, if the affected child is aborted, then that loss will make room for a normal one who would otherwise not have been born, so that in considering the benefits of abortion we ought not to neglect the gain of existence for the normal child.

4. There are the welfare and rights of the wider community to be considered: the tremendous strain placed upon the limited medical and financial resources of the community in caring for the severely defective child, and the right of other members of the community not to be unduly burdened by the conscious and free decisions of the parents. Furthermore, the problem of overpopulation appears not only on the level of the individual family unit but also on that of the society as a whole; for if there is only a limited number of individuals the environment can support, it would seem best that only those most capable of enjoying life be allowed to fill the available positions.

5. There is the genetic health of the species to be considered. By not aborting a child before his birth, we commit ourselves to the care of him after his birth; and this care, thanks to modern technological developments, can often not only save his life but even allow him to reach adulthood with a chance of reproducing and thus of passing on his genetic defect to his progeny. In the past, nature herself weeded out genetic defectives, and their death or serious incapacitation meant that their defect ended with them. This may have been a harsh way of preventing a serious deterioration of the gene pool, but it was effective; and unless we humanely but effectively imitate the workings of nature in this respect, our descendants will find themselves with a gravely compromised genetic endowment, the result of our well-intentioned but often misguided attempts to relieve human suffering. If we are truly concerned for the relief of human misery, the argument continues, we would do best to devote our limited economic and medical resources to the detection *in utero* of genetic disease and the

termination of those pregnancies found to be defective or to be seriously at risk, thus freeing our resources for investment in other pressing areas of human need.

These arguments on behalf of abortion for reasons of genetics are certainly powerful and are among the strongest arguments offered in support of abortion. Nonetheless, many persons would find these arguments insufficient to justify abortion. They would argue that a good end cannot justify a wrong means and that selective abortion represents a violation of our basic human responsibilities and of society's duties to its members.

Anti-abortion Responsibilities

The opponents of abortion would point to four major responsibilities in showing the moral difficulties with selective abortion:

1. The state has the duty to promote the fundamental principles of justice by providing equal protection and equal treatment for all members of society. Society's responsibility is to function as a just society in which the happiness of each of its members is deemed of equal worth and the life of each accorded equal respect. Such an attitude must be distinguished from, and in fact is opposed to, what has been called the "substitution mentality." The latter holds that killing X to replace that individual with Y is perfectly appropriate, since Y has simply been substituted for X. But the principle of justice being appealed to here would oppose such a substitution, since killing X in order to substitute Y is to treat X and Y with maximum inequality.

2. Each person has the responsibility to teach a true understanding of the value of personhood. This involves teaching by word and example that the value of the human being transcends the person's acceptance by society, that human worth cannot be measured in terms of costs and benefits to society. It is our responsibility to affirm that a human life is worthwhile even when it fails to meet particular standards of human normalcy or perfection, and that the subnormal are members of the human community just as surely as are their more fortunate brothers and sisters.

3. All have the duty to inculcate moral virtue, to encourage, and

strive for, moral growth. No virtue in our day is more neglected and in greater need of emphatic teaching than is the virtue of self-restraint. Many persons consider it old-fashioned, at the very least, to admit that although one *could* achieve one's goals *were* one willing to employ all available means, one exercises self-restraint and does not choose to employ certain means which are deemed to be morally evil. There are other virtues that go beyond what is required in strict justice: attitudes of active concern, compassion, and care for those who are less fortunate. The virtue of justice requires the equal treatment of equals; the virtue of benevolence requires that this treatment be loving, generous, and self-sacrificing.

4. Society has the responsibility to recognize limits on its power and to appreciate its proper role. The individual does not exist solely for the sake of the whole; rather, the greater society exists in order to promote the good of the individual person and of the smaller society, the family. It is the serious obligation of society, therefore, never to endanger the existence of the family structure by threatening or infringing the rights of married couples to beget and raise children according to sound moral and religious principles. Furthermore, society must strive to contribute positively to the welfare of the family by constantly seeking to preserve and promote that attitude of trust on the part of the child that is so necessary for growth to personal, moral, and spiritual maturity.

Implications of Selective Abortion

The opponents of selective abortion see it as the expression of a mentality that feels itself competent not only to make judgments about the relative worth of individual human lives but also to act upon such judgments by killing those individuals whose lives are held to be of little value. As such, abortion for reasons of genetic defect seem to the opponents of abortion to represent nothing less than an attack on what has been called "the belief in the radical moral equality of all human beings, the belief that all human beings possess equally and independent of merit certain fundamental rights, one among which, of course, is the right to life" (Kass, 1973). From the reasons given to justify selective abortion, it is possible to discern that in place of the belief in the radical moral equality of all human beings there has been substituted a belief in inequality based upon various social and individual considerations. From within this framework, an individual is to be judged in terms of a cost/benefit analysis: the cost of allowing him to live is assessed along with the projected social benefit of doing so; and unless the individual's net balance of benefit over cost is greater than a required minimum, his life is judged unworthy of preservation and his direct killing can be justified and even declared obligatory. (See Chapter 3 for a discussion of various concepts of human personhood.)

One of the most disturbing features of this cost/benefit analysis to the opponents of abortion is that all too frequently only economic considerations are brought into play: short shrift is given to a reflection about consequences that cannot be weighted in economic terms, such as the effects of the policy of selective abortion on the virtues of self-sacrifice and care. Furthermore, for the proponents of a cost/benefit approach to human worth the qualities for which a human life is judged good and worthy are such characteristics as intelligence, independence, self-direction and self-control, productiveness, and physical normalcy and attractiveness. The qualities disregarded in these considerations are the abilities to love and receive love, to trust, the virtues of courage, patience, and endurance. What is conveyed is an ideal of the perfect human being as one who is able to direct his own affairs and rely on his own abilities so that he costs his society little, one who because of his attractiveness pleases and does not trouble others or does not remind them of their mortality, one who because of his abilities can be expected to contribute to the welfare of others. The opponents of selective abortion see it as replacing the ideal of human equality with a pragmatic ideal of human perfection measured in terms of social acceptability, an ideal which has no limits and may be made more and more demanding.

Opponents of the practice of selective abortion fear that it has implications even for the lives of those who are already born. The reasons given for abortion in cases of genetic defect have a postnatal as well as a prenatal application. In some respects the arguments supporting infanticide for reasons of genetic defect are stronger than those supporting abortion: in the case of infanticide there is less risk of falsely positive or falsely negative tests, and a greater opportunity to assess the gravity of the defect. The opponents of abortion fear that if we are concerned to eliminate defective individuals, we may not restrict ourselves to killing only those whose defects were detectable and detected before birth. Post-natal accidents and disease are just as capable of destroying the normalcy of an individual and of making him unwanted and a burden on society as are prenatal difficulties: there is not one of us who is not "at risk" of being reduced to a condition similar to that of the individual with a genetic defect. The proponents of abortion view as absurd this fear of a more widespread practice of killing following from the acceptance of abortion and in this they may be correct; but the recent history of the shifting attitudes toward abortion should provide us with an object lesson in how quickly moral opinions can change. As recently as the early 1960's, opposition to abortion was widespread and seemingly unalterable. The opponents of abortion fear that changing attitudes toward abortion herald further profound changes down the road, alterations in our beliefs about the proper treatment of defective individuals of all ages. This fear may or may not be warranted, but it is indicative of the complex and far-reaching issues the practice of selective abortion raises for society.

The changes of attitudes toward abortion have been abetted by a subtle linguistic change. Terms which heretofore had a clear meaning and legitimate use suddenly have taken on a special connotation. Words like "embryo" and "fetus" which in context would have been understood to mean *"human* embryo" and *"human* fetus" without any minimizing significance, are now understood to refer to something *less* than human when referring to the "product of human conception" (another of those masking phrases), that is, to a human child. Formerly, physicians and biologists employed these terms to identify certain stages in the development of the human child (eg., "embryo" — from about 14th day to end of second month; "fetus" — from beginning of 3rd month to birth). These words did not lessen the reality of the fully human entity that came into being at the time of fertilization. As John Noonan rightly points out, these terms are now used as a kind of linguistic legerdemain to remove the humanity from the human fetus (Noonan, 1979). The intra-uterine child can be aborted with impunity because by a sinister use of words, that child no longer is a person but a thing.

Genetic Screening

The provision of a genetic screening network, as desirable as it may be, raises significant moral questions. In the first place, it seems likely that the existence of a national screening program for a wide range of diseases will increase social expectations that individuals who are at risk for being carriers will be tested for carrier status and that fetuses at risk for being affected will be antenatally diagnosed and aborted if tests are positive. A problem will arise when a prospective parent refuses to be tested or when a pregnant woman refuses to undergo antenatal diagnosis.

There are psychological burdens that may be associated with knowing that one is a carrier, and the person may feel incapable of dealing with this kind of personal information. Or, a forty-year-old woman may be aware that she is at somewhat of a risk for giving birth to an abnormal child and yet not be worried by the prospect and would not choose to abort even if she knew the child was affected. If there exists a diagnostic program designed to test such cases, and if the program has been presented to the public as a means of reducing the social costs of caring for affected children, then there arises the question of what the social attitude would be toward a person who did not choose to avail herself of the proffered services and as a result produced an affected child who consequently must be a drain on the resources of the society. Why, it may be asked, should society bear the cost of a woman's or a couple's irresponsibility? It may be suggested, for example, that medical insurance programs should not bear the costs of the genetically defective children of parents who refused the services of carrier testing, contraceptive advice, sterilization, prenatal diagnosis, or abortion (Easley and Milunsky, 1975). There is a problem, then, raised by the danger that reproductive decisions will tend to be taken out of the hands of the couple and placed in those of the state. What is at stake is the moral issue of whether the state should have the right to make such reproductive decisions for families.

If the existence of a screening program may lead to social intolerance of those who choose not to enter such a program, it may likewise lead to an increased intolerance of those born defective. The claim is asserted or implied that without such a program, a large number of affected children will be born. It is hoped that by the program's introduction this number will be significantly reduced. But individuals with genetic defects will still be born: spontaneous mutations will continue to occur, many diseases will remain untestable, some parents will refuse to enter the program, there will be instances of falsely negative diagnoses, etc. Genetically defective individuals will become more rare, but they will not disappear; and as they become more uncommon it seems reasonable to fear that society may grow even less tolerant of the abnormal and imperfect. As long as there is no widespread detection program, being born defective is simply a most unfortunate occurrence; but with such a program, being born defective becomes somebody's fault. Thus, the affected individual may go through life not only carrying the burden of a genetic defect but also as one whose very existence is held to be the result of culpable negligence. A person's recognition that society blames his parents for having him would be an awesome awareness, and could not have but a profound effect on his appreciation of himself.

The proposed program of a nation-wide system of screening and diagnosis could also have a serious effect on the self-awareness of those who are normal, those for whom the prenatal tests were negative. Such a person would know that he is alive only because he is not defective. He would be aware that his parents would have aborted him had he been less than perfect. He would possess the realization that he was accepted not simply for what he was, this unborn child, but partially because he met certain standards. It might be objected that the child need not know this, need not be told about his being tested prenatally. Certainly it would be possible to keep this fact from many, but it could not be kept from all. The national program would still exist, knowledge of it would become commonplace, and later pregnancies would continue to be diagnosed.

Another moral issue to be raised is the problem of discrimination. One of the most common uses of the technology of screening programs has been to detect carriers of sickle-cell anemia, a disease confined almost exclusively to blacks. Many members of the black community in this country have questioned why the stigma of genetic disease should be placed on them (Whitten and Frischhoff, 1974). There are at least three replies that are pertinent. First, screening programs for other groups have been proposed or implemented, such as tests for Tay-Sachs and PKU. Second, the sickle-cell anemia program was developed simply because there are available tests for carrier status. Programs for screening for other diseases would be developed were similar tests available. Third, the sickle-cell anemia program was developed not to attach any genetic stigma to blacks but to relieve their suffering. But in spite of the truth and relevance of these points, there does remain the fear that large-scale screening programs may foster a discriminatory mentality which implies superior and inferior races or groups within out society.

Finally, a few more moral concerns must be mentioned in passing. What safeguards can be instituted to protect basic human rights — such as informed consent and confidentiality — when large numbers of people are involved in a genetic screening program? Should afflicted individuals be told they are carriers for a genetic condition for which there is no adequate treatment currently available and for which there may be a social stigma, e.g., sickle-cell anemia? Are massive genetic screening programs the best way of using scarce medical and economic resources? Since large segments of the population lack even basic nutritional and medical care, should not such persons receive these basic needs before programs are mounted to detect genetic defects, for which, in many instances little can be done?

Each of these questions relative to genetic screening deserves extensive reflection, both privately and publicly, since large segments of the population are potentially involved. Discussions of these problems have been carried on during the last decade but no universally acceptable policy has yet emerged. (See Murray, 1972; Institute of Society, Ethics and the Life Sciences, 1972; Lappé, Roblin and Gustafson, 1974; National Reearch Council, 1975; and Milunsky and Annas, 1976.)

Parents, Counselors and Society

It is possible to outline various moral questions which the existence of genetic defects raises for parents, genetic counselors, and for society as a whole. Thus, the following three sets of questions can be asked of parents:

1. Do parents ever have a serious responsibility *not* to procreate? If they do have such an obligation, *to whom* do they have this responsibility? Do they owe it to themselves, or to their present children, or to society, or to the unconceived child himself? We have seen there is a problem with saying that it would be better for the defective child himself were he never born, for who is in a position to make this judgment about another being's life? Can we justify a decision to have no children on any other basis?

2. If the parents decide not to have another child, what means are

110

legitimate? Natural Family Planning methods are sometimes difficult to use; would sterilization or artificial means of contraception be permissible in such a case?

3. If the woman is pregnant and chooses to undergo amniocentesis, how can she justify taking a risk with her unborn? If prenatal diagnosis is not therapeutic for the fetus, how can she justify forcing another individual to run risks that are not for his benefit and are without his consent?

Genetic disease raises these five special problems for the counselor:

1. If he opposes abortion or believes that artificial contraception or sterilization is wrong, what are his responsibilities to his client? Should he engage in nondirective counseling and propose these as alternatives without advising against them? Or does he have a responsibility to present his moral views? These problems are further complicated: in light of the fact that many Catholics — lay, religious and priests — hold that for a sufficiently grave reason, contraceptive and sterilization technologies can be morally justified, how should such a counselor advise this client who is at high risk for begetting children with a serious inherited disease?

2. Does the counselor have a responsibility to disclose all relevant information to his client, or may he withhold some particular piece of information as not being in his client's best interest? Is it up to him to make such judgments about his client's interests?

3. What are the counselor's responsibilities toward those who are not his client but whose interests are vitally affected by information gained within the privileged setting of the doctor-patient relationship? Is it ever permissible to disclose information against the wishes of his client? If so, to whom: to his spouse, his siblings, civil authorities?

4. If he believes that his expertise is being misused, for example, when parents seeking a boy wish to know the sex of the fetus, does he have an obligation to refuse to assist them? What responsibilities does he have to see to it that technology is not misused?

5. What are the counselor's responsibilities toward society? Does he have an obligation to disclose information that might be useful to society as a whole? Ought the genetic health of

mankind be one of his primary concerns? Should he place the common good above the welfare of his patient? Does he have a responsibility to speak out against trends that he sees as dangerous, or are his obligations only to his patient?

Genetic disease also raises these four problems for the society as a whole:

1. What are the society's responsibilities in the matter of selective abortion? Should it be encouraged, or tolerated, or discouraged, or made illegal?

2. What are the responsibilities for the care of affected individuals? Should the fact that they were not aborted be relevant in deciding whether to provide public funds? What responsibilities does the society have to provide free counseling and diagnostic services?

3. What attitudes and values should be fostered by the society? What understanding of the value and nature of personhood should be encouraged? How should the society look upon affected individuals whether born or unborn? What should society's attitude be toward the mentality of substitution?

4. What right does the society have to make decisions in the matter of procreation? Does society have the right to decide about the conception and birth of defective children, and should these decisions be compulsory? Is it permissible to require sterilization to prevent the conception of affected children? Should the birth of genetically defective children be made illegal?

Summary

This chapter began with the listing of a number of reasons for selective abortion based on genetic considerations. In response to these reasons, responsibilities of individuals and of society were outlined which underline the moral difficulties of selective abortion. In addition, the implications of a cost/benefit analysis approach to genetic disease was shown to have serious negative implications for society. Significant moral questions of genetic screening were pointed out. Finally sets of moral issues facing parents, counselors, and society were briefly stated to indicate the moral perplexities associated with genetic disease. They will be dealt with in the following chapters, the first of which will examine the individual Christian's response to the moral issues.

Chapter 6

The Individual Christian Witness

Introduction

The preceding chapter identified many of the moral issues associated with genetic medicine while two earlier chapters presented a variety of perspectives on the nature of humanness. This review was important because an individual's response to moral issues arising from the presence of genetic defects will in large part be determined by that person's view of the world, the perceived meaning and purpose of human existence, and the values seen as primary. Most people can come to an agreement about the basic principles of morality: prohibitions against killing, stealing, lying, etc. But it would be naive to expect similar agreement on the applications of these principles to each particular case. How a person applies these basic principles to the concrete situation depends upon that individual's vision of the place of human beings in the universe. Only within this vision of the whole does human existence take on meaning. Consequently, a Christian's vision of the purpose of life will greatly influence the manner in which tribulations are met.

Individual Christian Responsibility

The Christian message is directed toward all human beings, for Christ died for all and God desires the salvation of all. That message of hope in Christ, communicated by the Apostles, is continuously proclaimed to the world by the Church, the community of believers. The Church, however, is present to the world not only in its official capacity as a moral teacher but also and perhaps more intimately and effectively through the lives and actions of its individual members. As the Second World Synod of Bishops indicated:

> The members of the Church, as members of society, have the same right and duty to promote the common good as do other citizens. Christians ought to fulfill their temporal obligations with fidelity and competence. They should act as leaven in the world, in their family, professional, social, cultural and political life. They must accept their responsibilities in this entire area under the influence of the Gospel and the teaching of the Church. In this way they testify to the power of the Holy Spirit through their action in the service of men in those things which are decisive for the existence and the future of humanity. While in such activities they generally act on their own initiative without involving the responsibility of the ecclesiastical hierarchy, in a sense they do involve the responsibility of the Church whose members they are (Gremillion, 1976, p. 521).

A similar recognition of the right and responsibility of the individual believer is expressed in the documents of Vatican II.

> Laymen should also know that it is generally the function of their well-formed Christian conscience to see that the divine law is inscribed in the life of the earthly city. From priests they may look for spiritual light and nourishment. Let the layman not imagine that his pastors are always such experts, that to every problem which arises, however complicated, they can readily give him a concrete solution, or even that such is their mission. Rather, enlightened by Christian wisdom and giving close attention to the teaching authority of the Church, let the layman take on his own distinctive role (Vatican II, 1965b, #43).*

In relation to the area of genetic diagnosis and counseling, these remarks imply that believers have the responsibility "to live their lives in its entire reality in accord with the evangelical principles of personal and social morality which are expressed in the vital Christian witness of one's life" (Gremillion, 1976, p. 523).

Parents, medical technicians, nurses, genetic counselors, theologians, scientists, legislators, all bear a proportionate responsibility of making their involvement in genetic diagnosis and counseling a

---

*All future reference to this document in this chapter will be cited by paragraph number only.

faithful witness and reflection of the values in which they believe. Of this list of concerned participants, only the parents' and genetic counselors' roles are considered to some detail in this study because, generally, these are the persons most directly involved in the decision process. The individual witnessing and fidelity of parents and counselors to their deepest faith convictions is an absolutely vital and indispensable part of the total Church's responsibility in the area of genetic disease.

These profound faith convictions were summarized in Chapter 4. They can be stated as four basic truths:

1. Left to itself, the world is in bondage to sin and suffering;
2. But God became flesh in Christ to save the world from slavery to sin through his dying on the cross and rising again;
3. The Christian is called to imitate Christ's self-sacrificing love for the world as a means of carrying out God's salvific plan;
4. Through the power of his Holy Spirit promised by Christ to his followers at the Last Supper the Christian receives the power of living the life of Christ.

These truths provide the basis for every Christian's life, bestowing meaning and purpose on that life and providing hope and encouragement to face the difficulties which confront the Christian seeking to serve God faithfully. The remainder of this chapter, accordingly, considers some of the issues associated with genetic defects to which Christian parents and Christian genetic counselors will need to bring their faith-vision.

Christian Parents' Response to Genetic Defects

The consideration of the Christian parents' response to the actual or potential presence of genetic disease in their midst includes 3 parts: (1) the value of married love and the family as described in documents of the Vatican Council II; (2) the problems relating to a decision not to procreate; and (3) Christian parents and genetic defects.

The Value of Married Love and the Family

The Fathers of the Vatican Council II were concerned to go beyond an enunciation of general principles and to speak about specific forms of Christian activity. This section contains a brief review of the values that are particularly relevant to the Christian who has been called to act as a co-creator with God in the generation of new members for his Kingdom. These values will be a base for dealing with the difficult and complex issues surrounding genetic counseling.

The Pastoral Constitution on the Church in the Modern World states simply and clearly the primary importance of the family: "Among the social ties necessary for man's development some correspond more immediately to his innermost nature — the family, for instance, and the political community; others flow rather from his free choice" (#25). Since the family flows from human beings' basic nature and since God is the author of human nature, the existence of the family is an element in God's plan. "The well-being of the individual person and of both human and Christian society is closely bound up with the healthy state of conjugal and family life" (#47). By a personal and irrevocable consent a man and a woman mutually surrender themselves for the sake of the good of each other, of the children, and of the larger society. This consent establishes a bond that is sacred and independent of human decision.

> For God himself is the author of marriage and has endowed it with various benefits and with various ends in view: all of these have a very important bearing on the continuation of the human race, on the personal development and eternal destiny of every member of the family, on the dignity, stability, peace and prosperity of the family and of the whole human race (#48).

A man and a woman encounter Christ through the sacrament of marriage. Christ abides with them so that through their mutual self-sacrifice they will grow into that kind of love for one another which Paul took as a model of Christ's love for his Church (Eph. 5:22-25). Christian marriage goes beyond a merely human contract, entering into the divine sphere by means of both its goal and its activity.

> Authentic married love is caught up into divine love and is directed and enriched by the redemptive power of Christ, with the result that the spouses are effectively led to God and are helped and strengthened in their lofty role as fathers and mothers. Spouses, therefore, are fortified and, as it were, consecrated for the duties and dignity of their state by a special sacrament; fulfilling their conjugal and family role by virtue of this sacrament, spouses are penetrated with the spirit of Christ, and their whole life is suffused by faith, hope and charity; thus they increasingly further their own perfection and their mutual sanctification, and together they render glory to God (#48).

Marriage by its very nature is ordered both to good of the spouses as well as to the procreation and education of children. By the example and prayer of the parents children are guided in the path of virtue and holiness and are provided with abilities necessary for life within the larger community. "Married couples should regard it as their proper mission to transmit human life and to educate their children; they should realize that they are therefore cooperating with the love of God the Creator and are, in a certain sense, its interpreters" (#50).

More recently, the Pontifical Commission for the Revision of the Code of Canon law has proposed the following wording for the first canon of the section on marriage:

> The matrimonial covenant, by which a man and a woman constitute between themselves a communion of the whole of life, which by its nature is ordered to the good of the spouses and the procreation and education of the children, has been raised by Christ the Lord to the dignity of a sacrament (Morrisey, 1979).

This statement represents an interesting shift from earlier formulations as it places the "good of the spouses" in first place. The implications to be drawn from that remain to be seen. At present, it suffices to say that the needs of the spouses and of the children must be in balance when evaluating the impact of genetic disease on a family.

The transforming love brought to the world by Christ animates every true Christian. "This love is not something reserved for important matters but must be exercised above all in the ordinary circumstances of everyday life" (#38). Christian parents who are called to the imitation of Christ will accept with confidence the difficulties and sufferings that arise within the life of a family, knowing that they lack no spiritual gift as they wait for the revelation of the Lord (1 Cor. 1:7) and "that God makes all things work together for the good of those who have been called according to his decree" (Rom. 8:28). In the light of the cross, suffering takes on meaning. "By suffering for us he not only gave us an example so that we might follow in his footsteps, but he also opened up a way. If we follow his path, life and death are made holy and acquire a new meaning" (#22). Parents know that they are bound to encounter pain, tribulation and sorrow for themselves and their children. But because they have died with Christ, they look forward to the resurrection and live this earthly existence with the conviction that nothing in heaven or earth can separate them and their loved ones from the love of God that comes to them in Christ Jesus (Rom. 8:35-39).

117

Children and the Decision Not to Procreate

The whole structure of family life is directed toward assisting the couple to cooperate with the creative love of God who through them will increase the human family. This role of co-creator is to be exercised responsibly and requires making procreative decisions only after prayerful submission to God. The Vatican Council II mentions a number of considerations the couple should keep in mind as they reach a decision in common (see #50):

1. Their own good and the good of the conjugal union
2. The good of their children, those already born and those yet to come
3. Their financial and other material resources as these relate to wider social conditions and trends
4. Their spiritual development
5. The good of the Church and of civil society.

This decision must be made by the couple themselves, recognizing that they are to be judged by God. This means that the couple are not free simply to follow their wishes in the matter but that they must be ruled by their consciences as they are in conformity with the divine and natural laws of God and the teaching authority of the Church. This divine law provides the basis for true married love, protects it, and leads it to fulfillment. "Whenever Christian spouses in a spirit of sacrifice and trust in divine providence carry out their duties of procreation with generous human and Christian responsibility, they glorify the Creator and perfect themselves in Christ" (#50).

The Council recognized that couples in certain situations may find that the number of their children should not be increased, at least for a time. The question of the means that may legitimately be employed in carrying out this decision then arises. Although condemning abortion and infanticide, the Council did not give any detail other than that the faithful "are forbidden to use methods disapproved of by the teaching authority of the Church in its interpretation of the divine law" (#51). Most readers will recall that the reason for this reticence was that at the time the document was being prepared (1965), the Church was awaiting a papal pronouncement on the matter and the Council Fathers did not wish to speak until Pope Paul VI had presented his statement. This pronouncement was made in the form of an encyclical letter, *Humanae Vitae,* promulgated to the universal Church on July 25, 1968.

In this encyclical Paul VI declared that the Church in accordance with constant doctrine "teaches that each and every marriage act must remain open to the transmission of life" (Paul VI, 1968, #11). After excluding procured abortion as morally impermissible even if performed for therapeutic reasons, the Pope then excluded direct sterilization, whether permanent or temporary, and "every action which, either in anticipation of the conjugal act, or its accomplishment, or in the development of its natural consequences, proposes, whether as an end or as a means, to render procreation impossible" (Paul VI, 1968, #14). If there are adequate reasons to space births, "The Church teaches that it is then licit to take into account the natural rhythms immanent in the generative functions, for the use of marriage in the infecund periods only, and in this way to regulate birth without offending the moral principles which have been recalled earlier" (Paul VI, 1968, #16). The basic position of Pope Paul as contained in these quotations is that it is wrong to *interfere* in any way with the marriage act in order to render it infertile.

His Holiness recognized that this teaching would be difficult for many, and in a spirit of charity he urged married couples to seek help from God in prayer and above all in reception of the Eucharist. "And if sin should still keep hold of them, let them not be discouraged, but rather have recourse with humble perseverance to the mercy of God, which is poured forth in the sacrament of Penance" (Paul VI, 1968, #25). *Humanae Vitae* represents a specification of some of the general values enunciated in *The Church in the Modern World* and is in no way inconsistent with the latter. Both documents are concerned to teach a basic truth: "that human life and its transmission are realities whose meaning is not limited by the horizons of this life only: their true evaluation and full meaning can only be understood in reference to man's eternal destiny" (#51).

Perhaps no other issue in modern times has so split the Church as the question of contraception and sterilization. While the magisterium has made its position clear by repeated affirmations of the teaching contained in *Humanae Vitae,* several prominent theologians (e.g., Curran [1978], Kosnik [1977], McCormick [1979] have seriously questioned the methodology and/or some of the conclusions. Such questioning arose from strongly felt, and sincerely held, convictions on the part of the dissenters that the very values papal teachings were seeking to protect and promote would better be served by a modification of that teaching which would be more in accord with the existential needs of married couples in today's world.* This internal division has resulted in a degree of confusion among the faithful. Faced with many urgent problems and frequently crushing burdens, their procreative decisions are difficult enough to make. However, in matters of moral guidance, the Church's magisterium holds that the Pope and the bishops in union with him have the prime responsibility of teaching and interpreting what God has revealed regarding what one is to believe and how one is to live.

> But the task of giving an authentic interpretation of the Word of God, whether in its written form or in the form of Tradition, has been entrusted to the living teaching office of the Church alone. Its authority in this matter is exercised in the name of Jesus Christ (Vatican II, 1965a, #10).

Not only from the Church's teaching but also from their personal experience, a Christian couple know that God loves them and their children. In faith they know that God manifested that love for them first of all by sending his Son to die for them and then by sending the Spirit to give them the power to live the life of God. This life of God in the believer cannot be taken away by any human or superhuman power and transcends the imperfections of this life. Sustained by the grace of the Spirit, the Christian finds the necessary strength to deal with suffering and death, for it is in the weakness of man that God's power is brought to perfection. "Three times I begged the Lord that his might leave me. He said to me, 'My grace is enough for you, for in weakness power reaches perfection.' And so I willingly boast of my weaknesses instead, that the power of Christ may rest upon me" (2 Cor. 12:8-9). Christian parents are committed to accepting the challenge of the cross. One aspect of that challenge is that there may be undertakings which human power may be able to accomplish but which are contrary to God's will and consequently should not be done. Such affirmation of the power of the cross will perhaps be viewed by others as "complete absurdity," but Christians believe that in such affirmation God's power will be revealed and they will be saved.

Parental Responsibilities

The specific cases of genetic diseases cited earlier (pp. 31-50) provide a good basis for an examination of the responsibilities of

---

*For a discussion of this issue, see Atkinson and Moraczewski, 1979.

Christian parents. For convenience, these areas of responsibility may be grouped under seven headings:

1. The responsibility of the parents themselves to decide
2. The good of married love and of children
3. Abortion and the mentality of substitution
4. The decision about future children
5. The choice of means of limiting conception
6. The decision to perform amniocentesis
7. The responsibility to warn others

These headings provide a convenient outline for the reflections which ensue.

First, the Church and civil society have obligations in assisting the couple to arrive at responsible decisions concerning procreation and to support them in those decisions, but "it is the married couple themselves who must in the last analysis arrive at these judgments before God" (#50). These decisions must be arrived at by husband and wife together. They should be made only after prayerful consideration and submission to the law of God and the teaching authority of the Church. In addition to the information and professional advice of the genetic counselor, the couple may also have a responsibility to seek a spiritual counselor in the matter.

Because of the complexity of genetic inheritance, some parents may wish to avoid making the decision and thrust it upon some other person. Furthermore, the decision may have agonizing consequences in the shape of a child doomed to die within a few years and/or requiring continuous care (e.g., Tay-Sachs pp. 32-34 or neural tube defects pp. 45-47). Nonetheless, parents faced with such painful procreative decisions can, in the process of making an informed choice, grow as Christian persons. It is in such decisions that a Christian understanding of the role of suffering becomes especially important.

Ultimately, it remains the couple's decision, whether made responsibly or irresponsibly, and the couple ought to recognize that no one else can or should make that decision for them.

Second, in coming to a responsible decision, the couple must simultaneously affirm the two primary goods of marriage: the love between the spouses and the children who are the fruits of that love. The love that binds man and wife is so holy that Paul called the marital union the "great foreshadowing" of Christ's love for his body, the

Church (Eph. 5:32). Christian parents cooperate with divine love when responsibly they give birth to children and raise them to be members of God's family. While it is desirable to have healthy children, Christians will value and love nonetheless those children who may be affected with some genetic defect. Secular values tend to promote the concept of the "perfect infant" which meets the tolerance specifications set by current notions of perfection. As a consequence, severely handicapped children may be shunned and unloved by their parents in such a culture.

Tendency of some parents will be to place the afflicted child in an institution. When the child is so severely handicapped that home care is physically impossible or places such a heavy burden on the parents that family life becomes intolerable, such a decision is appropriate. But some genetic diseases have a great range of mental and physical disability. Down's syndrome (pp. 49-50) is an example where in many instances the child may be raised at home. In making that decision the parents need to consider the impact this would have on the afflicted child, on the other children and on themselves. All other things being equal, a handicapped child reared in the atmosphere of a loving family fares much better. While in most instances it is the mother who has the greatest contact with the genetically afflicted child, it is important for the mutual love of the spouses that the husband have adequate caring contact with that child.

Third, a Christian couple faced with an unborn child diagnosed for a severe genetic defect will find certain options foreclosed. The dignity of the human person is an inherent dignity that comes to the human being precisely because that person is known and loved by God. This dignity, as the Sacred Scriptures teach and Church pronouncements affirm, exists prior to birth. Thus, the abortion of the unborn offspring is an attack on that dignity, at once inherent and transcendent.

During his visit to the United States, Pope John Paul II strongly reaffirmed the Church's tradition that direct abortion for whatever reason is absolutely reprehensible (John Paul II, 1979b). Today, with an apparent sensibility to the presumed preferences of individuals, an increasing number of people are advocating the thesis that it is better for a child not to be born at all than live with the heavy burden of severe physical and mental handicaps (e.g., Fletcher, Joseph, 1978). Apart from the fact that there is no empirically objective way in which an evaluation can be made as to whether such individuals would choose non-life over life as a handicapped person, there is the arrogance of adults who would venture to make such a judgment for the unborn child. Granted that children afflicted with Tay-Sachs (pp. 32-34), cystic fibrosis (pp. 34-36) or a neural tube defect (pp. 45-47), for example, are unable to experience much of human life, the frequent limitations of their mental awareness makes it difficult to assess the extent of their self-awareness and of the subjective dimensions of their suffering.

However, the Christian understanding of life and suffering provides a framework for dealing with these complex and painful issues. That Christian perspective holds that even the life of an afflicted child is good. Human life, when imperfect and a cause of suffering, is still not to be scorned, for the meaning and value of a human being transcends the conditions of this life. The suffering, death, and resurrection of Christ, into which Christians are incorporated by their baptism, is the primary fact in terms of which all the events of this life must be interpreted. With this faith-vision Christian parents are encouraged not to avoid suffering by aborting the infant or rejecting the child.

In instances like the one involving a muscular dystrophic child (pp. 36-38), a "mentality of substitution" is gradually becoming prominent. Since the muscular dystrophy is an X-linked recessive disease (only the male offspring — 50% — will manifest the affliction), there are those who advocate aborting all males and preserving the females when the couple is identified to be at risk for muscular dystrophy. But each person is an unduplicable, irreplaceable and truly unique being in God's Providence. No substitution is possible since one person is not equivalent to or commensurate with another. Accordingly, a person may not be discarded in favor of a healthier substitute.

Fourth, the Church recognizes that if parental decisions are to be made responsibly, Christian parents have an obligation to take into consideration a number of factors: "their own good and the good of their children already born or yet to come, an ability to read the signs of the times and of their own situation on the material and spiritual level, and, finally, an estimation of the good of the family, of society, and of the Church" (#50). The Church also recognizes that after taking these factors into consideration the couple may responsibly arrive at the conclusion that the number of children should not be increased (#51). Case #4 (pp. 36-38) would seem to provide an example of such a situation. There is legitimate concern for the marital relationship and also for the care of the sick child already born. Other considerations relating to the financial and emotional burdens of caring for another child should it be affected are also relevant. The decisions about whether to risk having an affected child can only be made by the parents themselves, but the values taught by the Church might very well lead the couple to conclude that they have a serious obligation not to have further children. In coming to such an important decision, the couple may have the obligation to seek the advice of a confessor or other Christian advisor.

Some genetic diseases, such as those associated with an autosomal dominant condition (see p. 8), present a carrier parent with a very high risk (one in two) of conceiving a child with the disease. Examples of that situation are Huntington's Disease (pp. 38-42), neurofibromatosis (pp. 42-44) and Marfan's syndrome (pp. 44-45). In addition, some of the chromosomal translocation defects (pp. 47-49) which involve multiple congenital anomalies are also situations of very high risk (one in two). When Down's syndrome is associated with increasing maternal age (pp. 49-50), the risk can become significant after 35-40 years of age (about one in forty).

In these and similar cases, couples at risk need to consider whether or not they have an *obligation* not to procreate any additional children. No simple rule exists for making the determination. With increased knowledge there is usually increased responsibility. A couple faced with such a decision needs to consider not only its family but society as well. The particular disease for which the two are at risk enters into the calculus. Huntington's Disease (pp. 38-42) involves an inevitably progressive neurological degeneration with a relatively late onset, usually around age thirty. In contrast, neurofibromatosis (pp. 42-44), although slowly progressive, is not fatal, allows a normal lifespan and activities, and normally involves only cosmetic alteration. More serious than the last mentioned is Marfan's syndrome (pp. 44-45), which shortens somewhat the lifespan (to about forty or forty-five years) and results in a variety of skeletal and cardiovascular problems with some danger of eventual blindness. When a decision is finally made, it should involve a prudential evaluation of all these factors against a faith background. At the same time, acknowledgement should be made that the *perception* of risk can vary markedly. One couple may seek a risk of 1/40 as slight, while another will consider it too likely a possibility. Similarly, there will be a wide divergence on estimating the burden a particular genetic disease will place on the individual and on the family. Consequently, these variable can have a significant impact on the moral evaluation by the couple and their decision.

The conclusion that it would be wrong to have additional children does not require and should not be thought to imply any judgment to the effect that it would be better for the child not to have been born. No couple has the obligation to conceive all the children they could possibly conceive, even if they know that their children would all be healthy and happy. The responsibility to have children must always be balanced against other responsibilities already noted. Thus, the decision of non-carrier parents to have no more children does not presuppose or require any judgment to the effect that another child would be better off never having existed. But if this is the case with non-carrier couples, it is no less true of carrier couples. The emotional, financial, and spiritual burdens of having an affected child, burdens that are assumed by the couple and the family, by the Church and civil society, are in themselves sufficient to justify the decision to bear no further children.

Fifth, the fact that a particular decision is justified does not imply that *any means* of implementing the decision is thereby justified. For example, the decision by a couple who have had previous experience with muscular dystrophy (pp. 36-38) not to have any defective children would not justify their decision to abort all males: a good end does not justify an evil means. Nor could the good that would be achieved by sterilization or the use of contraceptive devices justify those procedures according to authentic Church teaching. A good end justifies the use of a means only if that means is already morally good, or at least neutral. The authentic Church teaching stated in *Humanae Vitae* and consistently repeated thereafter by Paul VI and John Paul II is precisely that those procedures undertaken for the purpose of preventing conception are themselves morally wrong (Paul VI, 1968, ##11-14). The Fathers of Vatican II clearly point out the guide in these matters. "In questions of birth regulation the sons of the Church, faithful to these principles, are forbidden to use methods disapproved of by the teaching authority of the Church in its interpretation of the divine law" (#51). The Church recognizes that this teaching for many couples faced with the prospect of genetic defect will be an extremely difficult one to follow. Not only will it be difficult because of personal and social pressures on the couple, but also because of the division within the Church regarding the conditions which might justify the use of contraceptive or sterilizing technologies (Atkinson and Moraczewski, 1979).

For those Catholics who already accept a dissenting position with regard to the use of contraception and sterilization, the risk of generating a child with a genetic defect will probably provide a serious reason for resorting to one or other of those technologies. Those, however, who faithfully accept the papal teaching on the subject, such will be tormented by the crosscurrent of conflicting opinions and by the gravity and urgency of the situation.

A Catholic couple who prudently have made the decision not to bear additional children because of the high risk of begetting a genetically defective child, but who decline the use of contraception and sterilization are faced with the alternative of avoiding another conception by natural means exclusively. This choice raises the problem that natural methods are often considered unreliable. Part of the problem seems to be the notion held by many that natural family planning methods (NFP) are uncertain. This notion seems in part due to the identification of NFP with calendar-rhythm methods which are not totally reliable for some couples.

Since the couple rightly views the absence of conception as imperative, effectiveness of the method is of utmost importance. When the newer methods of natural family planning (e.g., Sympto-thermal) *are properly employed at all times,* their effectiveness is at least equal to the use of the "combined Pill" (Kippley and Kippley, 1979).* In addition, there is the advantage of no side effects such as those frequently experienced with the use of non-natural methods (Moraczewski, 1980).

Urging medical scientists to improve these natural methods of family planning, the Magisterium continues to hold fast today to its traditional teaching in this matter. Couples who find themselves forced to curtail additional child-bearing need to give serious heed in faith to the teaching authority of the Church. At the same time, they

---

*This assertion, nonetheless, will need to be reviewed in light of careful additional studies in the comparative efficacy of various methods of limiting births.

should obtain *competent* training in the use of the newer methods of natural family planning and then use them conscientiously. The Couple to Couple League, for example, has used a thorough training program to certify its 250 couples who presently teach NFP in over 40 states (see Kippley and Kippley, 1979). The guidance of a wise and prudent spiritual counselor will aid the couple in dealing with these difficult and painful problems with love and trust.

Sixth, it has already been noted that amniocentesis as a prenatal diagnostic technique is not usually followed by any therapeutic procedure which would make it beneficial for the child. This is easily seen in the cases of Tay-Sachs and muscular dystrophy (pp. 32-34; 36-38), which are at present untreatable. Since amniocentesis involves some risk for the unborn, the question arises whether it could be morally justified if no adequate therapy exists for the defect which is being tested. Case #4 (muscular dystrophy, pp. 36-38) provides at least one reason to believe that amniocentesis can have a therapeutic consequence. The case illustrates the tremendous anxiety a couple may experience when faced with the prospect of bearing a child with a genetic defect. Such anxiety may have serious implications for the gestational development of the unborn. For Mrs. A to know she was carrying a female child would be of great benefit not only to Mrs. A but also indirectly to the unborn girl. It seems, then, in those situations where the condition is untreatable, that if amniocentesis provides a reasonable hope of relieving deep and crippling anxiety, it could be justified on the basis of functioning as an indirect form of therapy for the unborn.

A second reason that may, under certain conditions, justify amniocentesis in nontreatable cases is that the advance warning provided could assist the physician and parents in preparing for the child. Necessary medical arrangements could be made for special care and the parents' expectations more likely would be realistic. The child would benefit from more appropriate care and lower chances of emotional rejection by the parents for they would have had time to work through their feelings. At the same time, recognition should be given to the other possibility that such advance warning may have the opposite effect and increase rejection feelings. Hence some consideration should be given to these possibilities, as well as to the risk to the unborn child, before the parents accept or reject amniocentesis.

There is a third argument that might be employed to justify the use of amniocentesis in certain cases even though the defect being tested for is currently untreatable. Essentially, the argument states that amniocentesis might be justified in certain cases where the parents concluded that they would have no trouble in justifying the amniocentesis to the individual after he had grown and reached mature years. This conclusion is based on the following considerations.

In the recent literature there has been much discussion about the moral legitimacy of nontherapeutic experimentation on children, experimentation not expected to benefit the children who are themselves the subjects of the experiment. This debate throws light on the question of amniocentesis, for although the latter procedure is not experimental, it is a technique that exposes a nonconsenting human being to some risk that may not be justifiable by appeal to offsetting benefits for that human being. On the one side is the position of Paul Ramsey (Ramsey, 1970), who denies the moral legitimacy of nontherapeutic experimentation on children. Opposing Ramsey is Richard McCormick (McCormick, 1974), who argues that such experimentation is legitimate because children *would* consent if they *could* and they *would* consent because they *ought to*. Ramsey rejects this position because, he says, it violates the child, treating him as though he were an adult when in fact he is not an adult but a child.

It is not to the purpose here to examine these arguments, but only to show how the two positions suggest a middle view relevant to the question of amniocentesis. Ramsey's and McCormick's positions suggest the following middle ground: nontherapeutic experiments on children are justified provided that — in light of the risks — one would have no problem justifying them to the individuals once they have grown up. The child is not treated as an adult, but what is done to him is done with a view to what he will say once he grows into an adult. Again, the point here is not to decide which experiments would be legitimate, but only to suggest this position as a possible means of dealing with the problem of amniocentesis: those amniocenteses may be justifiable which one would have no problem justifying to the individual after he has been born and attained maturity. This suggestion does not solve all the relevant moral problems, for it does not say when one would have no problem justifying the procedure to the adult, but it does indicate that amniocentesis might be justified even if it were not of clear therapeutic benefit.

Parents, then, will have honestly to consider the welfare of their unborn in deciding whether the relief of their anxiety is sufficiently beneficial to the child to warrant the risk (see pp. 18-20). Here again, how the objective, quantitatively stated risk associated with amniocentesis, namely, 1.5% of increased rate of spontaneous abortion, is *perceived* by a couple will greatly influence a judgment. While it is conceivable that the determination will be negative, an affirmative answer in certain cases seems not at all unreasonable. The burden of responsibility rests upon the couple to make that decision after prayerful reflection and consultation with experienced advisors.

Seventh, it seems that parents who discover that one child is afflicted with a genetic disease may very well have a serious responsibility to warn the siblings and other concerned persons. Christian love is to love neighbor as oneself, and certainly one's relatives are particularly important "neighbors." In Case #4 (pp. 36-38), Mrs. A's relatives were apparently aware of the risk of muscular dystrophy, but in many of the other cases mentioned the family members may not have been so informed. No hard and fast rules can be set here, for it is conceivable that a brother or sister might not be able to bear the burden of such knowledge or would be unable to use it properly. Again, the decision ought to rest with the couple, who must make it after prayer and perhaps consultation with a spiritual advisor. It is clear, however, that if the couple believes that the siblings could benefit from that knowledge, they have a responsibility to disclose that information, even though such disclosure might be painful to themselves or others.

A particularly distressing situation is that arising from Huntington's Disease (pp. 38-42). Because of the late onset of the disease — around thirty years of age — the afflicted will usually not be aware of his sickness until after entry into marriage and one or more children. As an autosomal dominant condition, the disease causes the one affected parent to transmit it to 50% of the children.

A person in this situation has an understandable reluctance about communicating such information to others. In particular, the reluctance could harden into a determination to remain silent if a marriage or job is at stake. A potential spouse might perhaps decline to contract marriage once the ramifications of the diseased state were known. Similarly, an employer might be reluctant to give a person afflicted with Huntington's disease greater responsibility and authority, because of the uncertainty of that individual's future.

The responsibility for revealing the presence of the disease varies. In the case of notifying an employer, it would seem that so long as the afflicted person was not placing himself or others (including his corporation) in some kind of jeopardy, he could remain silent until he began to experience symptoms of the disease. The genetic counselor would be able to monitor the progress of the disease and notify the patient when the neurological defect reached a level of significant functional disability. In regard to marriage, actual or potential, the patient has an obligation to communicate his actual condition. Before marriage, the future spouse has a right to know that the prospective partner has Huntington's disease and that within a few years the condition will manifest and progressive neurological degeneration begin to show. In making a decision, a prospective spouse would need to be informed fully and accurately of the probable course of the disease and its significance. Should the patient's medical status be learned after marriage, the spouse should be informed since the couple will need mutually to make decisions regarding whether to have children and the means of achieving the desired goal.

In concluding this discussion of the challenges genetic defects present to Christian parents, it can be noted that some alternatives are morally foreclosed: human beings are not morally free to do whatever can be done, but only what is consistent with the will of God as best they can ascertain it. "Do not conform yourselves to this age but be transformed by the renewal of your mind, so that you may judge what is God's will, what is good, pleasing and perfect" (Rom. 12:2). Particularly in the area of suffering, especially that of their children, are parents challenged to their limits. Armed with a Christian view of suffering they will be able to perceive how their suffering can have some meaning. As a consequence they will be able to deal with their problems more constructively.

In those areas that admit of possible moral alternatives, decisions must be made: (1) by both husband and wife; (2) with correct and adequate information; and (3) after prayerful consideration and wise spiritual guidance. Ultimately, notwithstanding all the genetic and spiritual counseling, only the couple can decide for themselves. Such parents will view their decisions from the standpoint of whether they are consistent with the transcendent meaning of human existence as revealed by Christ. In the realization that they are loved by God and redeemed by Christ, and that God's gift of the power of the Spirit is sufficient for their weakness, Christian parents will find strength and consolation.

The Christian Genetic Counselor

The Christian Health Professional

Genetic counselors who are Christians share the professional ideals and vocational responsibilities of all Christian health professionals. Many of the values already discussed have special relevance for Christians, who are committed to the care of the sick:

1. The transcendent value and dignity of all human life
2. The unique value of the family
3. The meaning of suffering and death in God's salvific plan
4. The final vindication of life over death as promised by Christ's resurrection
5. The grace that comes to the Christian to bear his burdens
6. The responsibility and power of the Christian to imitate Christ in his sacrificial love
7. The special responsibility to care for the troubled, the sick, the infirm, and the defenseless.

Christian health professionals have a most high calling; for if the grief and anguish of human beings are to be the grief and anguish of the followers of Christ, then in no way can these burdens be more directly assumed than by caring for the brother or sister at the time of his or her gravest spiritual and physical need. The prophecy is Isaiah, "It was our infirmities he bore, our sufferings he endured," was fulfilled in Christ (Mt. 8:17).

Health professionals who take to themselves the spiritual and physical suffering of their neighbors in a spirit of Christ-like sacrifice and care become other Christs to the troubled world, bringing the good news of healing where it is needed most. Thus, health professionals have special responsibility to appreciate the sufferings of others and to bear them in an understanding and gentle way.

The Council was concerned to emphasize that it is the responsibility of the laity "to be witnesses to Christ in all circumstances and at the very heart of the community of mankind" (#43). As citizens of the world, they are not to become satisfied with meeting the minimum requirements of their chosen field but should strive to attain true excellence in whatever task they have before them. They are to cooperate with others who show similar concerns. And most important of all, "their task is to cultivate a properly informed conscience and to impress the divine law on the affairs of the earthly city" (#43). Health professionals and others should seek guidance and spiritual strength from their pastors, but they should not expect an answer to be provided for every problem. Health professionals must come to their own conclusions about many difficult questions, while accepting guidance from Christian wisdom and attending to the teaching authority of the Church.

The Council was most concerned to teach that a person's responsibilities as a follower of Christ cannot be separated from professional duties. It is a mistake to think that

> we may immerse ourselves in earthly activities as if these were utterly foreign to religion, and religion were nothing more than the fulfillment of acts of worship and the observance of a few moral obligations. One of the gravest errors of our time is the dichotomy between the faith which many profess and the practice of their daily lives. As far back as the Old Testament the prophets vehemently denounced this scandal (cf. Is. 58:1-12), and in the New Testament Christ himself threatened it with severe punishment (cf. Mt. 23:3-33; Mk. 7:10-13). Let there, then, be no such pernicious opposition between professional and social activity on the one hand and religious life on the other (#43).

Christians must not conform themselves to the secular values so predominant in our culture today, but must be transformed by the renewal of their mind so that they think and act as Christ.

The Christian Genetic Counselor

Three major responsibilities of the Christian genetic counselor will now be discussed: (1) the acquisition and use of scientific knowledge and technical skills; (2) full disclosure and confidentiality; (3) nondirective counseling.

Each of these areas involve the responsibility of the counselor to a number of different individuals and groups. The first relates primarily to the counselor's responsibilities to the profession and to the community, but it also involves obligations to clients as well. The second and third are concerned specifically with duties regarding the counselor's clients even if they also relate to the wider community as well. None of the counselor's obligations can be neatly categorized, for all the responsibilities to society must always be viewed in terms of their implications for the care of clients.

The Acquisition and Use of Scientific Knowledge and Technical Skills — Vatican II's *Pastoral Constitution on the Church in the Modern World* makes it clear that the Christian counselor must see his work as a good and as part of the divine plan. Growth in scientific knowledge and in technological sophistication, if pursued in a morally proper manner, are means by which man pursues the divine call to master and subdue nature for the achievement of truly human purposes (#36). The use of this knowledge for the relief of human suffering is a great good. The Christian counselor, therefore, should "not be satisfied with meeting the minimum legal requirements but will strive to become truly proficient in that sphere [i.e., the area of professional activity]" (#43). By commitment to professional excellence the counselor displays Christ's concern for all persons and will also work with others who share a commitment to the relief of human suffering.

It was noted earlier in this chapter that the Fathers of Vatican II were most concerned to emphasize that a Christian's professional responsibilities cannot be separated from the obligations shared with all Christians: "to be witnesses to Christ in all circumstances and at the very heart of the community of mankind" (#43). Therefore, in addition to the acquisition of professional expertise, the counselor has a responsibility to develop a well-formed Christian conscience by prayer and consultation with wise and experienced spiritual advisors. The Christian counselor must be more than an accomplished technician, for the concurrent responsibility is nothing less than "to impress the divine law on the affairs of the earthly city" (#43). Thus, the counselor possesses a most serious obligation to be concerned about the moral implications of various proposed policies, and to speak out should it be apparent that any social policy or proposal is inimical to the rights of others or to the common good.

Some of the issues that should be of special concern to the Christian genetic counselor and about which he or she should be well informed, technically and ethically, in virtue of their vocation are:

1. Abortion and social attitudes toward handicapped persons
2. Infanticide
3. Society's responsibilities in the case of handicapped people

4. The meaning and significance of personhood
5. The correct balancing of individual vs. societal goods
6. The right of families to make procreative decisions
7. The implications of suggested screening programs
8. The use of antenatal diagnosis for sex determination
9. The effectiveness of Natural Family Planning by couples who are strongly motivated and properly informed and instructed.

"The social order and its development must constantly yield to the good of the person, since the order of things must be subordinated to the order of persons and not the other way around" (#26). By proclaiming this as a value for the profession and the wider community, the counselor is able to protect the privileged status of servant to individual clients, responsible directly for their good and only indirectly for the good of the wider community. In addition, by working for such an ordering of values the counselor also fulfills an obligation to the wider community to promote principles of justice, benevolence, and compassion; to raise the moral level of a society; and to protect the rights and dignity of its members. No social good is more important than the good of the individual, and the quality of no society can be higher than the quality of life of its members. Thus, in asserting a primary responsibility to the clients' welfare, the counselor best serves the wider community.

The next two discussions treat specific aspects of the counselor's service to the welfare of patients.

Confidentiality and Full Disclosure — In the discussion of Case #5 (pp. 38-42), a number of moral and legal issues were raised in connection with the requirements of confidentiality and full disclosure: is it ever right to disclose, contrary to the wishes of the client, information gained within the privileged setting of the counseling session? Is it ever permissible to withhold information from the client if the counselor believes this is in the best interest of the client?

The legal situation with respect to breach of confidentiality appears to be that the counselor faces liability for a breach of confidence and probably will not be liable should the counselor choose to remain quiet (see Appendix for a full discussion of the legal aspects of genetic counseling). It is true that a California court held a psychiatrist liable for failing to warn a third person that the patient had expressed threats against the person (the *Tarasoff* decision, 1976), but it seems unlikely that the courts would extend this to include the responsibility of genetic counselors to warn their clients' spouses or siblings that they are at risk for transmitting a genetic defect. Furthermore, although one might wish to refrain from the absolute prohibition of breach of confidentiality, it would seem that the counselor's primary *moral* responsibility to the client requires that confidentiality be respected. The genetic counselor should not be blamed for the client's misuse of information.

Can a counselor withhold information from a client? A counselor might at the beginning of an interview inform the client that some information must be withheld if it is deemed that the possession of such would be detrimental to the client's welfare, or that particular information might be disclosed if it is believed to be necessary for the well-being of others (see Moraczewski, 1976). Nevertheless, the counselor would still be legally bound by the ordinary standards of clinical practice, and would probably be required to disclose any information directly requested by the client. From a moral point of view, the counselor could conceivably be justified in failing to volunteer data if there were good reason to believe that disclosure would be harmful to the client and would not provide sufficient offsetting benefits. This would not, however, justify deception. Nor would it justify refusal to respond to an explicit request for information, even if the client had earlier agreed not to request that information. Respect for the moral autonomy of the client and for the primary responsibility of individuals to make their own decisions in matters of reproduction would seem to require that the counselor answer any questions straightforwardly and in a manner comprehensible to the client. Thus, it would appear that the counselor has a moral (and legal) responsibility to discuss, but not promote, even immoral alternatives (e.g., the use of contraception or abortion) with his client if they bear any reasonable relationship to the client's purposes and goals.

Nondirective Counseling and the Counselor's Moral Conviction — These last considerations raise the question of nondirective counseling. A problem arises because there are competing values. On the one hand there is the value of respect for the dignity of the human person and for each person's right to make informed, free decisions. There is also the value of the family and the right of the couple to make their own decisions in reproductive matters. On the other hand, there are the responsibilities of the Christian counselor not to separate religious and moral values from professional activity but rather to act as a leaven of society. A position must be developed that gives proper weight to these competing values.

Three alternative approaches may be hypothesized to deal with this conflict:

1. The counselor expresses his or her moral views and uses all appropriate means to assure that the client comes to what the counselor takes to be the morally correct decision

2. The counselor conceals his or her own moral views on the matter and simply provides technical information within the sphere of professional competence so that the client may make an individual judgment in the matter

3. While respecting the client's dignity and moral autonomy, the counselor expresses his or her moral and religious views and with the client's consent points out the morally significant aspects of various possible courses of action.

The problem with the third alternative is that it is in danger of collapsing into the first, but this should not be seen as an argument for the second alternative, since that approach cannot be reconciled with #43 of the *Church in the Modern World*. It is true, for example, that the discussion of abortion as a possible outcome of the counseling process does not by itself imply that the counselor approves of abortion as morally good or even as morally neutral. But to discuss alternatives without presenting the counselor's values and even once raising moral questions is hardly consistent with the responsibility to impress the divine law on the affairs of the secular city. The fear that the counselor will use the superior status of position to force particular values on the client is a legitimate one. The answer to this is not to eschew discussion of values entirely but to deepen the counselor's sensitivity to the sufferings of the client. The counselor's Christian responsibility is to become more Christ-like in the carrying out of professional duties and to deal with each client in a manner which combines technical competence with an ability to deal wisely, compassionately, and effectively with the anguish, doubts and guilt feelings of the client.

For a Catholic couple who in their own conscience accept contraception and/or sterilization as a morally acceptable means of controlling births for a serious reason, the genetic counselor, although personally adhering to the papal teaching on these matters, is not there to render a moral adjudication. Such a genetic counselor may have as clients a couple who in their own conscience do not accept that teaching. They feel free to employ those techniques when there is serious reason (e.g., genetic disease) to do so. What should be the counselor's stance when they seek professional advice? Clearly, the counselor is not sought out as a spiritual guide. Various responses are possible. Hence, on the one hand, the counselor is not obliged to dissuade them from their position. On the other hand, the counselor may state his or her own beliefs on the matter prudently in the context of professional concern and/or may send them to another counselor whose views would be more congruent with the couples' values.

But what does the counselor do when the Catholic couple agonizes over two conscientious decisions: (1) not to have any additional children, and (2) to be faithful to the Church's official teaching? A reasonable course to follow would be to reinforce the couple in both decisions and to assist them in locating a resource where they could be taught competently and correctly the most effective natural family planning methods. Referral to a sensitive and well-informed spiritual advisor who is faithful to papal teaching would also be of great assistance to the couple.

The counselor has a serious responsibility to those who come in need seeking help. That need should be seen by the counselor as not limited to, but transcending, the medically significant facts of the situation for, in some respects, more important than the medical problems occasioned by genetic defect are the moral problems raised. The client needs to make decisions based on medically correct information but far more than this is the need to make decisions that are consistent with the will of God. The client may come to the genetic counselor for medically important information, but to provide only this type of data is to render only a partial service. Again, to "compel" morally correct decisions is not the counselor's responsibility; but the counselor as teacher and advisor must be more than simply a technician if responsibilities as a Christian are to be carried out. Thus, the counselor should be willing to counsel with anyone who comes in need, including those with whom moral views are not shared. To restrict the acceptance of clients to those who share the counselor's moral and religious values would be to deprive others of his or her special moral and religious gifts. But for the same reasons, the counselor must deal with others in such a way that they might benefit not only from his or her professional expertise but also from the counselor's vocation as a Christian. How the counselor best clarifies his or her moral views to the client is a matter for the counselor's prudential conscience informed by prayer, professional experience, and consultation with wise spiritual advisors. The client should never go away unclear about the counselor's moral convictions or believing that the counselor is indifferent to moral questions.

The fact that many amniocenteses are performed with the possibility of abortion in mind need not necessarily be a reason for the counselor to refuse advising the client to undergo that particular diagnostic procedure. In some instances, discussed above, amniocentesis can be justified for reasons other than selective abortion. If amniocentesis is considered, the counselor must make use of the opportunity to counsel with the client about the morally significant aspects of the decision. The counselor should be conscious of the possibility of scandal being taken, that those who are uninformed about the nature of his or her intentions may take the performance of antenatal diagnosis to be an affirmative expression for selective abortion. Thus, the counselor has a serious responsibility, not only to the client but also to members of the wider community to minimize the danger of scandal by explaining his or her purposes — at least to the client and to those working in the clinic. The counselor needs to explain the therapeutic benefits of antenatal diagnosis and the fact that he or she uses the opportunity to counsel with the client about moral issues. The counselor, then, should be forthright about what is being done, concealing the purposes from neither the client nor from members of the wider community.

It is conceivable that some will find objectionable this approach to counseling, labelling it as "directive" and contrary to the highest canons of the profession. Such a charge is, in effect, demeaning to the profession, reducing it to a technical enterprise that fails to deal with the moral needs of the client and of society. It is conceivable that one of the conditions for the counselor's employment at a center will be that all such forms of counseling be avoided. If brought to this, the counselor will be faced with a difficult decision about whether the good that can be achieved as a "neutralized" genetic counselor is worth the limitation of the freedom to exercise prudently his or her Christian responsibilities in a professional field.

Summary

Individual Christians, be they parents or genetic counselors, are clearly called to witness to their faith by the Fathers of Vatican II. But confronted with the often grim reality of suffering and pain as associated with genetic disorders, Christian parents are challenged to affirm the transcendent value and dignity of all human life. Tempted as they might be to despair in face of crushing problems, their faith gives them an access to interpreting the pain and disabilities of their children and their own sufferings in light of Christ's own life and revelation.

Similarly, Christian genetic counselors are called on to witness to that same faith and hope. No matter with whom they deal in their profession, they have the responsibility to employ their technical skills and faith perspective in order to aid their clients in making the best moral decision possible considering the particular circumstances of the cases.

However, the Christian parent or counselor does not stand alone. The Church's institutions are mandated to speak forth in the areas where people are troubled and in pain. Accordingly, the next chapter will deal with the witness given by agencies of the Church.

Chapter 7

The Institutional
Christian Response

Introduction

The Church as an institutionalized body of Christians is a complex entity, not only because of its numerous and varied institutional groupings but also because it is a divine-human organism. The Church is alive. It grows, develops and adapts to a great variety of cultural and geographical settings without ever losing its essential identity. In its institutional adjustments to environmental changes there is usually a time-lag often to the dismay of its less patient members. At the same time, its inertia protects it from merely adapting to a transitory situation. In the field of health in general, and in the area of genetic medicine in particular, the Church is now challenged to meet some new problems fraught with human pain and suffering.

In this chapter, we will consider the institutional Church's response to these current problems involving genetic disease. In particular, consideration will focus on three aspects of the Church: (1) the Church as the christian community, (2) the Church in its official teaching body, the bishops, and (3) the Church as found in its various health care institutions.

The Church as the Christian Community

As a visible organization and spiritual community the Church existing in the world is to travel the journey with the human race and to share the same earthly lot. But the Church is to be more than a companion with the world. As stated by the Fathers of Vatican II, the Church "is to be a leaven and, as it were, the soul of human society in its renewal by Christ and transformation into the family of God" (Vatican II, 1965, #40)*. In order to guide the human family in its quest for God, the Church has a most serious obligation to read the signs of the times and interpret them in the light of the gospel. If there are trends that lead toward the development of true personal, moral, and spiritual values, then this should be encouraged. On the other hand, if there are tendencies that threaten to violate these fundamental values, then the Church should speak out in word and deed in concerned opposition to them. Above all, the Church should take care that it speaks in terms that are intelligible to everyone (see #4):

> Bishops, to whom has been committed the task of directing the Church of God, along with their priests, are to preach the message of Christ in such a way that the light of the Gospel will shine on all activities of the faithful. Let all pastors of souls be mindful to build up by their daily behavior and concern an image of the Church capable of impressing men with the power and truth of the Christian message. By their words and example and in union with religious and the faithful, let them show that the Church with all its gifts is, by its presence alone, an inexhaustible font of all those resources of which the modern world stands in such dire need. Let them prepare themselves by careful study to meet and play their part in dialogue with the world and with men of all shades of opinion (#43).

The Church has many forms of presence and witness in carrying out its overall mission to bring Christ's teachings and example to bear on the health care ministry in general and on the question of genetic diagnosis and counseling in particular. It is present as a moral teacher, i.e., as an institution committed to an honest search for and communication of the fundamental moral values that should guide efforts, programs, and decisions in this area. It is present through individual believers whose lives and actions witness to these values. It is also present in a more public and corporate form, as a health care

---

*Hereafter in this chapter, the number in parenthesis will refer to the paragraph number in *Pastoral Constitution on the Church in the Modern World.*

institution that provides, through its medical services, a concrete expression of these values.

The recent developments in genetic diagnosis and counseling have generated great interest because of the hope they offer for the enriching of human life. One of the important responsibilities of the Church is to share the good news about the meaning and value of human life as revealed in the teachings of Jesus Christ. The essence of that message affirms that:

> Human life is a precious gift from God; that each person who received this gift has responsibilities toward God, toward self and toward others; and that society, through its laws and social institutions, must protect and sustain human life at every stage of its existence. Recognition of the dignity of the human person, made in the image of God, lies at the very heart of our individual and social duty to respect human life (NCCB, 1975, pp. 1-2).

The correct implementation of this vision of human life for new medical insights and scientific developments is not always immediately evident. Serious study, research, experimentation, dialogue, and reflection are often required before appropriate conclusions can be reached.

The Church in its Official Teaching Body, the Bishops

It is a major responsibility of the Church in its role as proclaimer of the "good news" to bring a Christian perspective and understanding of the meaning of human existence to bear on the vitally important area of human life and health. The Church carries out its responsibility in this regard in a variety of ways but generally under the guidance and leadership of the bishops: "The moral evaluation of new scientific developments and legitimately debated questions must be finally submitted to the teaching authority of the Church in the person of the local bishop, who has the ultimate responsibility for teaching Catholic doctrine" (NCCB, 1971).

This overall responsibility of the official Church to provide moral guidance and leadership in this area entails serious commitment to meeting the following responsibilities.

1. It has the duty to manifest and arouse in Christians a genuine awareness of the far-reaching implications of genetic decisions. If Christian compassion is not to be a hollow claim, Catholics in general and the bishops in particular cannot remain unin-

formed or indifferent to the promises and perils which genetic diagnosis and counseling introduce.

2. It has the duty to articulate as clearly as possible the fundamental human and Christian values that are at stake in the issue of genetic diagnosis and counseling.

   a. A Christian has reverence for the transcendent meaning and dignity of every human life. The basic Christian orientation must be a respect for life coupled with a commitment to the sustaining of human life and the fostering of the development of human life from the moment of conception.

   b. A Christian has a positive appreciation of the Christian responsibility to use human imperfection and suffering as an opportunity for growth.

   c. A Christian has a special sensitivity and compassion for the weak, underprivileged, defenseless, or defective members of the human family. This sensitivity must extend not only to the unborn but also to the parents and counselors in their endeavor to gather, assess, and cope with the data at hand in the light of their human and Christian responsibilities.

   d. A Christian accepts the responsibility to exercise prudent control over the processes of human life. This involves in particular the responsibility of the parents to seek expert guidance in the begetting, bearing, and raising of their children.

   e. A Christian has a sensitive appreciation of the multiple responsibilities of the parents, the counselor, the Christian community, and civil society in the presence of genetic defects.

3. The Church has the duty to recognize the ambiguity, inadequacy, and incompleteness of our present knowledge of many aspects of these issues which necessarily render our present answers tentative and inconclusive. This calls for a recognition of the limitations of the official Church's ability to give detailed and specific responses in highly complex matters. A proper appreciation of the many unanswered and presently unanswerable aspects of these questions should call forth the kind of interdisciplinary dialogue and mutual respect advocated by the Council Fathers of Vatican II (#43).

4. It has the duty to encourage and support the serious work of

scientists, theologians, and experts in other disciplines searching for more complete answers to the problems that remain unresolved. This implies an openness to and respect for serious scientific evidence and solid theological argument even when such is not in complete harmony with or does not fully corroborate current official teaching on an issue. This dialogue must extend itself beyond the community of scholars to consultation with Judaism and other Christian bodies as well as with those with no specific ecclesial allegiance.

5. It has the duty to provide educational opportunities that will enable individual Christians to reach informed and conscientious decisions reflecting the Christian reverence for life. Such education will include the fostering of respect for the freedom of the well-formed Christian conscience to reach decisions in agreement with the person's deepest convictions.

6. It has the duty to help create the kind of public policy in the legislative, judicial, and administrative areas that will most effectively protect and ensure the realization of these values. An appreciation of the educative force of law which powerfully influences societal attitudes and behavior make this an especially important area of responsibility.

One specific example of the Bishops' role in dealing with the problems associated with genetic disease is the *Pastoral Statement of U.S. Catholic Bishops on Handicapped People* (November 16, 1978). In this statement the bishops enunciate a number of principles and outline the responsibilities of the Church at three levels: parish, diocesan, and national.

In this regard the Bishops clearly state the Church's responsibility to imitate Jesus:

Concern for handicapped people was one of the prominent notes of Jesus' earthly ministry. When asked by John's disciples, "Are you 'He who is to come' or do we look for another?" Jesus responded with words recalling the prophecies of Isaiah: "Go back and report to John what you hear and see; the blind recover their sight, cripples walk, lepers are cured, the deaf hear, dead men are raised to life, and the poor have the good news preached to them" (Mt. 11:3-5). Handicapped persons become witnesses for Christ, His healing of their bodies a sign of the spiritual healing He brought to all people.

"Which is less trouble to say, 'Your sins are forgiven' or 'Stand up and walk?' To help you realize that the Son has authority on earth to forgive sins" — He then said to the paralyzed man — "Stand up! Roll up your mat, and go home" (Mt. 9:5f.).

The Church that Jesus founded would surely have been derelict had it failed to respond to His example in its attention to handicapped people (NCCB, 1978, p. 2).

Many handicapped persons are such because of a genetic defect while others became handicapped because of some accident, usually subsequent to birth. But whatever may have been the origin to their condition, their rights as human persons and as Christians are clear. Although some may feel a natural shyness or reluctance in dealing with handicapped people, these feelings must not prevent Christians from working vigorously to provide the necessary and rightfully expected assistance.

It is not enough merely to affirm the rights of handicapped people. We must actively work to realize these rights in the fabric of modern society. Recognizing that handicapped individuals have a claim to our respect because they are persons, because they share in the one redemption of Christ, and because they contribute to our society by their activity within it, the Church must become an advocate for and with them. It must work to increase the public's sensitivity toward the needs of handicapped people and support their rightful demand for justice. Moreover, individuals and organizations at every level within the Church should minister to handicapped persons by serving their personal and social needs (NCCB, 1978, p. 3).

If the efforts of the Church at all levels to assure that the rights of handicapped persons are fully recognized and implemented are successful, then the conscience level of society will have been that much elevated. Furthermore, the fear and suspicions of such persons will be diminished in the mind of the public because many handicapped persons who were once shunned as "untouchables" are seen capable of leading a reasonably happy and productive life. In turn such improvement in public attitude toward the handicapped may very well lessen the call for abortion as a "solution" for genetically defective fetuses.

The Church in its Health Care Institutions

In addition to the responsibilities that flow from its mission as a moral teacher, the Church's compassion and concern for those in need have compelled it to reach out through Church-sponsored health care and social service agencies and provide for special needs to the extent of its means and resources. The provision of such services has never been viewed as the Church's primary responsibility, but wherever unmet needs could be served and the Church was able to respond, compassionate service has always been regarded as an integral part of its mission.

In addition to serving the health care needs of people in an immediate and concrete way, the Church's presence through its health care institutions has brought other distinct advantages to its overall mission:

1. Church-sponsored health care institutions give credibility and convincing proof of the Church's concern for the needy by providing a powerful corporate witness to the values which it possesses.
2. Such institutions furnish a needed challenge and alternative in the United States to public institutions where the emphasis accorded the right to privacy results often in the prevailing of a morality of the least common denominator.
3. Such institutions provide a base from which the Christian value system can have a voice to influence public policy, legislation, and regulatory agencies with an effectiveness which personal witness alone would never accomplish.

These considerations make it a matter of extreme importance that the Church continue its institutional presence and witness in a matter so vital as genetics for the future of the human race.

The question at issue is how the Church can best fulfill its mission as witness to the gospel message by its institutional presence. One of the most significant points of disagreement has been whether Catholic health facilities should permit amniocentesis on their premises. The argument opposing such provision is based on the assumption that most women today undertake amniocentesis with abortion con-templated in the event of a positive diagnosis. The argument is two-fold:

1. By providing amniocentesis the hospital is cooperating with the abortion plans of the woman.
2. The provision of amniocentesis would be a source of scandal for the community.

The position of this study is that the objections, although reasonable, do not provide an adequate basis for a blanket condemnation of providing antenatal diagnostic facilities. In the first place, not all antenatal tests presuppose or imply an intent to abort. Some are morally legitimate as offering therapeutic benefits for the unconsenting unborn such as determining the condition of the fetus when there is cause for concern. Second, the provision of such facilities can permit an opportunity to counsel with the couple about the morality of certain courses of action. Thus, one of two options may be open to the Catholic health facility. The first of these is to permit all antenatal diagnostic tests that provide hope of therapeutic benefit for the child or that could be justified to him after he has reached maturity. A second option is that of providing tests for all couples requesting them on the understanding that the couple would receive moral as well as technical counseling and the wider community would be informed of the reasons for such tests being provided. The fact is that abortions are often prevented by resort to prenatal diagnosis (see Case #4, pp. 36-38) since about 95% of amniocenteses performed in the United States do not terminate in an abortion (NICHD, 1979). It should be clear, however, that the second option can be justified only if:

1. The intent is to save lives or to protect the health of the fetus;
2. The couple receives moral counseling;
3. The danger of scandal is countered by efforts at educating the general public.

The first option provides less opportunity for abuse and for scandal, but this advantage seems more than offset by the disadvantage that there is less opportunity to provide moral counsel to couples who are most in need of it. Assessments of the dangers of abuse and of scandal may vary from case to case, but unless these dangers are rather high, the second option would appear preferable.

Closely related to the question of amniocentesis is the problem associated with the use of contraceptive devices or permanent sterilization when one or other is the physician's recommendation. Because some genetic diseases result in significant physical and/or mental disabilities, as for example, Huntington's disease (see pp. 38-42), or Down's syndrome due to advanced maternal age (see pp. 49-50), with a concurrent high risk of begetting such a child, many genetic counselors maintain that the best way to manage that situation is for the woman to be sterilized. This can place the Catholic hospital or clinic in a difficult position in light of the repeated teaching of the Church's Magisterium. Should a Catholic health facility permit such contraceptive sterilization to take place within its walls?

As part of larger problems, this issue can only be treated here in a very limited way. (For a fuller discussion, see Atkinson and Moraczewski, 1979.) The Church's official teaching is clear: Catholic health facilities, as a matter of policy, are not to assist in direct, contraceptive sterilizations (NCCB, 1971, 1977; Sacred Congregation, 1975). The sterilization is considered contraceptive when the direct intent is to prevent conception. The desired good effect is obtained precisely because another conception is not possible. No matter how laudable or necessary — such as preventing the conception of a genetically defective child — the official teaching does not seem to allow an exception.

But the document from the Sacred Congregation for the Doctrine of the Faith regarding sterilizations in Catholic hospitals (1975) after stating its prohibition of sterilizations, does allow exception by way of material cooperation:

a) Any cooperation institutionally approved or tolerated in actions which are in themselves, that is, by their nature and condition, directed to a contraceptive end, namely, that the natural effects of sexual actions deliberately performed by the sterilizied subject be impeded, is absolutely forbidden. For the official approbation of direct sterilization and, *a fortiori,* its management and execution in accord with hospital regulations, is a matter which, in the objective order, is by its very nature (or intrinsically) evil. The Catholic hospital cannot cooperate with this for any reason. Any cooperation so supplied is totally unbecoming the mission entrusted to this type of institution and would be contrary to the necessary proclamation and defense of the moral order.

b) The traditional doctrine regarding material cooperation, with the proper distinctions between necessary and free, proximate and remote, remains valid, to be applied with the utmost prudence, if the case warrants.

c) In the application of the principle of material cooperation, if the case warrants, great care must be taken against scandal and the danger of any misunderstanding by an appropriate explanation of what is really being done (see Sacred Congregation, 1975, p. 118).

While this teaching seems clear enough, problems and divisions of opinion have arisen around the matter of material cooperation and its applications in these hard cases. In an attempt to clarify the issue, the National Conference of Catholic Bishops in the United States issued a commentary (NCCB, 1977). In that commentary it emphasizes that a distinction must be made between the reason for the sterilization and the reason for the cooperation. These may not be the same:

> In judging the morality of cooperation a clear distinction should be made between the reason for the sterilization and the reason for the cooperation. If the hospital cooperates because of the reason for the sterilization, e.g., because it is done for medical reasons, the cooperation can hardly be considered material. In other words the hospital can hardly maintain under these circumstances that it does not approve sterilizations done for medical reasons, and this would make cooperation formal. If the cooperation is to remain material, the reason for the cooperation must be something over and above the reason for the sterilization itself. Since, as mentioned above (n. 2), the hospital has authority over its own decisions, this should not happen with any frequency (p. 7, #4).

Consequently, a Catholic hospital faced with the necessity of making a decision as to whether or nor it could permit this or that particular contraceptive sterilization to take place, must make a prudential judgement regarding the presence and gravity of an extrinsic reason for permitting the operation to take place. Such a reason might be one which would lead to closing down the obstetrical services or even the hospital itself. In making such a decision, the administrator and/or Board of Trustees should also consider the presence or absence of other hospitals within a reasonably accessible distance, the nature of the civil community which the hospital is serving, and previous analogous experiences in the region. Guidance should also be sought from the local Ordinary.

A Catholic health facility in its witness to the Christian faith renders numerous services to the people it serves. It has serious and heavy responsibilities regarding the health of its surrounding community. Consequently, its single actions must be assessed against the totality of health care delivery it provides.

Among the manifold services such Church-related institutions would be expected to provide in relation to the question of genetic diagnosis and counseling could be listed the following:

— Adequate education and material sustenance for women so that they may choose motherhood responsibly and freely in accord with a basic commitment to the sanctity of life;
— Nutritional, pre-natal, childbirth, and post-natal care for the mother, and nutritional and pediatric care for the child throughout the first year of life;
— Intensified scientific investigation into the causes and cures of maternal disease and fetal abnormality;
— Continued development of genetic counseling and gene therapy centers of perinatal intensive care facilities;
— Extension of adoption and foster care facilities to those who need them;
— Pregnancy counseling centers which provide advice, encouragement, and support for every women who faces difficulties related to pregnancy;
— Counseling services and opportunities for continuation of education for unwed mothers;
— Special understanding, encouragement, and support for victims of rape;
— Continued efforts to remove the social stigma that is visited on the woman who is pregnant out of wedlock and on her child (NCCB, 1975, p. 6).

In addition to these activities, Church-related institutions would also appropriately be expected to provide morally acceptable alternatives to sterilization. Natural Family Planning clinics and NFP teacher training are important services to meet that need (Kippley & Kippley, 1979).

The Church through its leaders, the bishops, provides basic Christian moral guidance. At various levels of the Church organization, responsibilities need to be recognized and programs implemented to provide concrete assistance for handicapped persons and for their parents. Research into the identification, cause and appropriate treatment of genetic disease needs to be strongly encouraged and promoted. Catholic health care facilities can provide truly competent genetic counselors and well-equipped facilities while at the same time being sensitive to the moral issues involved.

Summary

In numerous ways the Church through its various institutions can assist and supplement the efforts of individual Christians to bear witness to Gospel values in dealing with the difficult human problems associated with genetic disease. The bishops are challenged to provide moral leadership not only by bearing witness to the faith of which they are the custodians and ministers but also in encouraging other institutions and scientists to find morally acceptable ways to prevent these diseases and to discover new treatments or improve currently available therapies.

Working with the bishops, Catholic health facilities are challenged to provide appropriate facilities for genetic diagnosis and counseling when circumstances allow this to be done in a morally acceptable manner. In addition, as Catholic health centers, these institutions can provide a variety of health-related services including well organized Natural Family Planning clinics.

The magnitude of the problems presented by the treatment and care of patients who are handicapped, whether by genetic disease or by some prenatal or post-natal trauma, is such that the Church in its various institutions is not able to deal with them adequately. Consequently, the Church rightly looks to civil society for assistance. The following chapter, hence, will deal with society's responsibilities in the matter of genetic diseases.

Chapter 8

Christian Expectations Regarding Civil Society's Responsibilities Toward Genetic Defects

Introduction

The previous two chapters have dealt with the manner in which Christians, individually and collectively, are challenged to respond to the problems posed by the genetic diseases. In this final chapter, attention is turned to the role of civil society in aiding individuals, families and institutions to deal with some of the heavy burdens that can result from the various genetic diseases. To accomplish this end, the material will be divided into three parts: (1) principles, (2) expectations regarding societal responsibilities, and (3) partial realization of expectations. Of necessity, the treatment will be condensed.

Principles

The transcendent dignity of the individual human person that forms the basis for so many values provides guidelines for society's obligations. Social existence is not something accidental or accessory to human beings. It is only through their dealings with others that persons are able to develop their capabilities and attain their true destiny. "Insofar as man by his very nature stands completely in need of life in society, he is and ought to be the beginning, the subject and the object of every social organization" (Vatican II, 1965b, #25)*.

---

*Hereafter in this chapter, the number in parentheses will refer to the paragraph number in Vatican II, 1965b.

Human persons are not made for the benefit of society, but society ought to be constituted to aid individuals in attaining their natural and supernatural ends. "The social order and its development must constantly yield to the good of the person, since the order of things must be subordinate to the order of persons and not the other way around" (#26). Therefore, the fundamental rights of human persons are inalienable and cannot be taken from them by any appeal to the greater good. Many of these rights have already been enumerated (see above, pp. 86-88). They include the right to life, the right to what is necessary for a fully human existence, the right to choose a state in life and to set up a family, the right to privacy, and the right to act in conformity with his moral and religious conscience.

The common good may be defined as "the sum total of social conditions which allow people, either as groups or as individuals, to reach their fulfillment more fully and more easily" (#26). Because all social institutions must work for the betterment of persons, it is the serious obligation of society to promote the common good. Indeed, the Council Fathers go so far as to say that the promotion of the common good is society's reason for existence.

> Individuals, families, and various groups which make up the civil community, are aware of their inability to achieve a truly human life by their own unaided efforts; they see the need for a wider community where each one will make a specific contribution to an even broader implementation of the common good. For this reason they set up various forms of political communities. The political community, then, exists for the common good: this is its full justification and meaning and the source of its right to exist. The common good embraces the sum total of all those conditions of social life which enable individuals, families, and organization to achieve complete and efficacious fulfillment" (#74).

The Council declared that the family is "a school for human enrichment" (#52). The welfare of the family grounds the well-being of the individual and the larger communities of Church and State (#47).

> Everyone, therefore, who exercises an influence in the community and in social groups should devote himself effectively to the welfare of marriage and the family. Civil authority should consider it a sacred duty to acknowledge the true nature of marriage and the

family, to protect and foster them, to safeguard public morality and promote domestic prosperity. The rights of parents to procreate and educate chilren in the family must be safeguarded (#52).

Governments should take care not to put obstacles in the way of family, cultural or social groups, or of organizations and intermediate institutions, nor to hinder their lawful and constructive activity; rather, they should eagerly seek to promote such orderly activity (#75).

It is the responsibility of the civil community to exercise its power "within the limits of the moral order and directed toward the common good" (#74). The meaning and value of the individual human life and of the family transcend their significance for the social group just as God's plan for human beings transcends their earthly existence. This fact, that the value of human persons and the integrity of the family cannot be comprehended merely in social terms, means that there are limits placed upon what society may legitimately do. It is only by recognizing these limits and respecting the inviolability of the human person and family that society functions in accordance with God's will.

Expectations Regarding Societal Responsibilities

The responsibilities of civil society follow directly from what has been said. First, society has a responsibility to promote a true understanding of the dignity of the human person. This dignity is one that cannot be reduced to considerations relating to the individual's talents and value for society or to personal attractiveness and acceptability by society. The fact that a person will require a costly series of treatments does not detract from the individual's value as a person. Nor does the fact that the person is in some way abnormal or less than perfect tend in any way to lessen personal dignity and worth. The Declaration of Independence holds these truths to be self-evident: that all humans are created equal and endowed by their Creator with inalienable rights, among them the right to life, liberty, and the pursuit of happiness. It is the function of government to preserve and protect these rights. Thus, at the foundation of our government's right to exist is its responsibility to teach and promote the true dignity of the human person, to protect the fundamental moral equality of all human beings.

Following from this first responsibility of government, there is a second responsibility to oppose abortion and infanticide and euthanasia as violations of the inalienable right to life. This responsibility becomes acute in the case of abortion or infanticide for reason of genetic defect, because such practices mark off a group of humans as second-class citizens, as beings not worthy of the full protection of the law. The *Roe* and *Doe* decisions accomplish precisely this, and they do so without even attempting to justify calling the unborn nonhumans. "We need not decide the difficult question of when human life begins," wrote Justice Harry Blackmun in the majority opinion for *Roe v. Wade* (1973). A society concerned for the fundamental principles of justice has a responsibility to oppose the discriminatory treatment of human beings who are weak and defenseless, unwanted, or afflicted.

If abortion is so opposed to the basic moral equality of all human beings, it would seem incumbent on society to oppose abortion of individuals with genetic defects, as it would be to oppose infanticide for the same reason. It may be that the woman herself sees nothing morally wrong with selective abortion, but a clear conscience by itself can never be sufficient to justify permitting a person to act in accordance with it. An individual who sees nothing wrong with child abuse or who believes that children below a certain age are simply the property of their parents to be disposed of at will cannot claim freedom from restrictive law on the grounds of a good conscience; for there is the overriding consideration of the harm done to the violated child and to the society that would permit such practices. Furthermore, if the toleration of selective abortion is so violative of the rights of individuals and threatens the very existence of a humane society, then it would be difficult to see how it could be the *obligation* of society to provide prenatal diagnostic facilities also for women contemplating abortions. Society might well have an obligation to provide those facilities as a service to women who are not contemplating abortion but who choose to employ medical technology in an effort to save their unborn children. Then the provision of such facilities for women contemplating abortion might be justified by the principle of the double effect without being obligatory.

A third responsibility of civil society is to espouse a proper relationship between individual rights and the good of others. This means that a society must recognize limits on its power, that the collective good of the society must be subordinated to the good of the individual member even when society possesses the power to assert the collective will over the individual. Furthermore, members of society should recognize that the good of all is dependent on the respect for the rights of the individual, and that a society that would subordinate the rights of a few for the sake of the good of the many stands in danger of using similar justifications for sacrificing the rights of any of its members.

Fourth, society has a responsibility to care for those who are less fortunate and less perfect than others. Society cannot guarantee happiness for all its members, and happiness is not a God-given right of anyone, but the Declaration of Independence does declare that the "pursuit of happiness" is an inalienable right, that each person has a right to seek happiness and to possess the minimum conditions necessary for that pursuit. Whether or not a person with a genetic defect has a right to the reception of care is not dependent on utilitarian calculations related to the actual attainment or maximization of happiness by that individual. This right is prior to all such calculations of general benefit and is rooted in the fundamental dignity of the human person. The quality and extent of that care to which a handicapped person has a right will depend, of course, on the economic and technical resources actually available in a particular region, state or nation. No doubt tensions will arise when the government has to decide how to allocate its limited resources. The severely handicapped may require life-long care and institutionalization. In order to do this, the government may find it necessary to cut back other programs deemed to be of lesser national importance. Such decisions will reflect the hierarchy of values which motivate legislators' decisions as well as indicating, ultimately, the dominant values of society at large.

Fifth, the civil society has a responsibility to protect the freedom of parents in the making of procreative decisions, provided that these decisions respect the rights of others. It is true that some decisions made by parents may in certain respects be harmful to the *interests* of others. For example, the procreative decision of parents — at risk for Down's syndrome — to have a child will mean that time and care will have to be given to an afflicted child; time and care which in part could have been devoted to others. But this cannot be a justification for a general restricting of those decisions because many, if not most, decisions in favor of some persons will have some detrimental effect on the interests of others. It is only when the *rights* of others are violated that infringement of freedom can be justified. A society can exist only if its members are willing to bear with the decisions of others that may adversely affect them. A good society places a high enough value on responsible and free decisions that it is willing to tolerate some harmful consequences in individual instances. Also, members of society should recognize that it is very much in their interest that the community respect this sphere of individual freedom.

What is society's clear responsibility is the fostering of a loving attitude of concern for affected individuals and the provision of moral and financial support for the parents and others upon whom the responsibility of care primarily rests. While it may be that a cost/benefit analysis would show the desirability of providing free prenatal diagnostic facilities for all women desiring them, for enough defective individuals might be detected and aborted under such a program that its cost would be more than offset by the amount of money and effort that could thereby be diverted from the care of defective individuals, such purely pragmatic calculations must not be allowed to determine social policy.

Above all, society has a responsibility to see to it that the parents and family of an affected child are not abandoned. It is all too easy for a society to say, "You had your chance to abort the child and you refused to do so; now you've made your bed and must lie in it." We have already mentioned the responsibility of the individual couple to prevent the conception of a seriously affected child; but it is absolutely impossible to prevent all such occurrences, for spontaneous mutations happen every day. Faced with the existence of an affected individual, whether or not through the "culpable" failure of the parents, society has a responsibility to promote care of the child through public and private institutions. Society must see to it that the affected child, already disadvantaged by its defect, it not further disadvantaged by societal neglect. Families often respond in a most generous fashion to the birth of an affected child, but unfortunately the same can not always be said of society's approach. The handicapped are oftentimes shunted off into some out-of-the-way institution, there to be forgotten by society's more fortunate members. To be in favor of life, society must be as much and more concerned about what happens to the individual after birth as before. Society can promote a deeper concern for the more humane treatment of all human beings by fostering research into the causes and cure of genetic disease, care of the unborn, and greater opportunities for treatment of those born.

Sixth, the civil society may, depending on its resources, have a responsibility to develop screening programs to detect carriers for certain specified genetic defects. Nevertheless, it is vital that these programs be conducted in such a manner that the autonomy of the parents is not endangered, discrimination against certain groups is not encouraged, and adverse attitudes toward handicapped persons are not fostered. If such programs generate these abuses, they should be modified or even abandoned. Such a recommendation may not be palatable to a community that subscribes to materialistic values. But the most important human values, as the history of mankind records and the Christian message teaches, are not the material values of health, wealth, and security, but the moral and spiritual values of human dignity, wisdom, compassion, generosity, courage, justice, and self-sacrifice. It is the obligation of Christians and of all peoples to work for these material values, for they are true goods flowing from the goodness of their Creator. But their value cannot justify subordinating the moral and divine law in their pursuit.

Partial Realization of Expectations

An adequate history of United States government involvement in the care of the handicapped remains to be written. However, even a cursory study of various government enactments indicate an increasing involvement in, and support of, the mentally and physically disadvantaged.

In 1978 several pieces of Federal legislation were enacted which were amendments to existing laws and regulations. Public Law 95-602 (1978) introduced amendments to the Rehabilitation Amendments of 1973 (P.L. 93-112) which in turn had completely revised the Vocational Rehabilitation Act dating back, through five revisions, to the Smith-Fess Act of 1920 (Gettings, 1975).

The 1973 Amendments provided, among other items that:

1. Vocational rehabilitation services be extended for additional two years with ceilings of $650 million (FY 1974) and $680 million (FY 1975).
2. State agencies give priority to "those individuals with the most severe handicaps."
3. State agencies develop for each client an individualized written program (Gettings, 1975).

On November 6, 1978, President Carter signed into law the Rehabilitation Amendments (State of Minnesota, 1979). This act extends state grant funding for an additional four years but after the 1979 figure ($808 million) it interlocks the increases with the Consumer Price Index and sets an upper limit for each fiscal year, peaking at $972 million for FY 1982. Another important provision of the 1978 Legislation is the establishment of a National Institute of Handicapped Research which will have the responsibility to administer all research pertaining to handicapped individuals and to disseminate its findings.

Yet another important element of P.L. 95-602 is Title V which includes Amendments to the Developmental Disabilities (DD) Services and Facilities Construction Act. Among the provisions is a new definition of "Developmental Disability" which can serve to show the extent of persons covered by these amendments. Thus:

> The term 'developmental disability' means a severe, chronic disability of a person — which is attributal to a mental or physical impairment or combination of mental and physical impairments; is manifested before the person attains age twenty-two; is likely to continue indefinitely; results in substantial functional limitations in three or more of the following areas of major life activity: (i) self-care, (ii) receptive and expressive language, (iii) learning, (iv) mobility, (v) self-direction, (vi) capacity for independent living, and (vii) economic self-sufficiency; and reflects the person's need for a combination and sequence of special, interdisciplinary, or generic care, treatment, or other services which are of lifelong or extended duration and are individually planned and coordinated (Minnesota, 1979, p. 6).

There are many other Federal Programs which are available for serving the handicapped. Among these are such acts as Education Amendment, Federal Highway Acts, Amtrack Improvement Act, Community Services Act, Health Program Extension Act, etc. (Gettings, 1975).

From these brief remarks, it can be seen that the Federal Government has indeed taken an active interest in the needs of the handicapped persons. Whether the appropriations are adequate to meet the needs is another question. The formation of a National Institute of Handicapped Research (NIHR) is a good omen. With adequate funding and competent staffing the NIHR is in a position to extend our understanding of the causes, prevention and treatment of crippling handicaps. Whether their origin is prenatally due to defective genes or whether it is post-natally due to some accident is of little consequence. The information of each will benefit the other. Eventually, it may become possible to correct the defective gene at the most fundamental level, but this awaits the development of a nascent science, genetic engineering. Meanwhile, research funded by the federal and state governments should be vigorously encouraged by the Church so that better treatment, palliative at least, of those persons handicapped by genetic defect will be available.

Summary

As developed in this chapter, the magnitude of the task of providing adequate care for those affected by genetic disease exceeds the resources of individual Christians and the Church. Justly, the Church expects civil society to carry out its appropriate responsibilities. Basing its expectations on the dignity of the human person as an individual and as a member of society, the Church looks to civil society to promote the unique and imponderable worth of each individual person. Society is also expected to protect human life at all stages of its development, to provide for the less fortunate, to foster basic freedoms including the right to make procreative decisions, and to promote those conditions and values which will guard and enhance family life. In the United States, state and federal governments have made some progress in providing aid and programs to assist the handicapped. However, the support provided by current federal legislation is still insufficient. The Church needs vigorously to encourage legislators to pass improved laws which will more effectively meet the needs of the handicapped persons.

BIBLIOGRAPHY

Alter, M. "Anencephalus, Hydrocephalus and Spina Bifida: Epidemiology with Special Reference to a Suvey in Charleston, S.C." *Archives of Neurology* 7: (1962) 411.

Aristotle, *Politics,* I, 2. 1253a. In Vol. VI: *Politics and Poetics of The Student's Oxford Aristotle,* edited and translated by W. D. Ross. London and New York: Oxford University Press, 1942.

Ashley, O. P., Benedict M. "A Critique of the Theory of Delayed Hominization." In *An Ethical Evaluation of Fetal Experimentation: An Interdisciplinary Study,* edited by Donald G. McCarthy and Moraczewski, O. P., Albert. St. Louis: Pope JOHN XXIII Medical-Moral Research and Education Center, 1976, pp. 113-133.

Ashley, O. P., Benedict M. and O'Rourke, O. P., Keven D. *Health Care Ethics – A Theological Analysis.* St. Louis: The Catholic Hospital Association, 1978.

Atkinson, Gary M. "Persons in the Whole Sense." *American Journal of Jurisprudence* 22: (1977) 86-117.

Atkinson, Gary M. and Moraczewski, Albert S. *A Moral Evaluation of Contraception and Sterilization: A Dialogical Study.* St. Louis: Pope John Center, 1979.

Bergsma, Daniel ed. *Birth Defects; Atlas and Compendium.* Baltimore: The National Foundation, 1973.

Bowman, B. H. and Mangos, J. A. "Cystic Fibrosis." *New England Journal of Medicine* 294 (17): (April 26, 1976) 937-938.

Callahan, Daniel. *Abortion: Law, Choice and Morality.* New York: Macmillan, 1970. _____ . "Search for an Ethic: Living with the New Biology." *The Center Magazine* 5: (July/August, 1972) 8.

Chamberlain, J. "Human Benefits and Costs of a National Screening Program for Neural-Tube Defects." *Lancet,* 1978, ii, 1293.

Christian, Francis. "Technological Reproduction: The Moral Question of Extra-Corporeal Conception and Gestation in Human Reproduction." Unpublished Dissertation, University of Louvain, 1975.

Church in the Modern World. See Vatican II, 1965b.

Cleary, S.J., Francis X. "Biblical Perspectives on Suffering." *Hospital Progress,* December 1974, pp. 54-58.

Clow, C. L.; Fraser, F. C., Laberge, C. et al. "On the Application of Knowledge to the Patient with Genetic Disease." In Vol. 9 of *Progress in*

Medical Genetics, edited by A. G. Steinberg and A. G. Bearn. New York: Grune and Stratton, Inc., 1973.

Connery, John R., S. J. *Abortion: The Development of Roman Catholic Perspectives,* Chicago: Loyola Press, 1977.

——————. "Morality of Consequences: A Critical Appraisal" in Curran, Charles, *Moral Norms and Catholic Tradition.* Paramus, New Jersey: Paulist Press, 1978.

——————. "Abortion and the Duty To Preserve Life" *Theological Studies* 40: (June, 1979) 318-33.

Curran, Charles E.

1968. *A New Look at Catholic Morality.* Notre Dame, Ind.: Fides Publishers.

1969. "Natural Law and Contemporary Moral Theology." In *Contraception: Authority and Dissent,* edited by Charles E. Curran. New York: Herder & Herder, pp. 151-175.

1974. *New Perspectives in Moral Theology.* Notre Dame, Ind.: Fides Publishers.

1975. *Ongoing Revision: Studies in Moral Theology.* Notre Dame, Ind.: Fides Publishers.

1978a. "After *Humanae Vitae:* A Decade of Lively Debate." *Hospital Progress,* 59 (7): (July) 84-89.

1978b. *Issues in Sexual and Medical Ethics.* Notre Dame, Ind.: University of Notre Dame Press.

Day, N. and Holmes, L. B. "The Incidence of Genetic Disease in a University Hospital Population." *American Journal of Human Genetics* 25: (1973) 237.

Doe v. Bolton, U. S. Sup. Ct. 22 Jan. 1973; 410 U. S. Rept. 179-223.

Dyck, Arthur. "An Alternative to the Ethic of Euthanasia." In *To Live and to Die,* edited by Robert H. Williams. New York: Springer-Verlag, 1973, pp. 98-112.

Easley, R. and Milunsky, A. "The Economics of Prenatal Genetic Diagnosis." In *The Prevention of Genetic Disease and Mental Retardation,* edited by Aubrey Milunsky. Philadelphia: W. B. Saunders Co., 1975, pp. 442-455.

Editorial. "The Risk of Amniocentesis." *Lancet,* 1978, ii, 1287-1288.

Engelhardt, Jr., H. Tristram. "The Beginnings of Personhood: Philosophical Considerations." *Perkins Journal of Theology* 27: (Fall, 1973) 20-27.

Epstein, C. J. and Golbus, M. S. "The Prenatal Diagnosis of Genetic Disorders." *Annual Review of Medicine* 29: (1978) 117-28.

Erbe, R. W. "Principles of Medical Genetics." *New England Journal of*

Medicine 294:7 (February 12, 1976) 381-385; 294, 9: (February 26, 1976) 480-482.

Federal Register, August 14, 1979, 47732-47734.

Fienman, N. L. and Yakowac, W. C. "Neurofibromatosis in Childhood." *Journal of Pediatrics* 76: (1970) 339.

Fletcher, John. "The Brink: The Parent-Child Bond in the Genetic Revolution." *Theological Studies* 33, 3: (September 1972) 457-485.

_____ . "Ethics and Amniocentesis for Fetal Sex Identification." *New England Journal of Medicine* 301, 10: (September 6, 1979) 550-553.

Fletcher, Joseph.

1960. "The Ethics of Personality: Morality, Nature and Human Nature." In his *Morals and Medicine.* Boston: Beacon Press, pp. 211-228.

1970. "Technological Devices in Medical Care." In *Who Shall Live,* edited by Kenneth Vaux. Philadelphia: Fortress Press, pp. 115-42.

1972. "Indicators of Humanhood: A Tentative Profile of Man." *Hastings Center Report* 2, 5:1-4.

1974. "Four Indicators of Humanhood: The Inquiry Matures." *Hastings Center Report* 4:4-7.

1978. "Pediatric Euthanasia: The Ethics of Selective Treatment for Spina Bifida." In *Decision Making and The Defective Newborn,* edited by Swinyard, Chester A. Springfield, Ill.: Charles C. Thomas.

Ford, S. J., John C., and Grisez, Germain G. "Contraception and the Infallibility of the Ordinary Magisterium." *Theological Studies* 39:258-312.

Frigoletto, F. D., Jr. and Griscom, N. T. "Amniography for the Detection of Fetal Myelomeningocele." *Obstetrics and Gynecology* 44: (1974) 286.

Fuchs, Josef. *Natural Law: A Theological Investigation.* New York: Sheed & Ward, 1963.

_____ . "The Absoluteness of Moral Terms." *Gregorianum* 52 (1971): 415-458.

Gaudium et Spes. See Vatican II, 1965b.

Gerald, P. "Sex Chromosome Disorders." *New England Journal of Medicine* 294 (1976): 706-708.

Gettings, Robert M. *3rd Congress: Federal Laws and Regulations Affecting the Handicapped.* Arlington, Va.: National Association of Coordinators of State Programs for the Mentally Retarded, Inc., 1975.

Goetz, C. G. and Weiner, W. J. "Huntington's Disease: Current Concepts of Therapy." *Journal of the American Geriatrics Society* 27, 61 (1979): 23-26.

Golbus, M. S., Loushman, W. D., Epstein, C. J., et al. "Prenatal Genetic Diagnosis in 3000 Amniocentesis." *New England Journal of Medicine* 300 (1979): 157.

Gremillion, Joseph. *The Gospel of Peace and Justice: Catholic Social Teaching Since Pope John.* Maryknoll, NY: Orbis Books, 1976.

Grice, G. R. *The Grounds of Moral Judgment.* Cambridge: Cambridge University Press, 1967.

Grisez, Germain G.
1964. *Contraception and the Natural Law.* Milwaukee: Bruce.
1970a. *Abortion: The Myths, the Realities, the Arguments.* Washington, D.C.: Corpus Books.
1970b. "Toward a Consistent Natural-Law Ethics of Killing." *American Journal of Jurisprudence* 15:65-96.
1978. See Ford, S. J., John C. and Grisez, Germain G.

Grisez, Germain G. and Boyle, Jr., Joseph M. *Life and Death with Liberty and Justice,* Notre Dame, Ind.: University of Notre Dame Press, 1979.

Grisez, Germain G. and Shaw, Russell. *Beyond the New Morality: The Responsibilities of Freedom,* Notre Dame, Ind.: University of Notre Dame Press, 1974.

Gustafson, James. "Genetic Engineering and Normative Humanity." In *Ethical Issues in Biology and Medicine,* edited by Preston Williams. Cambridge, Mass.: Schenkman Publishing Company, 1973, pp. 46-58.

Hamerton, J. L. *Human Cytogenics.* Vol. I, New York: Academic Press, Inc., 1971.

Häring, Bernard. *Medical Ethics.* Notre Dame, Ind.: Fides Press, 1972.

Hauerwas, Stanley. "The Retarded and the Criteria for the Human." *Linacre Quarterly* 40 (November 1973): 219.

—————. *Vision and Virtue.* Notre Dame, Ind.: Fides Publishers, 1974.

Heschel, Abraham, *Who Is Man?* Stanford, Cal.: Stanford University Press, 1965.

Hook, E. and Henly, K. "Height and Seriousness of Crime in XYY Men." *Journal of Medical Genetics* (14 (1977): 10-12.

Hopkins, Gerard Manley, No. 60, "The Blessed Virgin Compared to the Air We Breathe," ln. 34, In *Poems,* ed. by W. H. Gardner, 1948, 34d edition, Oxford University Press. See Bartlett's Familiar Quotations, 14th ed., p. 803.

Howard v. Lecher, 53 App. Div. 2d 420, 386 N. Y. S. 2d 460 (1976); aff'd, 42

N.Y. 2d 109, 366 N. E. 2d 64, 397 N. Y. S. 363 (1977).

Howell R. R. and Stevenson, R. E. "The Offspring of PKU Women." *Social Biology*[18] *(1971): 19.*

Humanae Vitae. See Paul VI, 1968.

Institute of Society, Ethics and the Life Sciences: Research Group on Ethical, Social and Legal Issues in Genetic Counseling and Genetic Engineering. "Ethical and Social Issues in Screening for Genetic Disease." *New England Journal of Medicine* 286 (May 25, 1972), pp. 1129-32.

Institute of Society, Ethics and the Life Sciences, Task Force on Death and Dying. "Refinements in the Criteria for the Determination of Death." *Journal of the American Medical Association* 221 (July 3, 1972): 53.

Jacobs, P. A.; Melville, M.; and Ratcliffe, S. "The Cytogenic Survey of 11,680 Newborn Infants." *Annals of Human Genetics* 37 (1974): 359.

Janssens, Louis. "Personalist Morals." *Louvain Studies* 3 (Spring 1970): 12.

John Paul II.
1979a. March 4, *Redeemer of Man (Redemptor Hominis).* Washington, D.C.: United States Catholic Conference.
1979b. Homily October 7 on the Capitol Mall, *Origins,* Vol. 9, No. 18, October 18, 1979, p. 278-80.

Jonas, Hans. "Against the Stream" In *Philosophical Essays: From Ancient Creed to Technological Man.* Englewood Cliffs, NJ: Prentice-Hall, 1974, pp. 138-139.

Kaback, Goldie Ruth. *Guidance and Counseling Perspectives for Hospital Schools of Nursing.* New York: National League for Nursing, Inc., 1958.

Karlsons v. Guerinot, 57 App. Div. 2d 73, 394 N.Y.S. 2d at 933 (1977).

Kass, Leon R. "The Implications of Prenatal Diagnosis for the Human Right to Life." In *Ethical Issues in Human Genetics: Genetic Counseling and the Use of Genetic Knowledge,* edited by Bruce Hilton et al. New York: Plenum Press, 1973, 185-199.

Keane, S. S., Philip S., *Sexual Morality: A Catholic Perspective.* New York: Paulist Press, 1977.

Klawans, H. L., Jr.; Paulson, G. W.; Riegel, S. P. *et al.* "Use of L-Dopa in the Detection of Presymptomatic Huntington's Chorea." *New England Journal of Medicine* 286 (1972): 1332.

Knauer, Peter. "The Hermeneutic Function of the Double Effect." *Natural Law Forum* 12 (1967); 132-162.

Knox, W. E. "Phenylketonuria." In *Metabolic Basis of Inherited Disease,* edited by J. B. Stanbury, J. B. Wyngaarden and D. S. Frederickson. New York: McGraw-Hill, 1972.

Kosnik, Anthony R. Chairperson; with Carrol, William; Cunningham, Agnes; Modras, Ronald; and Schulte, James. *Human Sexuality: New Directions In American Catholic Thought*. New York: Paulist Press, 1977.

Lappé, Marc, Roblin, Richard O., and Gustafson, James M. "Ethical, Social, and Legal Dimensions of Screening for Human Genetic Disease." In *Birth Defects*. Original articles series, X, edited by Daniel Bergsma, Miami, Fla.: Symposia Specialists, 1974.

Lebacqz, Karen A. "Prenatal Diagnosis and Selective Abortion." *Linacre Quarterly,* 40, 2 (May 1973): 109-127.

Lejeune, J.; Gautier, M.; and Turpis, R. "Etude des chromosomes somatiques de neuf enfants mongoliens." *Comptes Rendus de l'Academie des sciences* (Paris) 248 (1959): 1721-22.

Littlefield, John W. "The Pregnancy at Risk for a Genetic Disorder." *New England Journal of Medicine* 282 (1971): 627-628.

Lonergan, Bernard. "Dimensions of Meaning." In *Collection: The Papers by Bernard Lonergan, S. J.* New York: Herder and Herder, 1967, pp. 252-267.

_____ . "The New Context of Theology." In *Theology of Renewal.* New York: Herder and Herder, 1968, pp. 34-46.

Lubs, H. A. and Ruddle, F. H. "Chromosomal Abnormalities in the Human Population: Estimation of Rates Based on New Haven Newborn Study." *Science* 169 (1970): 495-497.

McCarthy, Donald G. and Moraczewski, Albert S., O.P., eds. *An Ethical Evaluation of Fetal Experimentation: An Interdisciplinary Study.* St. Louis: Pope John XXIII Medical-Moral Research and Education Center, 1976.

McCormick, S. J., Richard A.

1972. "The New Directives and Institutional Medico-Moral Responsibility." *Chicago Studies* 11 (Fall): 305-311.

1973a. *Ambiguity in Moral Choice.* 1973 Pere Marquette Theology Lecture. Milwaukee, Wis.: Marquette University.

1973b. "Notes on Moral Theology." *Theological Studies* 34:53-102.

1974a. "Proxy Consent in the Experimental Situation." *Perspectives in Biology and Medicine* 18:2-20.

1974b. "To Save or Let Die: The Dilemma of Modern Medicine." *Journal of the American Medical Association* 229:172-176.

1976a. "Notes on Moral Theology." *Theological Studies* 37:70-119.

1976b. "Experimentation in Children: Sharing in Sociality." *Hastings Center Report.* (December) pp. 41-46.

1977. "Notes on Moral Theology." *Theological Studies* 38:57-114.

1978. "Notes on Moral Theology." *Theological Studies* 39:76-138.

1979. "Notes on Moral Theology." *Theological Studies* 40(59-112.

McKusick, V. A. *Mendelian Inheritance in Man.* 5th ed. Baltimore: Johns Hopkins University Press, 1978.

Mangan, Joseph. "Ethical-Theological Aspects of Direct Abortion." In *Theological Studies* 31 (1970): 128.

Marks, F. Raymond and Salkovitz, Lisa. "The Defective Newborn: An Analytic Framework for a Policy Dialog." In *Ethics of Newborn Intensive Care,* edited by Albert Jonsen and Michael J. Garland. San Francisco and Berkeley: A joint publication of the Health Policy Program, School of Medicine, University of California at San Francisco and the Institute of Governmental Studies, University of California at Berkeley, 1976, pp. 97-124.

Marten, P. M.; Smith, D. W.; and McDonald, M. J. "Congenital Anomalies in the Newborn Infant, Including Minor Variations." *Journal of Pediatrics* 64 (1964): 357.

Massachusetts Department of Public Health: Cost-benefit analysis of newborn screening for metabolis disorders, *New England Journal of Medicine* 291 (1974): 1414.

May, William E.

1975. *Becoming Human: An Invitation to Christian Ethics.* Dayton, Ohio: Pflaum Press.

1977. *Human Existence, Medicine and Ethics.* Chicago: Franciscan Herald Press.

1979. "The Natural Law and Objective Morality: An Historical Perspective." Symposium on Principles of Catholic Moral Life. Washington, D.C., June 17-21, 1979 [in press].

May, William F. "The Sacral Power of Death in Contemporary Experience." In *Perspectives on Death,* edited by Liston O. Mills. Nashville, Abingdon Press, 1969.

Medical Research Council Working Party on Amniocentesis. "An Assessment of the Hazards of Amniocentesis," *British Journal of Obstetrics and Gynecology,* 1978, 85, suppl. 2.

Milunsky, A. *The Prenatal Diagnosis of Hereditary Disorders.* Springfield, Ill.: Charles C. Thomas, Publishers, 1973.

_____ . *The Prevention of Genetic Disease and Mental Retardation.* Philadelphia: W. B. Saunders Co., 1975.

Milunsky, A. and Annas, G. J. *Genetics and the Law.* New York: Plenum Press, 1976.

Milunsky, A. and Atkins, L. "Prenatal Diagnosis of Genetic Disorders: An Analysis of Experience with 600 Cases." *Journal of the American Medical Association,* 230 (1974): 232.

Monteleone, Patricia and Moraczewski, O. P., Albert. "Prenatal Diagnosis of Genetic Disease" In Hilgers, Thomas W., ed., *Abortion and Social Justice,* Revised edition in press 1980.

Moraczewski, Albert S. "Ethical Aspects of Genetic Counseling." In *Psychiatry and Genetics,* edited by Michael A. Sperber and Lissy F. Jarvik. New York: Basic Books, 1976.

Mounier, E. *Personalism.* Notre Dame, Ind.: Notre Dame University Press, 1975, p. 11.

_____ Op. cit., p. 23.

Murray, Robert F., Jr. "Problems Behind The Promise: Ethical Issues in Mass Genetic Screening." *Hastings Center Report* 2 (1972): 10-13.

National Conference of Catholic Bishops.

1971. *Ethical and Religious Directives for Catholic Health Facilities,* Washington, D.C.: United States Catholic Conference; Reprinted by The Catholic Hospital Association, St. Louis, 1975.

1975. *Pastoral Plan For Pro-Life Activities,* Washington, D.C.: United States Catholic Conference.

1976. *To Live in Christ Jesus: A Pastoral Reflection on the Moral Life.* Washington, D.C.: United States Catholic Conference.

1977. *Commentary on Reply of the Sacred Congregation for the Doctrine of the Faith on Sterilization in Catholic Hospitals.* Washington, D.C.: United States Catholic Conference.

1978. *Pastoral Statement of U.S. Catholic Bishops on Handicapped People.* Washington, D.C.: United States Catholic Conference.

National Institute of Child Health and Human Development. *Antenatal Diagnosis,* Report of a Consensus Development Conference. Bethesda, Maryland: National Institutes of Health, April 1979, p. I-4.

National Research Council. Committee for the Study of Inborn Errors of Metabolism. *Genetic Screening: Programs, Principles, and Research.*

Washington, D.C.: National Academy of Sciences, 1975.

NCCB. (See National Conference of Catholic Bishops.)

Nelson, James B. *Human Medicine: Ethical Perspectives on New Medical Issues.* Minneapolis: Augsburg Publishing House, 1973.

The New American Bible. Washington, D.C.: Confraternity of Christian Doctrine, 1970.

NICHD. (See U.S., DHEW, National Institute of Child Health and Human Development.)

Nitowsky, H. M. "Genetic Counseling: Objectives, Principles and Procedures." *Clinical Obstetrics and Gynecology* 19, 4 (December 1976): 919-940.

Noonan, Jr., John T. *A Private Choice – Abortion in America in the Seventies.* New York: The Free Press, 1979, pp. 146-152.

O'Connell, Thomas E. *Principles for a Catholic Morality.* New York: The Seabury Press, 1976.

Omenn, G. S. "Prenatal Diagnosis of Genetic Disorders." *Science* 200 (May 26, 1978): 952-958.

O'Rourke, O. P., Keven D. "An Analysis of the Church's Teaching on Sterilization." *Hospital Progress,* May, 1976, pp. 68-75.

_____ . See Ashley, O. P., Benedict M.

Outler, Albert. "The Beginnings of Personhood: Theological Considerations," *Perkins Journal of Theology* 27 (1):31, Fall, 1973.

Pannenburg, Wolfhart. *What Is Man?* Philadelphia: Fortress Press, 1970.

Paul VI. *Humanae Vitae (On the Regulation of Birth)* (July 25, 1968). In *Encyclical of Pope Paul VI Humanae Vitae On the Regulation of Birth and Pope Paul VI's Credit of the People of God.* Study Club Edition. New York: Paulist Press, 1968, pp. 3-24.

Philip, J.; Lundstein, C.; Owen, D.; and Hurshborn, K. "The Frequency of Chromosome Aberrations in Tall Men with Special Reference to 47 **XYY** and 47 **XXY**." *American Journal of Human Genetics* 28 (1976); 404-411.

Polani, P. E. "Incidence of Developmental and Other Genetic Abnormalities." *Proceedings of the Royal Society of Medicine* 66 (1973): 1118.

Powledge, T. A. and Fletcher, J. "Guidelines for the Ethical, Social and Legal Issues in Prenatal Diagnosis." *New England Journal of Medicine* 300, 4 (1979): 168-172.

Pyeritz, R. E. and McKusick, V. A. "The Marfan Syndrome: Diagnosis and Management." *New England Journal of Medicine* 300, 14 (April 5, 1979): 772-777.

Ramsey, Paul.

1968. "The Morality of Abortion" in *Life or Death: Ethics and Options,* Labby, Daniel, editor, Seattle: University of Washington Press, p. 69.

1970. *The Patient as Person.* New Haven and London: Yale University Press.

1976. "The Enforcement of Morals: Nontherapeutic Research on Children." *Hastings Center Report,* (August) pp. 21-30. "Children as Research Subjects: A Reply." *Hastings Center Report,* April, 1977. pp. 40-42.

Regan, August. "The Worth of Human Life." *Studia Moralia* 6 (1969): 207-77.

Riccardi, V.M. *The Genetic Approach to Human Disease.* New York: Oxford University Press, 1977.

Roe v. Wade, U. S. Sup. Ct. 22 Jan. 1973; 410 U. S. Rep. 113-178.

Rosenberg, Leon, M.D. "Medical Genetics: Progress and Problems." In *Genetic Responsibility: On Choosing Our Children's Genes,* edited by Mark J. Lipkin, Jr. and Peter T. Rowley. New York: Plenum Press, 1974.

Rowley, P. T.; Marshall, R.; and Ellis, J. R. "A Genetical and Cytological Study of Repeated Spontaneous Abortion." *Annals of Human Genetics* 27 (1963); 87.

Sacred Congregation for the Doctrine of the Faith. "Document about Sterilization in Catholic Hospitals (March 13, 1975)." Reprinted in *Linacre Quarterly* 44 (1977): 117-118. Cited in text as 1975.

Scheler, Max. *Man's Place in Nature.* Boston: Beacon Press, 1961.

_____ . *Vom Umsturtz der Werte.* Cited by Alfons Deeken in *Process and Permanence in Ethics: Max Scheler's Moral Philosophy.* New York: Paulist Press, 1974.

Schüller, Bruno. *Die Begründung sittlicher Urteile: Typen ethischer Argumentation in der katholischen Moraltheologie.* Düsseldorf: Patmos Verlag, 1973.

Scriver, C. R. and Efron, M. L. "Disorders of Proline and Hydroxyproline Metabolism." In *The Metabolic Basis of Inherited Disease,* edited by J. B. Stanbury, J. B. Wyngaarden and D. S. Frederickson. New York: McGraw-Hill, 1972.

Scriver, C. R.; Laberge, C.; Clow, C. L.; and Fraser, F. C. "Genetics and Medicine: An Evolving Relationship." *Science* 200 (1978): 946-952.

Simpson, N. E., Dallaire, L., Miller, J. R., *et al.* Prenatal Diagnosis of Genetic Disease in Canada: Report of a Collaborative Study. Canadian Medical

Journal 115 (1976): 739.

Sloan, H. R. and Frederickson, D. S. "Gm2 Gangliosidosis: Tay-Sachs Disease." In *The Metabolis Basis of Inherited Disease,* edited by J. B. Stanbury, J. B. Wyngaarden, and D. S. Frederickson, New York: McGraw-Hill, 1972.

Sly, W. S. "What is Genetic Counseling?" *Birth Defects* 9 (1973): 5.

Smith, David W. *Recognizable Patterns of Human Malformation: Genetic, Embryologic and Clinical Aspects.* Vol. 7 2d ed. Philadelphia: W. B. Saunders Co., 1976, pp. 368-69.

Smith, David W. and Wilson, Ann C. *The Child with Down's Syndrome.* Philadelphia: W. B. Saunders Co., 1973.

Sorenson, J. R. "Counselors, Self Portrait." *Genetic Counseling* 1 (1973): 31.

State of Minnesota. *Developmental Disabilities News Letter* 4, 2 (Spring, 1979).

Tarasoff v. Regents of the University of California, 1976, 17 CAL 3d 425, 551 P. 2d 334, 131 California Reporter 14.

Thielicke, Helmut. *Theological Ethics.* Vol. I: *Foundations.* London: Black, 1968 (Also Philadelphia: Fortress Press).

_____ . "The Dictor as Judge." In *Who Shall Live?* edited by Kenneth Vaux. Philadelphia: Fortress, Press, 1970.

Thompson, J. S. and Thompson, M. W. *Genetics in Medicine.* Philadelphia: W. B. Saunders Co., 1976.

Tooley, Michael. "A Defense of Abortion and Infanticide." In *The Problem of Abortion,* edited by Joel Feinberg. Belmont, Cal.: Wadsworth Publishing Company, 1973, pp. 51-91.

Tracy, David. *The Achievement of Bernard Lonergan.* New York: Herder and Herder, 1970.

U.S., DHEW, National Institute of Child Health and Human Development (NICHD).
1976. National Registry for Amniocentesis Study Group. "Midtrimester Amniocentesis for Prenatal Diagnosis." *Journal of the American Medical Association* 236: 1471-1476.
1979. "Task Force Report: Predictors of Hereditary Disease or Congenital Defects (Draft)." Consensus Development Conference on Antenatal Diagnosis, Bethesda, Md., March 5-7, 1979.

Vatican Council II.
1965a. *Dogmatic Constitution on Divine Revelation (Dei Verbum)* (18 Nov. 1965). In *Vatican Council II: The Conciliar and Post Conciliar Documents,*

edited by Austin Flannery, O.P. Northport, N.Y.: Costello Publishing Company, 1975, pp. 750-765.

1965b. "The Pastoral Constitution on the Church in the Modern World" *(Gaudium et Spes)* (7 December 1965). *Ibid.,* pp. 903-1002.

Vaughan, V. C. and McKay, R. James. *Nelson Textbook of Pediatrics.* Philadelphia: W. B. Saunders Co., 1975.

Whitten, C. and Frischhoff, J. "Psychosocial Effects of Sickle Cell Disease." *Archives of Internal Medicine* 133 (1974): 681-689.

Appendix

Genetic Counseling
and Tort Liability

by Patrick J. Kelley*

*Another version of this paper was published in The Washington University Law Quarterly (1979). The author thanks Professors Frank W. Miller and Jules B. Gerard for their helpful comments on an earlier draft of this paper. Appreciation is also expressed to Miss Mary J. Cosgrove for her constructive suggestions in preparing this appendix.

Introduction

A number of special problems arise in applying traditional principles of tort law to the special problems involved in genetic counseling.[1] One of the main purposes of genetic counseling is to provide couples at risk of producing a defective child with the information needed to decide whether to avoid giving birth to a child. If there is some flaw in the genetic counseling process, then, the result may be the birth of an unwanted defective child. Any unwanted birth, whether of a normal or a defective child, could conceivably lead to two different law suits against one who could have prevented that birth: (1) the parents could sue, claiming that the unwanted birth and subsequent responsibilities of parenthood caused them serious harm in the form of physical pain, emotional distress, and economic loss; (2) the child himself could sue, claiming that his birth caused him to have to put up with a life filled with physical and mental pain. For convenience, commentators have labeled the law suit by the parents an action for "wrongful birth," and the law suit by the child an action for "wrongful life."[2] No one in the United States asserted either kind of claim until 1934.[3] Since then, a number of both kinds of law suits have been brought to the courts.[4] Accordingly, Section A of this appendix analyzes the special problems of defining the scope of the duty in genetic counseling cases, while Section B discusses the standard of care and the special problems of deliberate concealment or disclosure of diagnosis in genetic counseling cases.

Special Problems in Defining the Scope of Duty in Genetic Counseling Cases

"Wrongful Life" Cases

In wrongful life cases the defendant is accused of wrongful conduct in *failing to prevent the avoidable conception or birth* of the plaintiff; the defendant is not accused of causing specific avoidable physical harm to the plaintiff. Thus, a suit by a child born because the defendant doctor negligently failed to diagnose rubella in the pregnant mother in time to afford her the opportunity to abort would be a suit for wrongful life,[5] as would a suit by a child against a doctor for negligently performing an abortion.[6] On the contrary, a suit by a child against the manufacturer of a drug for injury to him *in utero* caused by his mother's taking the drug while pregnant would not be a suit for wrongful life, nor would a suit against a physician who negligently transfused plaintiff's mother with incompatible RH blood prior to plaintiff's conception, thereby causing plaintiff harm when later conceived.[7] Each of these four hypotheticals shares a common characteristic: the plaintiff at the time of the defendant's wrongful act and at the time of the resulting injury could have had no conscious expectations about the defendant's conduct. In order to grant redress for harm caused by conduct insufficiently respectful of the plaintiff's personal dignity, the courts use a standard of general community expectations about appropriate conduct, embodied in the reasonable person standard.

Ordinarily in a wrongful life suit the defendant's conduct is contrary to the expectations of the plaintiff's parents. The question then is whether that conduct can also be said to have wronged the infant plaintiff. When the older tort categories that focused on the nature of the plaintiff's interest were replaced by the modern division of torts into categories that focus on the character of the defendant's conduct, the legal relevance of plaintiff's interest changed. Formerly it was a basis for determining when a private injustice had occurred; now it is formally useful only in determining whether there were compensable damages flowing from defendant's negligence. It is not surprising, then, that the principles of the law of damages have figured prominently in the arguments for and against recognizing the wrongful life cause of action.

Three different interests of the plaintiff have been isolated and used to formulate arguments for and against recognition of the proposed 'wrongful life' cause of action. The first and most obvious interest is the plaintiff's interest in not being born under certain unfavorable conditions such as with birth defects or as illegitimate. In each of the cases in which this was seen by the court as the plaintiff's interest (every wrongful life case[8] except two)[9] the court rejected the proposed cause of action. Commonly, the courts relied on the following argument, elaborated in an article by G. Tedeschi:[10]

> Under traditional tort standards, recovery in negligence requires a showing of damage. Damage is loss or detriment, determined by comparing the present position of the victim with his ideal position had the injurious event not occurred. There can be no damage in a wrongful birth case because it is logically impossible to say that plaintiff has suffered a loss or detriment when the ideal position for purposes of comparison is one in which plaintiff would not exist.[11]

Tedeschi's argument depends on the claim that the notions of loss and detriment logically entail some kind of continuity of personal identity. Thus, Tedeschi concludes that "the aphorism that 'it would be better for man not to have been born' . . . may be given some meaning by interpreting it as a finding that the balance between happiness and misery in life is negative . . . but not literally as a comparison of a person's condition with the condition of non-being, as in the latter state there is neither happiness nor misery whatsover."[12] Tedeschi's statement that it is *logically* impossible to discover damage in a wrongful life case may thus be too strong. At bottom, his argument reduces to the claim that the loss or detriment required in the negligence cause of action must be a loss to an identifiable person who would exist in the absence of the defendant's wrongful conduct, but without some harm he now suffers.

In a 1973 article by Professor Alexander Capron[13] there is a shift from the plaintiff's viewpoint to that of someone else. He argues that the infant plaintiff in a wrongful life case should have a cause of action because the defendant's negligence deprived the plaintiff's parents of their right to make an informed decision about whether to have the child. According to Capron, the child can sue, even though only the parents' interests seem at stake, because the parents make that decision on behalf of the child. Capron solves the problem of turning an injury to the parents' interests into an injury to the child only by the assumption that the parents in deciding not to have a child are acting on behalf of and in the interests of the child they decide not to have. This assumption, however, breaks down. If the purported interest in not being born cannot be related to the child's personal dignity, it is difficult to see how the parents' decision not to have a child can be said to be made on behalf of and in the best interests of the child they decide not to have. Once the connection between the parents' reproductive decision and the interests of the children they decide not to have is severed, Professor Capron's argument reduces to the unpersuasive claim that the child should have a cause of action because the parents have been injured by the child's birth. This, of course, makes little sense.

In *Park v Chessin,* [14] a woman who had previously given birth to a child afflicted with polycystic kidney disease who subsequently died consulted with a physician who advised her that inasmuch as polcystic kidney disease was not hereditary the chance of her delivering a second child afflicted with the disease were "practically nil". Based on her doctor's advice, Hetty Park and her husband, Steven, sought to conceive a second child. They were all but guaranteed that this child would escape the ravages of polycystic kidney disease. Tragically, a second child similarly affected was born to them and lived for two and one-half years before succumbing to the disease.

The parents brought suit against the defendant physician, seeking damages on behalf of their infant for "wrongful life" and in their own right for the pecuniary expense they incurred for the care and treatment of their child until her death.

The defendant physician moved the court to dismiss the parents' petition for failure to state a cause of action. At the trial court level, over defendant's motion to dismiss, the court sustained the following causes of action: "wrongful life"; Hetty Park's emotional and physical injuries stemming from birth; and Steven Park's loss of his wife's services. At the intermediate appellate level, the court modified the holding of the trial court further by dismissing portions of Hetty Park's claim for emotional distress and Steven Park's claim for loss of his wife's services. Plaintiffs and defendants cross-appealed to the highest court of the State of New York. That court modified the previous lower court's decisions by dismissing all counts of plaintiffs' complaint except the count relating to the recovery of expenses incurred by the Parks for the care and treatment of their daughter until her death.

In *Park,* the court declined to fashion a remedy for the proposed tort of "wrongful life" noting that such a recovery demanded calculation of damages dependent on a comparison between the Hobson's choice* of life in an impaired state and nonexistence. In the opinion of the court, this is a comparison which the law is unprepared to make.

"Wrongful Birth" Cases

Arguments Based on Corrective Justice Theory

Arguments Favoring the Cause of Action — Parents in wrongful birth cases ordinarily allege that defendant failed to take steps to prevent the conception or birth of the child after expressly or impliedly undertaking to help the parents avoid conception or childbirth. For example, parents have sued druggists who negligently filled a prescription for birth control pills with tranquilizers[15] and doctors who negligently performed sterilization operations.[16] In such cases, the parents claim to have suffered a private injustice. The defendant who failed to perform his undertaking has frustrated their reasonable expectations, and the unwanted conception or birth of the child impairs important personal interests. The mother's interest in maintaining emotional and physical well-being may be harmed by the emotional and physical pain of pregnancy and childbirth. The parents' interest in economic well-being may be harmed by the costs of

---

*Apparent freedom of choice with no real alternatives.

pregnancy, childbirth and childrearing. The parents' interest in personal autonomy in making reproductive decisions may be harmed by the defendant's failure to provide information needed to make informed decisions or by defendant's failure to provide effective assistance in implementing reproductive choices. These interests are closely enough related to the parents' personal identities to support the conclusion that harm to these interests caused by conduct contrary to their reasonable expectations constitutes a private injustice. This conclusion is buttressed by an estoppel argument*. By undertaking to help the parents avoid conception or childbirth, the defendant recognized the importance of these interests to the parents. Defendant should then not be allowed to deny the importance of those interests in a subsequent law suit for failure to perform his undertaking.

Certain courts that rejected the cause of action used technical arguments drawn from the law of damages. A closer examination, however, reveals that underneath the damage arguments lie concerns for preventing wholesale injustice by courts possibly incompetent to sort out valid from invalid claims, and for preventing harm to third persons from recognizing the cause of action. The following discussion analyzes the technical damage arguments in terms of their relationships to these underlying concerns.

Compensatory Damage: Arguments Against the Cause of Action — Damages in tort cases are compensatory. The trier of fact† compares plaintiff's current position with the position he would have been in had defendant acted properly, and then determines the award needed to put plaintiff in that position.[17] Judges are not magicians, however. They cannot by decree restore a lost arm, or blot out pain and suffering. What they do in the case of a lost arm, to take one example, is to reckon the purely economic harm attributable to the loss (medical expenses, lost wages, impaired earning capacity) and then assign a dollar amount to compensate for the intangible, noneconomic detriment of pain and suffering, recognizing that any translation of pain into dollars is necessarily conjectural in the absence of a market for pain or its surcease.[18]

---

*Estoppel is a bar or impediment which precludes allegation or denial of a certain fact or state of facts, in consequence of previous allegation or denial or conduct or admission . . . . (Editor's note from Black's Law Dictionary — Revised Fourth Edition).
†Judge or jury.

The problem in applying the compensatory damages standard to wrongful birth cases comes from the special benefit rule. That rule, a simple elaboration of the basic principle of compensatory damages,[19] requires the trier of fact to determine compensable damages by subtracting from total damages the value of any special benefit conferred on plaintiff by defendant's wrongful conduct.[20] The special benefit rule is thus one device courts use to limit recovery to cases in which there is actual private injustice. In applying the special benefit rule to the wrongful birth case, the fact-finder would have to assign a dollar value to the intangible benefits of parenthood — the joy of watching a child develop and grow, the love given and the love returned — and then subtract that from the sum of the economic cost of giving birth to and raising a child and the dollar value of the pain and suffering of pregnancy, childbirth, and parenthood.

Problems with this calculation led the New Jersey Supreme Court to reject a wrongful birth action brought by parents of a defective child. The court reasoned that courts were incompetent to weigh the "intangible, unmeasurable, and complex human benefits of parenthood" against the "alleged emotional and money injuries" from parenthood of a defective child.[21] A Michigan appellate court attacked this reasoning in the leading case of *Troppi v. Scarf.*[22] In that case defendant pharmacist negligently filled plaintiff's oral contraceptive prescription with tranquilizers. The plaintiffs subsequently produced a normal, healthy, but unplanned child. Plaintiffs claimed damages for the wife's lost wages, for medical and hospital expenses, for the pain and anxiety of pregnancy and childbirth, and for the economic costs of rearing the child. The court argued that these claimed items of damages were the same as those courts have traditionally compensated. Courts have always trusted the trier of fact to value these items of damage. Furthermore, the trier of fact can be trusted to value the offsetting benefits since this involves precisely the same factual issues the Michigan courts had previously left to the trier of fact: under a prior interpretation of the Michigan wrongful death act parents were compensated for loss of the companionship and services of a deceased child. Since each individual item of damage or benefit entering into the calculation of net damages here had been entrusted to a trier of fact before, that calculation could safely be left to the trier of fact.

Troppi v. Scarf held that all legally recognizable elements of damage claimed by parents who had an unwanted child as a result of a pharmacist negligently supplying tranquilizers to the mother instead of the prescribed birth control pill may be weighed against the benefits parents enjoy from an unplanned child. Thus, application of the benefit rule does not automatically prevent recovery for expenses of rearing the unplanned child.

The court went on to hold that consideration of the mother's lost wages; medical and hospital expenses; pain and anxiety of pregnancy and childbirth and economic cost of rearing a child were properly within the competence of the fact finder and the element of uncertainty in net recovery did not render damages unduly speculative.

The *Troppi* court's argument succeeded by focusing one's attention on the individual components of the net damage calculation and away from the calculation itself. But that calculation is what all the trouble is about. The basic argument is that in wrongful birth cases courts cannot make accurately the determination called for by the special benefit rule. They therefore cannot sort out valid from invalid claims, and may cause more injustice than they cure. The *Troppi* court's arguments do not allay these fears. The *Troppi* court cited cases in which the courts allowed triers of fact to assign dollar values to relatively intangible items of damage when it was already clear, if plaintiff's version of what happened were believed, that defendant's conduct had harmed plaintiff. In each instance, the trier of fact was allowed to assign dollar values to intangibles in determining total, not net damages. Under those circumstances, the irreducibly conjectural character of the valuation would not bother the court. The risk of over-valuation of intangible elements of damage could justifiably fall on the wrongdoer who had clearly harmed plaintiff. If the intangible elements of damage were undervalued, at least the plaintiff's tangible economic loss was repaired, and the court had tried to make the plaintiff whole.

The wrongful birth case is different. To determine net damages the trier of fact must offset one intangible (the joy and love brought by the child) against the sum of another intangible (the sorrow and pain of pregnancy, childbirth and parenthood) and certain hard economic losses. Furthermore, in cases in which the unplanned or unwanted child is living with the parents at the time of the trial, the trier of fact must forecast the future to determine the intangible benefits and intangible detriments. Given these peculiarities in wrongful birth cases, the ordinary justification for letting the trier of fact determine intangible items of damage breaks down. The court cannot tell by examining plaintiff's version of what happened whether a jury believing plaintiff's evidence would find that defendant harmed plaintiff. The jury must offset one intangible against another before it can determine that the plaintiff was harmed at all. To delegate this determination to the jury would be to empower the jury to determine, by balancing values arbitrarily assigned to intangibles, whether the conditions exist for allowing the jury to assign values to intangibles. The need for judicial control over essentially law-making decisions thus justifies a special rule of law determining which kinds of cases can go the jury.[23]

A second feature of the net damage calculation that undercuts the *Troppi* analysis is the relationship between the offsetting intangibles. It is at once a fact and a mystery that the pain and the joy of parenthood are inextricably bound together. We worry about our children and grieve at their suffering and their failures because we love them. That love is the source of the joy and the sorrow of parenthood. Most parents would find it odd to be asked to figure up the joys on one side and the sorrows on the other, as if the one did not in some fundamental sense depend on the other. The courts that rejected a cause of action for wrongful birth, both before and after *Troppi,* seemed to reflect this common understanding that isolating and weighing the joys and sorrows of parentood is impossible.[24] One could object, of course, that separability may depend on the facts of the individual case. Judges should not enshrine their personal experience of parenthood in a general rule that would prevent other, less fortunate parents from proving that under their circumstances[25] the unplanned child was a net detriment.

The process of proving an unplanned child to be a net detriment raises a third objection to the net damage calculation. The child, a nominal stranger to the litigation, may be hurt. The judgment of liability in a wrongful birth case would stand as an official, public pronouncement that that child's existence was a net detriment to his parents, even after valuing all the love and joy he offers them. If the child ever discovered this judgment, his sense of worth and his relationship with his parents could be devastated.[26] This effect on the child points to a deeper flaw in the wrongful birth cause of action. As the court in *Coleman v. Garrison*[27] observed, judicial recognition that "under certain circumstances a child would not be worth the trouble and expense"[28] would tend to contradict our traditional affirmation of the ultimate value of each human life.

These three problems with the wrongful birth damage calculation provide weighty reasons for rejecting the proposed cause of action. Other weighty reasons support recognizing that cause of action. For example, the defendant's wrongful conduct frustrated the reasonable expectations of the plaintiffs and resulted in the unwanted birth of a child; the accompanying pain and expense of parenthood is pain and expense that plaintiffs had intended to avoid and that defendant undertook to help them avoid. If the child is defective, the increased pain and expense are even more compelling reasons for imposing liability.

The preceding discussion simply considered arguments which favor a cause of action and those which oppose a cause of action. The following material presents three positions which in different ways limit the amount of recovery rather than argue for an all or none stance.

Intermediate Positions: *(a) Recovery limited to damages from pain and expense of pregnancy and childbirth* – After *Troppi* most courts[29] and commentators[30] followed the Michigan court's lead and analyzed away the conflict of principles in the proposed wrongful birth cause of action. A number of courts, however, attempted to formulate intermediate positions that accommodate the competing principles. In *Coleman v. Garrison,*[31] a Delaware court argued that plaintiffs in wrongful birth cases should recover damages only for the expense and pain of pregnancy and childbirth. They should not recover damages for the expense of raising the child.

The *Coleman* court gave the following three reasons for its suggested rule: (1) The net damage from raising a child is necessarily speculative; (2) parents who keep an unwanted child instead of giving it up for adoption indicate their judgment that the benefits outweigh the detriments of parenthood; they should therefore be estopped from asserting otherwise; and (3) any judicial judgment that a child is a net detriment to its parents would be contrary to fundamental public morality.

In *Sherlock v. Stillwater Clinic,*[32] the Minnesota court reached a similar, though less drastic conclusion. It allowed the wrongful birth cause of action, but held that the benefits from the child's aid, comfort, and society were to be offset only against the costs of rearing the child. Parents who claimed damages only for the expense and pain of pregnancy and childbirth could therefore avoid any application of the special benefit rule.

The *Sherlock* court was moved by the harm to the child and the parent-child relationship from the parents' claim that the child was a net detriment. The court reasoned that this consideration could not justify rejecting the wrongful birth cause of action completely, but said it expected that parents would be deterred from seeking recovery for the costs of child-rearing by the court's special offset rule.

At first glance, the *Coleman* solution seems perfect. By turning the wrongful birth cause of action into one for 'wrongful pregnancy' the court can continue to affirm the ultimate value of human life while accommodating the traditional tort law demands for redress of injury caused by departures from customary and expected standards of behavior. On closer examination, however, the *Coleman* arguments appear flawed.

The stoppel argument[33] supporting the *Coleman* solution is unpersuasive. The mother may decide to keep the child both to avoid the heartache of giving up her child and to avoid the social disapproval visited on mothers who give their children up for adoption. One of the 'benefits' weighed by the plaintiffs in deciding to keep the child is the avoidance of a harm that would result from the alternative. Plaintiffs are forced to choose between unpalatable alternatives by defendant's wrongful conduct. The subsequent choice should therefore not estop the plaintiffs from claiming that the alternative chosen caused them harm.[34] Put simply, the avoidance of injury from giving up one's child for adoption is not an offsetting benefit of parenthood.

The 'special benefit' rule seems to require the court to subtract the benefits of parenthood from the damages even when damages are limited to the harms from pregnancy and childbirth, since parenthood follows pregnancy and childbirth. The *Coleman* and *Sherlock* courts thought otherwise: both courts emphasized that the Restatement of Torts[35] limits the special benefit rule to cases in which the interest benefited is the same as the interest harmed. The courts' attempt to separate the interest in avoiding pregnancy and childbirth from the interest in avoiding parenthood, however, is unconvincing. First, since separability can be shown only by emphasizing the possibility of giving up the child for adoption, whatever persuasive force the separability argument has derives from the seriously-flawed estoppel argument discussed above.[36] Secondly, the broad "same interest" language adopted by the Restatement to express a limitation on the special benefit rule goes beyond the cases on which the limitation was apparently based.[37] Those cases all dealt with the rule that damage to the use and enjoyment of plaintiff's land caused by an improvement on defendant's land could not be reduced by the increase in market value of plaintiff's land attributable to that improvement.[38] The increased market value is only a benefit to plaintiff in case he sells. If plaintiff chooses not to sell, there is no offsetting benefit, and defendant's wrongful act should not force plaintiff to sell to mitigate damages. The principle behind these cases is the same as that used above to reject the *Coleman* court's estoppel argument, and therefore undermines rather than supports the *Coleman* court's proposed rule.

Finally, the *Coleman* "wrongful pregnancy" rule seems to give just exactly the wrong result in an action against a genetic counselor for the birth of a defective child. Plaintiffs in that case were not particularly interested in avoiding the pain and expense of pregnancy and childbirth; what they wanted to avoid was the birth of a defective child. To allow damages for the pain and expense of pregnancy and childbirth and not for the special expenses attributable to the child's defect is to ignore completely both the plaintiffs' expectations and the specific interest harmed by defendant's conduct.

(b) Recovery limited to special expense attributable to birth defects — The Texas and Wisconsin courts adopted a second solution to the conflict of principles in the wrongful birth case. In those states the courts denied recovery in wrongful birth cases when the unplanned or unwanted child was normal and healthy.[39] When defendant's wrongful conduct kept the parents from seeking a eugenic abortion, the courts authorized recovery but limited damages to the special expenses occasioned by the child's defect.[40] The Wisconsin court gave no reason at all for this distinction.[41] The Texas court argued that, when the alleged injury is the birth of a normal, healthy child "the objection . . . is to an award based upon speculation as to the quality of life and as to the pluses and minuses of parental mind and emotion."[42] The objection thus does not apply when the child has birth defects: "The economic burden related solely to the physical defects of the child . . . lies within the methods of proof by which the courts are accustomed to

determine awards in personal injury cases."[43] The Texas court's reasoning is unpersuasive. Courts had previously rejected recovery in wrongful birth cases because they could not weigh the intangible benefits of parenthood against the intangible detriments. No one ever doubted that the courts could measure the tangible economic burden imposed by parenthood. In the eugenic abortion case, the measurable expense attributable to the child's defect would be added to the previously-measurable economic burden. The problem of weighing the offsetting intangible benefit of parenthood against the detriment of parenthood of a defective child would still remain.

Although the court's stated reasons seem inadequate, the result can be defended. Oddly enough, that defense would single out as a virtue what three prior commentators[44] thought was an error in the Texas position, namely, a comparison of parents in two conditions: the condition of parents with a defective child compared to that with a normal child. Defendant's wrong-doing resulted in the birth of a defective child, but did not cause the defect. If defendant had acted properly, plaintiffs would not have had the child. Thus, under the ordinary compensatory damage standard, the trier of fact would determine the extent of damages by comparing the present state of the plaintiffs — now the parents of a defective child — with the alternative state in which they would not have had the child. Instead, the Texas court compared plaintiff's present state with an impossible state in which they would have had a normal child. The Texas court thus adopted a new measure of damages contrary to the traditional compensatory damage standard.

This unusual measure of damages has two distinct advantages. First, under this standard, the jury does not have to weigh intangible benefits and detriments to determine whether there is legal injury. The court determines as a matter of law that there is injury, and asks the jury to measure only the tangible expense attributable to the child's defect. Second, since the jury is never asked whether, all things considered, the child is more of a burden than a joy to his parents, the court avoids the potentially damaging judgment that the child is a net detriment to his parents.

Any compromise can be attacked from two directions, and the Texas court's compromise is no exception. Those favoring denial of the wrongful birth cause of action under any circumstances would argue that the Texas approach avoids a case-by-case adjudication of net detriment by embodying in a legal rule the cruel judgment that a defective child is always a net detriment[45] while a normal child is always a net benefit. The Texas measure of damages was not intended to be compensatory under the ordinary tort standard, however, so it is difficult to see how the dinstinction between normal and defective children embodies any judgment that defective children as a class are net detriments to their parents. The Texas court simply recognized that most people would rather avoid the special anguish and expense associated with a defective child, regardless of the ultimate balance between benefits and burdens. By holding that the birth of such a child constitutes legal injury to those who wanted to avoid it, the court just protects the expectations of the parties, which are consistent with the common assumptions of the community. By adopting an avowedly noncompensatory measure of damages, the court provides a remedy for an obvious wrong while avoiding the unfortunate consequences of net detriment determinations under a rigid compensatory damage scheme.

One could respond by attacking the noncompensatory measure of damages. First, whenever the net compensatory damages are more than the costs occasioned by the child's defect, the defendant is treated unjustly, for he must pay more than the harm he caused. Conversely, whenever the net compensatory damages are less than the costs occasioned by the child's defect, the plaintiff is treated unjustly. Secondly, there is no basis in common-law damage principles for such a noncompensatory damage standard. Under our legal system, courts in tort cases do not impose noncompensatory punitive damages without first finding that defendant's conduct was malicious or outrageous.[46] The Texas noncompensatory standard is, then, an infringement on the legislative prerogative to impose fines for wrongful conduct.

In cases falling within the Texas rule, however, plaintiffs had indicated by their conduct that they wanted to be parents of a normal child, and defendant had undertaken to help them achieve that goal. If defendant had acted properly, plaintiffs would have had the opportunity to achieve that goal, either by contraception plus adoption or by an immediate abortion and a subsequent pregnancy. The Texas rule just attempts to put plaintiffs in the position they *expected* to be with defendant's help. The contract measure of damages — expectation damages — thus supports the Texas rule. Since the malpractice cause of action was originally a hybrid of tort and contract, based on the implied undertaking of a member of a common calling,[47] there are no serious obstacles to adopting a contract measure of damages when the tort measure of damages proves unsatisfactory. Moreover, since the proposed measure of damages attempts to put plaintiffs in the position originally intended by both parties, there is no injustice to either party in adopting the expectation standard.

Those in favor of recognizing the wrongful birth cause of action in all cases could argue that since the plaintiffs in the ordinary wrongful birth action indicated their intention not to have any children and defendant undertook to help them achieve that aim, the expectation damages argument supports a cause of action for wrongful birth of a normal child. Furthermore, insofar as the Texas compromise depends on community consensus that the unwanted birth of a defective child is a serious harm, one could just as well argue that the widespread use of contraception and abortion indicates a community consensus that, under certain circumstances, the unwanted birth of a normal child is a serious harm. The arguments used to defend the Texas compromise against attacks from one side thus eliminate any defense against attacks from the other side.

But this of course is not true. In the wrongful birth case for birth of a normal child, the expectation measure of damages is necessarily the same as the compensatory measure of damages: plaintiffs wanted to avoid the birth of any child. Thus, in that case there is no principled basis for avoiding the net compensatory damage calculation, with all its unfortunate consequences. Furthermore, the strength of the community consensus about the harm, or the severity of the harm, to the plaintiff's personal interest, or indeed upon the relative importance of the interest at stake, may differ greatly depending on whether the unwanted child is defective or normal. Rejection of the wrongful birth cause of action for birth of a normal child is not based on a logical deduction, but on a prudential judgment that the harm from authorizing the jury to make the net damage calculation outweighs the benefits from enforcing the expectations of the parties. One may reach a different judgment on this issue than the Wisconsin and Texas courts, but it seems clear that the court must weigh significantly different factors in deciding whether to allow a cause of action for wrongful birth of a *defective* child than it weighs in deciding whether to allow the cause of action for wrongful birth of a *normal* child. One cannot simply reject the Texas approach as internally inconsistent.

(c) Recovery limited to contraception wrongful birth cases — A court could allow the wrongful birth cause of action when defendant's conduct prevented contraception and bar the cause of action when defendant's conduct prevented an abortion. Before *Roe v. Wade*[48] and *Doe v. Bolton,* [49] the reasons for this distinction were persuasive. Most states prohibited abortion by criminal statutes that reflected the fundamental policy that all human life is precious. To allow recovery in tort for denial of the opportunity to abort would violate this fundamental public policy.[50] Furthermore, to prove that defendant's conduct caused injury, plaintiff would have to show that she would have aborted the child had defendant acted properly. Arguably, plaintiff could never prove that defendant's conduct was the proximate cause of plaintiff's injury while the state criminal law prohibited abortion.[51] In addition to these two arguments based on the abortion statutes, a third argument supports the distinction. The wrongful birth suit for denial of the opportunity to abort is potentially more damaging to the child and his relationship to his parents than the suit for contraceptive failure. The parents in the abortion case contend that they would have aborted *this* child had defendant acted properly. The child existed as a genetically independent, separate human being during pregnancy.[52] He can reasonably identify with himself in the womb.[53] The parents' revealed intention to abort is therefore a more serious threat to the child's sense of worth and his relationship with his parents than the parents' revealed intention to avoid conception in the contraception wrongful birth cases.

The Supreme Court in *Roe v. Wade*[54] and *Doe v. Bolton*[55] seemed to weaken the bases for this distinction by adopting guidelines that invalidated the criminal abortion statutes in all 50 states. Commentators[56] argued after *Roe* and *Doe* that the public policy and proximate cause arguments against the abortion wrongful birth cause of action fell with the statutes on which they were based.

To evaluate the commentators' arguments, one must first analyze the original arguments based on the criminal abortion statutes. Careful analysis shows that, at bottom, the proximate cause and public policy arguments are equivalent. A statute making abortion a criminal act need not have precluded an abortion: Plaintiff could conceivably prove by preponderance of the evidence that, had the defendant acted properly, she would have obtained a legal abortion outside the state or an illegal abortion within the state.[57] Since plaintiff might thus prove that the defendant's conduct was the cause in fact of her injury, the flat ban on recovery under the proximate cause rubric must be based on policy considerations that go beyond simple causation theories. The argument is that, since abortion is illegal and thus patently contrary to the public policy of the state, it is consequently contrary to the recognized public policy to award damages for the allegedly wrongful denial of the opportunity to abort. After *Roe* and *Doe,* then, the proximate cause-public policy arguments do not work because the state no longer has a public policy against abortion.

The problem with the commentators' argument is that it assumes the state legislatures repealed the criminal abortion statutes and thus rejected the prior public policy against abortions. Abortion on demand nationwide was adopted by judicial decision, not by democratic vote, however, so the question becomes whether the constitutional interpretation adopted in *Roe* and *Doe* precludes the states from implementing a public policy against abortion by distinguishing between abortion and contraception wrongful birth cases. The controlling case is *Maher v. Roe,*[58] in which the Court held that a legislative classification favoring childbirth over abortion which did not prohibit abortion was justified by the state's legitimate interest in protecting potential human life. The *Maher* argument could be applied to support the distinction between abortion and contraception wrongful birth cases: by the classification the state does not interfere directly with the pregnant woman's abortion decision; the state's legitimate interest in protecting potential human life therefore suffices to justify the distinction and it withstands an equal protection attack.

Plaintiffs in abortion wrongful birth cases would attempt to distinguish *Maher* by pointing out that in *Maher* the distinction between providing indigents with medical care for childbirth while not providing medical care for abortion can be supported by a public policy to protect potential human life: an indigent pregnant woman's decision whether to abort or carry to term may very well be influenced by the availability of free medical care for childbirth only. The distinction between abortion and contraception wrongful birth cases, on the other hand, cannot be supported by that public policy, since a pregnant woman's decision whether to abort or carry to term would not be influenced by the fact that she cannot recover damages from one who negligently or intentionally deprives her of the opportunity to abort, or who negligently performs an ineffective abortion. The only reason for the distinction, therefore, is hostility toward abortion, and a desire to punish those who would seek abortions. The classification is thus unconstitutional, even under the *Maher* analysis, for it interferes directly with the abortion decision by punishing those who would seek an abortion.

The weakest part of the plaintiffs' above argument is their contention that the classification is not supportable by the state's interest in protecting potential human life. If all that is required is a conceivable rational relationship between the classification and a legitimate state interest, the classification would be constitutional. Surely the legislature could reasonably assume that providing wrongful birth cause of action for contraception cases and not for abortion cases has some deterrent effect: some women might choose childbirth over abortion because the legal protection against malpractice is greater in childbirth; some women before conception might choose contraception rather than abortion as a family planning device because of the differences in legal protection against malpractice. Since there are alternative, more direct methods to achieve these goals (such as education about contraception) that impose less of a burden on the abortion decision, the distinction may not withstand any stricter scrutiny than the conceivable rational relationship test, but under *Maher* that is arguably the controlling test, and the proposed distinction is constitutional.

Alternative Theories Supporting the Wrongful Birth Cause of Action

Constitutional Arguments — One commentator[59] and two courts[60] have argued that courts that reject the cause of action for wrongful birth in either abortion or contraception cases unconstitutionally interfere with the woman's right to privacy recognized in *Griswold v. Connecticut,*[61] *Roe v. Wade,*[62] and *Doe v. Bolton.*[63] If this argument is correct, a court could not use the compensatory damage arguments analyzed above to reject the proposed cause of action for wrongful birth, and would have to recognize the wrongful birth cause of action.

The following two arguments support this conclusion. First, if defendant's wrong-doing precludes plaintiff from the opportunity to choose an abortion or an effective contraceptive, the state court's subsequent refusal to grant a damage remedy is a delegation of power to private individuals to bar access to abortion or contraception, similar to the spousal consent requirement held unconstitutional in *Planned Parenthood v. Danforth*.[64] This argument is unpersuasive. The spousal consent statute in *Planned Parenthood* flatly prohibited abortion unless the husband consented. Thus, a woman unable to get her husband's consent was forbidden to abort. Refusal to recognize a cause of action for wrongful birth, on the other hand, involves no *governmental* interference with the woman's constitutional right to contraception or abortion. The Constitution has never been held to require state courts to grant tort recovery for private interference with the exercise of constitutional rights. Furthermore, the defendants' conduct in wrongful birth cases could not meet the requirements of the federal civil rights statute[65] authorizing civil actions for certain private interference with federal constitutional rights.[66]

Secondly, the court's denial of the proposed wrongful birth case of action is arguably a denial of equal protection. To treat wrongful birth claims differently than other similar claims is to place an unequal burden on the exercise of the constitutional right to abortion and contraception that must be justified by a compelling state interest.[67] Since the arguments for and against recognizing such a cause of action are fairly evenly balanced,[68] no compelling state interest can be found. This argument, too, is unpersuasive. In *Maher v. Roe*,[69] the United States Supreme Court upheld the constitutionality of a state statute that authorized free maternity care for indigents but refused to fund non-therapeutic abortions for indigents. Since the distinction drawn between abortion and childbirth did not directly interfere with an indigent woman's constitutional right to decide whether to abort, the distinction was justifiable since it was reasonably related to a constitutionally-permissible purpose.[70] The same analysis applies here. The distinction between ordinary tort cases and wrongful birth cases does not directly interfere with a woman's constitutional right to choose contraception or abortion. Consequently, a rational relationship to any legitimate state purpose will justify the distinction. The purposes discussed above — avoidance of speculative damage awards, avoidance of injury to a third party from the litigation, avoidance of inconsistent judgments — are certainly legitimate state interests supporting the distinction between wrongful birth cases and other tort cases.

The constitutional arguments for recognizing the wrongful birth cause of action are seriously flawed. The cases recognizing a constitutional right to contraception and abortion thus merely reinforce the argument that parents in the ordinary wrongful birth case have suffered a private injustice through defendant's conduct contrary to the parents' reasonable expectations. Those constitutional cases do not require the court to recognize the cause of action.

Strict Liability Theories Supporting Wrongful Birth Cause of Action — The most popular argument against strict liability for medical accidents is the difficulty in proving that any particular result was caused by medical treatment rather than by the disease.[71] That argument probably does not apply in most wrongful birth cases. If the sterilization operation or the abortion procedure is not successful the subsequent birth of a child can be traced directly to defective, though perhaps non-negligent, medical care. Similarly, in genetic counseling cases, expert testimony could help the courts determine whether the genetic advice was 'defective.'

Both the "best cost-avoider" and the social insurance theories could be used to support imposition of liability on surgeons who fail to sterilize or abort successfully and on genetic counselors whose defective genetic advice resulted in the birth of a defective child. Under these theories, the court could impose liability without finding the defendant negligent. It would be enough under Calabresi's best-cost-avoider theory that the surgery was unsuccessful or that the genetic advice was defective. Liability should be imposed because the surgeon and the counselor are in better positions than their patients to act in order to avoid the unwanted result. It is enough under the social insurance theory, too, that the advice was defective or the surgery unsuccessful. Liability should be imposed because the surgeon and the genetic counselor can insure against liability for defective surgery or defective advice and can pass the cost of insurance on to those who benefit from surgery or genetic counseling.

Two arguments can be made against the strict liability proposal, however, based on the two general weaknesses in utilitarian theories: (1) their assumption that consequences are predictable, and (2) their justification of results that deny respect to individuals' personal dignity.

197

First, imposition of strict liability on surgeons and genetic counselors with either the best-cost-avoider theory or the social insurance theory could lead to unacceptable consequences neither intended nor predicted. The adoption of the social insurance theory in products liability law is an unsettling precedent. Increases in product liability losses led to dramatic increases in product liability insurance costs and the refusal of insurance companies to underwrite some kinds of product liability risks.[72] Implementation of the social insurance theory by adopting strict liability for surgeons and genetic counselors in wrongful birth cases runs the risk of forcing insurance cost so high that many potential defendants will be unable to obtain liability insurance and potential patients might be unable to obtain desired services. The imposition of a strict liability standard in wrongful birth cases could very well have unfortunate effects on the practice of surgery or genetic counseling itself. Since the most significant threat of liability is from suits by parents of defective children, genetic counselors might be inclined to resolve every diagnostic or counseling doubt in favor of the solutions (avoiding conception, aborting the possibly affected fetus) that would minimize the risk of liability, rather than promote the best interests of the patient.[73] Surgeons might refuse to perform sterilization operations, or increase the price of such operations dramatically.

Second, most importantly, however, imposition of strict liability on non-negligent genetic counselors seems to deny the counselor's and patient's claims to personal dignity. The counselor could claim that it is unfair to impose liability on him when his conduct fulfilled the reasonable expectations of his patient. To impose personal liability on him because he is a good insurance conduit or the best cost-avoider is not to treat him as a responsible moral agent within society but as a pawn in the utilitarian game.[74] Moreover, the patient who cannot choose lower-cost genetic counseling without built-in insurance against the results of defective counseling may claim that his personal autonomy has been impaired for no demonstrably good reasons.

Recent commentators have discussed extensively the question of strict liability for medical accidents. To date, however, no court has imposed liability under a strict liability theory. The risk of liability in wrongful birth cases comes primarily from the application of general malpractice theories.

Conclusion

The trend seems to be toward recognizing the wrongful birth cause of action under a malpractice theory either for all cases or, under the Texas-Wisconsin approach, only for the birth of defective children. Under either approach, of course, the genetic counselor is at risk. It therefore makes sense to examine in more detail the application of malpractice principles to genetic counseling cases.

Special Problems of Deliberate Concealment or Disclosure in Genetic Counseling Cases

The Standard of Care

Defining the Standard of Care in Malpractice Cases

The plaintiff in a negligence case must establish that defendant had a duty to exercise due care for the plaintiff's safety, that the defendant's conduct breached that duty, and that defendant's breach was the proximate cause of actual loss or damage to the plaintiff.[75] In professional malpractice cases, the duty to exercise due care arises when one holds oneself out as a professional and undertakes to provide professional services to another.[76] The courts hold that, in providing those professional services, the defendant has a duty to exercise the knowledge, skill, and care exercised by such professionals.[77]

The standard of due care is thus the customary standard of practice in the profession. In medical malpractice cases, for example, the standard "requires that the physician undertaking the care of a patient possess and exercise that reasonable and ordinary degree of learning, skill, and care commonly possessed and exercised by reputable physicians practicing in the same locality, or in similar localities, in the care of similar cases ..."[78] One need not be a physician to hold oneself out as a genetic counselor and engage in genetic counseling,[79] although most genetic counselors are licensed physicians.[80] That genetic counselors need not be licensed does not mean they can escape application of a professional standard of care in malpractice cases: under the basic professional malpractice theory, those who hold themselves out as genetic counselors will be required to possess the knowledge and exercise the skill and care of other reputable genetic counselors.

What services do genetic counselors undertake to provide? Two common threads run through the various definitions of genetic counseling: first, the genetic counselor as such undertakes to determine the risk of an hereditary disorder in a family, and second, the counselor undertakes to explain the magnitude of the risk and the burden of the disorder so that his clients can make an informed procreative choice.[81] Given this definition of the genetic counseling undertaking, the counselor's legal duty is clear: he must employ the knowledge, skill, and care ordinarily possessed by reputable genetic counselors to determine the risk of hereditary disorder and to explain the risk and the burden of the disorder to his clients. One need not resort to any social policy favoring autonomy in procreative decision making to justify imposition of this legal duty on genetic counselors,[82] for the duty derives from an understanding of what genetic counselors ordinarily undertake to do, and what a client therefore can reasonably expect from a genetic counselor.

The first part of the genetic counselor's undertaking — determining the risk of an hereditary disorder — can be characterized as "diagnosis," but only in an extended sense, since the genetic counselor as such does not diagnose a diseased or aberrant physical state, but "diagnoses" the risk of a hereditary disorder. (As physician, however, he may *diagnose* a genetic condition.) The similarity between this undertaking and the ordinary undertaking of physicians to diagnose a disease prior to treatment, however, suggests that standards similar to those developed in medical malpractice misdiagnosis cases will be applied in genetic counseling cases.[83] Thus, misdiagnosis alone should not be actionable, if a genetic counselor exercising the care and skill of reputable genetic counselors could have made the same judgment[84] but malpractice can be found when the counselor failed to order diagnostic tests that a prudent, skilled genetic counselor would order,[85] or if he failed to perform or interpret the tests with the skill and care of ordinary, reputable genetic counselors.

Application of the legal standard of care to the second part of the genetic counselor's undertaking — conveying risk and burden information to the clients — raises problems. The first question is whether the courts should defer to professional custom in setting the standard of care for disclosure. It could be argued that courts adopt professional custom as the standard of care in professional malpractice cases because the client who is not a professional can only be said to have a very general expectation about the way the professional will perform: the client expects the professional to exercise the care, skill, and knowledge of other professionals in providing the professional service. Without professional training, the client is not in a position to have any more specific expectations. Professional custom therefore is the appropriate measure of the client's expectations, and courts properly rely on professional custom to fill in the blanks in the agreement to provide professional services.[86] Moreover, a court that refuses to accept professional custom as the standard of care in professional negligence cases runs the risk of distorting future professional judgments in ways harmful to the professional's clients.[87]

These arguments do not justify adopting professional custom as the standard of care in judging the genetic counselor's disclosures to his clients, however. The genetic counselor undertakes to provide information about the risks and burdens of possible hereditary disorders so that his clients can make informed procreative choices. The risks and burdens themselves are matters for expert testimony and professional judgment, but the content of the disclosure and the manner of conveying those risks and burdens need not be. As to these, the client may have very specific expectations, unrelated to professional custom: the client expects the genetic counselor to disclose risk and burden information that a reasonable person would consider relevant to procreative choices. In addition, the client expects the counselor to do so in a way that will enable her or him to understand fully the risks and burdens and thereafter make an informed procreative choice.

Moreover, rejecting professional custom as the standard for the content and manner of disclosure runs little risk of adversely affecting the practice of genetic counseling: genetic counselors have no monopoly on understanding the factors relevant to procreative choices, so a jury's lay assessment of those factors is as likely to capture the reasonable expectations of the clients as expert testimony by genetic counselors; additional efforts by counselors to ensure that clients understand fully the technical risk and burden information would not be socially undesirable. In adopting a reasonable client standard for disclosure, however, courts should not imply that genetic counselors guarantee the success of genetic counseling. The counselor undertakes to exercise reasonable care to see that the client understands the risk and burden information presented; the counselor does not guarantee that the client will in fact understand fully. Thus, the question whether the client in fact understood fully is not dispositive; the court must always ask whether the counselor took reasonably prudent steps to make sure that the client understood.[88]

When Do Physicians Have Legal Duty to Provide Genetic Counseling?

The most troublesome problem in applying professional malpractice law to the practice of genetic counseling comes not in determining the standard of care for genetic counselors but in determining when physicians should be held to have a legal duty to provide genetic counseling. Two recent New York cases provide a convenient introduction to this troublesome problem.

Failure to Make Due Assessment of a Genetic Risk — In

Howard v. Lecher,[89] plaintiffs were husband and wife, both Jews of Eastern European ancestry. The defendant was an obstetrician who cared for the plaintiff wife during two pregnancies. Plaintiffs' first child was normal, but their second child was afflicted with Tay-Sachs disease, an autosomal recessive defect that causes progressive neurologic deterioration and early death. Jews of Eastern European origin are much more likely to be carriers of the recessive gene than others in the general population: 1 in 3,600 children born to Eastern European Jews has Tay-Sachs disease, while the incidence is only 1 in 500,000 in the general population.[90] Tay-Sachs carriers can be identified by a simple blood test. In a marriage between two carriers, the probability of producing an affected child is 1 in 4 for each conception. Affected fetuses can be identified by biochemical tests following amniocentesis (see page 32-34).

Plaintiffs in the *Howard* case claimed that defendant negligently failed to take a family history and thus failed to discover the common Eastern European Jewish ancestry of the couple. Discovery of that ancestry would have indicated the need to test both husband and wife for carrier status. Discovery that both were carriers would have indicated the need either for contraceptive measures or for amniocentesis to monitor each pregnancy and give the parents the opportunity to abort affected fetuses. Defendant's negligence thus resulted in the avoidable birth of a Tay-Sachs child.

The intermediate appellate court in *Howard* rejected the plaintiff's claim for damages for mental distress caused by witnessing the child's progressive deterioration and death. The narrow ground for this holding was the rule that one cannot recover for mental distress caused by defendant's negligent injury of another,[91] but the court went on to discuss an alternative broader ground:

> In addition, recognition of the claim for emotional harm herein would, in my opinion, constitute an unwarranted and dangerous extension of malpractice liability. Under the plaintiffs' theory as to what the law should be, an obstetrician in our ever-expanding heterogeneous and pluralistic society would have an absolute duty to conduct an exhaustive genealogical profile of both parents in order for him to counsel them as to the wisdom of the wife obtaining an abortion. If such should be the law today, then it might follow that tomorrow courts would require a physician to advise parents when extraordinary means of sustaining the vital processes of their child should be terminated.[92]

Failure to Provide Correct Genetic Information —The same intermediate appellate court that decided *Howard v. Lecher* decided the subsequent case of *Park v. Chessin*[93] (see above, p. 181). In *Park,* the defendant obstetricians attended the plaintiff mother during the birth of a baby in 1969. Five hours after birth the baby died of polycystic kidney disease, an autosomal recessive defect.[94] At that time, plaintiff husband and wife asked the defendants about the likelihood of their producing another child with a similar defect. Defendants told them that their chances of producing another such child were "practically nil," when in fact the chances were one in four for each subsequent pregnancy. The court held that the parents had a cause of action for damages caused by the birth and subsequent death of a second child with polycystic kidney disease. The court distinguished *Howard* on the ground that in *Park* the plaintiffs specifically asked for genetic counseling and reasonably relied on the defendants' response to that request. Since the defendants voluntarily undertook to provide genetic counseling, liability in *Park* would not impose additional affirmative duties on the ordinary obstetrician. In

Howard, on the other hand, liability "would have compelled all [obstetricians] to take lengthy genealogical histories of both parents, whether . . . affirmatively requested or not, whether the medical circumstances indicated cause for alarm or not, and all at the inevitable penalty of bearing the ultimate legal liability should the infant be born with a genetic deformity. . . . [T]o validate the parents' cause of action [in *Howard*] would make the physician a virtual insurer of the genetic health of newborns, ordinarily a mere fortuitous event."[95]

Other Cases of Negligence — The *Howard* and *Park* cases are obviously poles apart. A number of other cases fall somewhere in between a specific undertaking to provide genetic counseling and an ordinary obstetrical case. The most common intermediate cases are those in which parents present a child with physical or developmental problems to a physician for diagnosis and treatment. Parents may bring a child with Down's syndrome, or polycystic kidney disease, or cystic fibrosis, or sickle-cell anemia, to the physician. In such cases, accurate diagnosis of the child's condition would reveal its genetic origin and therefore provide important information relevant to the parents' future reproductive decisions.[96] Thus, a physician's negligence in fulfilling his primary undertaking to diagnose and treat the child's condition may result in the avoidable birth of another defective child. In many of these cases, courts could impose liability for wrongful birth without finding a specific undertaking to provide genetic counseling, since fulfilling the primary duty to exercise ordinary skill and care in diagnosing and treating the child's condition would have provided the necessary genetic information.

This analysis would not work for all cases, however. Once a physician has diagnosed a case of Down's syndrome, it may be unimportant for subsequent treatment decisions whether the child's condition is the common or 'regular' trisomy-21 in which the child has an identifiable, independent third chromosome, or is of the translocation type, in which the extra chromosomal material is attached to another chromosome and the affected individual's karotype shows the normal number of chromosomes. For genetic counseling purposes, however, the distinction is important. The risk of producing another child with trisomy-21 is small, while the risk of producing another child with translocation Down's syndrome may be as high as 1 in 3 if the mother is a carrier of the translocation defect[97] (see pages 49-50).

The distinction between the diagnosis and treatment undertaking and the genetic counseling undertaking may be legally unimportant in such cases, however. Patients expect their doctors to be experts on all kinds of medical matters. A physician who conveys any information about the genetic origin of the child's condition can reasonably expect the parents to rely on that information in making subsequent procreative choices. By providing such information that physician has thereby undertaken genetic counseling, and should be held to the legal duty to fulfill that undertaking competently or to refer to a genetic counselor. Once a court has decided to recognize the cause of action for wrongful birth, there seems little reason to refuse to extend the cause of action to cases of negligent failure to diagnose genetic disorders in affected children presented for diagnosis and treatment. If the defendant failed to meet the customary standards of sound medical practice, the plaintiff parents have suffered a grave private injustice. Liability for failure to diagnose genetic defect in a child presented for diagnosis and treatment would pose little danger of adverse social effects beyond those necessarily risked by recognizing the wrongful birth cases of action. The physician whose incompetence or carelessness caused plaintiff harm excites little sympathy.

The *Howard* case could, of course, be seen as just another case of negligent failure to diagnose genetic disease in an affected child. Under that characterization, the above arguments would apply equally to the *Howard* case, and the only relevant question would be whether defendant violated customary standards of sound medical practice.[98] The court in *Howard,* however, hit upon an important point that may serve to distinguish the case. Imposing liability on the obstetrician in *Howard* would recognize a radical shift in the nature of an obstetrician's undertaking. Obstetricians traditionally undertake to care for the mother and unborn child during pregnancy and childbirth to ensure that no harm befalls either.[99] The plaintiffs in *Howard* urged the court to recognize that obstetricians also undertake to discover untreatable fetal defects to enable the mother to abort defective unborn children. That changes the role of the obstetrician from that of protector of life and health of both mother and unborn child to that of eugenic abortion counselor. In that role, he may further the destruction of the unborn child, neither to protect the health or life of the mother (being pregnant with a defective child is, after all, not a disease) nor to protect the health or life of the unborn child, but simply in order to prevent the birth of a defective child. Imposing liability in *Howard* would force obstetricians to adopt this new role, a role inconsistent with the traditional obstetrical undertaking and the correlative reasonable expectation of patients who go to obstetricians.

Informed Consent Doctrine

One could argue that the obstetrician in *Howard* should be liable not because he breached a traditional undertaking of obstetricians, but because he failed to obtain the patient's "informed consent" to treatment. The modern doctrine of informed consent is a species of medical malpractice liability that grew out of the older tort rule that medical treatment involving touching of the patient is an actionable battery unless the patient consents.[100] To give legally valid consent, the patient need only be competent and understand what the doctor proposed to do.[101] The courts later broadened liability for treatment without "informed consent" by treating the question as one of malpractice rather than battery.[102] The courts assumed that physicians ordinarily explain to their patients not only the nature of proposed treatment but also the risk of the proposed treatment and alternatives to the proposed treatment.[103] A patient injured by treatment he agreed to without such full explanation should have a cause of action for damages if he would not have consented had he been given the additional information about risks and alternatives. A few courts have held that the standard of disclosure is not what the ordinary reputable physician would have disclosed but what the ordinary reasonable patient would have wanted to know before deciding whether to consent to the proposed treatment.[104] This last development has led to an outpouring of academic commentary supporting further refinements in the informed consent doctrine to protect the patient's personal autonomy in treatment decision from paternalistic physicians who think they alone should decide what treatment is to be given.[105]

The ordinary genetic counseling undertaking and the legal obligations of disclosure under the informed consent doctrine are superficially very similar. The genetic counselor undertakes to inform his clients of the risks and burdens of hereditary disorders so they can make informed procreative choices; the physician under the "informed consent" doctrine is obliged to inform his patients of the risks of proposed treatment and alternative methods of treatment so that the patient can make an informed treatment choice. The problem for those attacking the *Howard* decision is to convert that similarity into an argument that obstetricians have a legal obligation to discover untreatable fetal defects to enable the pregnant woman to choose a eugenic abortion.

Proponents have tried two alternative solutions to the problem. First, if one equates continuation of pregnancy with "treatment" under the informed consent model, the risk of giving birth to a defective child can be characterized as one of the risks of that treatment.[106] The ostetrician who fails to discover and disclose that risk of treatment has, therefore, breached his legal duty under the informed consent doctrine. The Texas court in *Jacobs v. Theimer*[107] accepted this argument, holding that the obstetrician failed to obtain informed consent to continuation of his patient's pregnancy when he failed to diagnose German measles in the early stages of pregnancy and consequently failed to inform the mother of the risks of rubella-induced birth defects. The dissent in the intermediate appellate court in *Howard v. Lecher*[108] made a similar argument. The *Jacobs* argument succeeds only by sleight of hand. We do not ordinarily consider pregnancy a disease, with childbirth and abortion as alternative "treatments."[109] Pregnancy is a natural condition, not a diseased state, and childbirth is the natural conclusion of pregnancy, not a treatment prescribed or administered by a physician. The risk of giving birth to a defective child is not the same as the risk of physicial harm to a patient posed by medical intervention: there is no physical harm to the mother, and childbirth itself is not medical intervention.

The need to distort ordinary language to bring the *Howard* case under the informed consent theory points to a deeper flaw in the argument. The original rationale for liability under the informed consent doctrine was that a patient had a right to decide whether to allow his physician to perform proposed treatment. The basic concern was the inviolability and dignity of the person: others may not do things to you without your permission. Requiring an explanation of the nature of the proposed treatment was not enough to protect fully this dignitary interest. A patient who mistakenly thought a particular treatment was absolutely safe, or who mistakenly thought it the only hope of curing his disease could very well argue that his consent was merely formal and that he would not have consented had he known the treatment's risks and alternatives. To fully protect the basic dignitary interest, then, courts must require that consent to treatment be knowledgeable, or 'informed' — given after consideration of the risks and alternatives to the proposed treatment.

This understanding of the dignitary basis for the informed consent theory underlies the decision of the court in *Karlsons v. Guerinot*.[110] In that case, defendant obstetricians were retained to care for the plaintiff wife during pregnancy. They knew she was 37 years old, that she had a thyroid condition, and that she had previously given birth to a "deformed child,"[111] yet, according to the plaintiffs, they failed to tell her of the risks of producing another deformed child and the availability of amniocentesis to detect certain genetic abnormalities. After the mother gave birth to a Down's child, the parents sued the obstetricians. The court held that a woman who continues a pregnancy because her obstetrician fails to diagnose a fetal defect or to inform her of the increased risk of fetal defects has no cause of action against the obstetrician for lack of informed consent to the continuation of her pregnancy. The court reasoned that the informed consent theory was best limited to cases "where the injury suffered arises from an affirmative violation of the patient's physical integrity and where nondisclosure of risks is concerned, those risks are directly related to such affirmative treatment."[112] The court relied in part on the origin of the informed consent theory in battery cases and in part on the statutory limitations on the informed consent cause of action[113] to support its holding.

One could, of course, criticize the *Karlsons* holding by urging a broader interpretation of the informed consent rationale. The purpose of the informed consent requirement is to insure patient's personal autonomy in making decisions that directly affect her life. The doctrine should therefore apply even when the doctor advises the patient that no treatment is necessary. Even then, when the doctor obviously proposes no invasive medical procedures, the patient would have to know the risks of doing nothing and the alternatives to inaction in order to make an informed decision about a matter vitally important to her. Otherwise, the doctor would simply be substituting his paternalistic medical judgment for the patient's judgment. Thus, in the *Karlsons* case, it would make little difference whether one characterizes childbirth as an alternative treatment for pregnancy, or just the natural consequence of doing nothing. The basic concern for patient autonomy underlying the informed consent doctrine would support application of the doctrine under either characterization.

The above argument depends on blurring one important point. The personal autonomy protected by the informed consent doctrine is the opportunity to choose knowledgeably among alternatives within the scope of the physician-patient relationship; it is not the opportunity to choose knowledgeably among every alternative open to the patient. Without this limitation, the informed consent doctrine would require a physician to become financial advisor, marital counselor, and interior decoration consultant. The informed consent doctrine can be applied when the doctor recommends no treatment because the patient originally went to the doctor for diagnosis and treatment of a particular condition. The decision not to do anything to treat that condition is therefore a decision within the understood scope of the physician-patient relationship. To apply the same analysis to the *Karlsons* case, however, one must first assume that obstetricians ordinarily undertake not only to diagnose the fact of pregnancy and take steps to protect the health of the mother and the child, but also to determine whether an elective abortion is advisable. The informed consent doctrine therefore cannot be used to finesse the basic question of the obstetrician's undertaking.

The Obstetrician's Traditional Undertaking

Two commentators have argued that an obstetrician's traditional undertaking includes the detection of untreatable fetal defects to provide information for the eugenic abortion decision. Professor Annas argued that an obstetrician has "a legal duty to fully inform [his patient] of any reason he has to believe that the fetus might be defective, and to further inform her of the existence of diagnostic tests that might identify precise genetic defects."[114] According to Annas, the obstetrician incurs this duty "because it is precisely this kind of information that the woman employed the physician to learn in the first place, *i.e.,* to learn all she could to help her have a healthy child."[115] A recent Note in the Yale Law Journal echoed this argument, asserting that "an obstetrician in his practice attempts to ensure, insofar as possible, that children will be born healthy"[116] [This argument is just a variation of the *Park v. Chessin*[117] argument that a child's right to be born healthy entails a duty to counsel abortion for defective fetuses.[118]]

Traditionally, obstetricians have undertaken to protect the life and health of the mother and the unborn child. To turn the undertaking to protect the health of the unborn child so that the child will, if possible, be born healthy, into an undertaking to ensure, by eugenic abortion counseling, that *only* healthy children will be born, is to play with words. This redefinition changes the obstetrician's undertaking to protect the life and health of the unborn child into an undertaking to counsel abortion and death for defective unborn children. The redefinition is therefore not an accurate characterization of the obstetrician's traditional undertaking.

It is true, of course, that obstetricians, as part of their traditional undertaking to protect the health and well-being of the mother, have attempted to determine under certain circumstances whether or not the unborn child is defective in order to reassure a worried mother or, alternatively, to prepare the mother emotionally for the shock of a defective child.[119] It could be argued that Professor Annas's proposed duty is but a recognition of this traditional undertaking in the context of improved techniques capable of detecting a greater number of fetal defects. But this argument raises a problem about the extent of recoverable damages.

If the plaintiffs' theory in a wrongful birth case is that defendant breached an undertaking to resolve the parents' doubts and fears, the recoverable damages could be limited, under a proximate cause rationale, to compensation for the emotional anguish that could have been avoided by earlier information about the child's defect, assuming the child would be born in any event. Under the traditional undertaking, that was the only harm the obstetrician undertook to prevent, and that is therefore the only harm he should be liable for if he breaches his undertaking.[120] The obvious counter-argument is that, given the current availability of eugenic abortion, breach of the traditional undertaking to resolve therapeutically the parents' doubts and fears can foreseeably preclude the parents from choosing a eugenic abortion. If the test of proximate cause is foreseeability of the resultant harm,[121] breach of the duty to resolve doubts therapeutically could give rise to a claim for the full damages caused by the birth of a defective child.

The basic question, then, is whether Professor Annas's proposed duty can be characterized as a simple extension, under changed circumstances, of the obstetrician's traditional undertaking to resolve therapeutically the parents' doubts and fears. The argument against this characterization would focus on the nature and risks of amniocentesis (see pages 15, 18).

According to many physicians, the risk of harm to the mother or the unborn child posed by amniocentesis overbalances the emotional benefits from knowing the child's status a few months early. As a rule, amniocentesis is not recommended simply to resolve a mother's fears about the child's possible untreatable disorders. The medical experts generally support amniocentesis only when the suspected disorder is treatable prenatally or when the mother would consider aborting a fetus with an untreatable defect.[122] In cases of suspected untreatable defects, then, the obstetrician ordinarily cannot justify suggesting amniocentesis by the traditional therapeutic undertaking to resolve the mother's doubts, although there may be individual cases where the procedure is warranted. Moreover, the need to justify amniocentesis by reference to possible therapeutic abortion of an affected unborn child underscores the argument that the duty proposed by Professor Annas is inconsistent with the obstetrician's traditional undertaking to protect the life and health of the unborn child.

It could be argued that the obstetrician's traditional undertaking is no longer the customary or expected obstetrical undertaking after the United States Supreme Court's decisions recognizing the pregnant woman's constitutional right to an abortion. Those decisions, plus the development of the means to diagnose certain genetic defects prenatally, have led obstetricians to adopt — and pregnant patients to expect — a new undertaking. Medical literature reflects this new development: Milunsky and Atkins, for example, have listed "indications" that a pregnant woman should consider amniocentesis.[123] The obstetrician's duty to keep up with recent medical developments reinforces the conclusion that obstetricians who fail to use professional skill to detect risks of fetal defects should be subject to liability for the subsequent birth of a defective child.[124] Furthermore, the fact that a "respectable minority" of obstetricians refuse to accept this role should not protect the defendant obstetrician, for the basis for the refusal is not medical judgment but personal moral opposition to abortion.[125] Conscientious opposition to abortion cannot absolve an obstetrician from the duty *simply to inform* a pregnant patient of the increased risks of fetal defect and the availability of amniocentesis, since providing such information does not require the obstetrician to act against his conscience by advising or participating in an abortion[126] (see p. 28-29; 135-138).

The problem with this argument for imposing a legal duty to investigate untreatable fetal defects is that it assumes there are medical indications for eugenic abortion, and that the judgment to recommend amniocentesis is therefore a medical judgment, as opposed to the purely moral judgment of an obstetrician who believes that eugenic abortion counseling is not and should not be part of the obstetrician's undertaking. But there are no medical indications for eugenic abortions: a woman pregnant with a defective child is not diseased, and abortion is not a cure for the child's defect. Both those who support and those who reject the notion that obstetricians should undertake to detect untreatable fetal defects to provide grounds for eugenic abortion, then, do so based on particular moral or social policy reasons unrelated to traditionally "medical" judgments. The Yale Note urges obstetricians to adopt that role because they have the knowledge needed to avoid the birth of defective children, with their accompanying economic harm to society.[127] One opposed to that position could argue that adopting the role of eugenic abortion counselor may well weaken the obstetrician's commitment to protect the life and health of the unborn child, with consequent lessening of trust between patient and physician and gradual decline in the quality of obstetrical care. If doctors' conduct influenced by the second policy view is legally irrelevant to the determination of obstetricians' customary undertaking because it is based on moral rather than medical grounds, surely doctors' conduct influenced by the first social policy should be, too.

Two Competing Practices — The problem for the law is this: in attempting to find the obstetrician's ordinary undertaking, one finds two competing practices. Some obstetricians may adopt the new role of eugenic abortion counselor and others may not. A patient may get a completely different kind of service from one obstetrician than she would get from another. The kind of service would depend on which obstetrician she chanced upon. Any particular patient could expect her physician to adopt the role of eugenic abortion counselor. That patient may well be aggrieved by her obstetrician's failure to fulfill her expectations, but the physician may believe that his patient only expected adherence to the traditional obstetrical undertaking.

Three Possible Resolutions to Mismatched Expectations —
A court could resolve this problem of mismatched expectations in one
of three ways. In the first way, the court could impose the legal duty
proposed by Professor Annas on the obstetrician, but allow the
obstetrician to avoid that obligation by expressly limiting the scope of
his undertaking.[128] This would provide redress for private injustice
caused by frustration of a patient's reasonable expectations, tend to
prevent future private injustice by frustration of patients' expectations, and put the burden of clarifying the patients' expectations on the
physician, who has more detailed knowledge about the practice of
obstetrics than the patient, and who also is in a better position to think
of raising the question than the patient.

In the second way, the court could refuse to impose the legal duty
proposed by Professor Annas on the obstetrician. This refusal could
be based on the argument that the courts can attach an implied
undertaking to the obstetrician-patient relationship only when that
undertaking is so universal that the court can assume that reasonable
parties would enter the relationship believing that was part of the
obstetrician's undertaking.[129] Since that is not so in the eugenic
abortion counseling case, the court cannot attach that undertaking to
the obstetrician-patient relationship. In choosing between these two
positions, the court could take into account the likely consequences of
adopting one or the other positions. Thus, the Yale Note's economic
consequences argument could be considered,[130] along with the
contrary argument about lessening the obstetrician's commitment to
preserving the life and health of the unborn child.

The third possible judicial approach would be to leave the
question of the obstetrician's undertaking to the jury whenever there
is credible expert testimony on both sides. This would be undesirable
for a number of reasons. The nature of the obstetrician's undertaking
is a question on which a patient is likely to have very specific
expectations. The relevant considerations are social and moral
judgments that do not require medical expertise. There is therefore
no need to delegate the decision to doctors. The practice of
obstetricians is relevant insofar as it conditions the actual expectations
of patients who go to them, but there is likely no consistent medical
custom here, and in any event, the court may refuse to give controlling
weight to medical custom here without running the risk of adversely
skewing therapeutic medical judgments. Finally, in times of

controversy over the obstetrician's role, when different patients may have different expectations about the obstetrician's role, both physicians and patients need a definite legal rule defining the implied scope of the obstetrician's undertaking, to avoid unfair surprise to either patient or doctor.

An obstetrician following the older traditions of the profession runs a risk. Some courts may decide that obstetricians have a legal duty to inform their patients of increased genetic risk and the availability of amniocentesis; some may leave the question of obstetrician's undertaking to the jury.

Three Options for Clarification of Expectations — To protect against future liability for failure to adopt the eugenic abortion counselor role, an obstetrician professionally and morally opposed to abortion may want to clarify the expectations of his patients at the start of the doctor-patient relationship. Even without the threat of liability, he may want to clarify his patient's expectations to avoid confusion and bad feelings. The obstetrician has at least three options open to him.

Under the first option, the obstetrician could explain that he will limit his services to care for the mother and unborn child during pregnancy, and that he considers both to be his patients. He will therefore not advise the mother during pregnancy about the probabilities or the detectability of untreatable birth defects. This approach preserves the doctor's moral and professional integrity and arguably protects him from liability, while giving fair notice to the patient that the scope of the obstetrical care he offers is narrower than she might otherwise expect. Nevertheless, there are serious problems with this approach. The obstetrician could not help a patient faced with a high probability of a defective child prepare emotionally and financially for that possibility. More importantly, perhaps, the patient's knowledge that her obstetrician would conceal information about the risks of birth defects would interfere with the doctor's ability to calm the sometimes overpowering fears that the child will have a serious birth defect. This approach may thus impair the obstetrician's ability to provide ordinary obstetrical care to his patients. Neither patients personally opposed to abortion nor patients willing to abort under certain circumstances may want this kind of obstetrical care. A court faced with such a case might therefore refuse to accept the self-imposed limitation on the scope of treatment. The court could hold that no patient who fully understood the implications of the limitation would agree to it and that such a limitation was therefore void as unconscionable.[131]

Under the second option, the obstetrician could explain to his prospective patient that, because of his professional opposition to abortion, he would only accept as patients women who would not consider abortion except to save their own lives. If the prospective patient indicated that that was her position, the obstetrician could then explain that he would accept her as a patient and advise her assuming that eugenic abortion was not an available option. The physician could thus freely discuss the probabilities of birth defects, but amniocentesis would be recommended only to detect treatable conditions, or rarely as therapeutic resolution of an uncertainty that seriously threatened the mother's emotional or physical well-being. This approach would thus enable the physician to preserve his moral and professional autonomy while providing adequate obstetrical care. Furthermore, it would give fair notice to the patient of the scope of treatment, and arguably protect the physician from liability in the situations discussed above. But this option, too, has its problems. It would tend to limit the practice of obstetricians opposed to abortion to those who share their views. This may be the inevitable and foreseeable result of the Supreme Court's abortion decisions, but the cost to society of dividing the community should at least be noted and mourned.

Moreover, an attack on the legal effectiveness of this approach could be made. A plaintiff suing for the obstetrician's failure to discuss the option of amniocentesis and selective abortion could argue that the physician's conditions on the scope of treatment are unenforceable if viewed as a contract. Under a contract analysis, the plaintiff would argue that the conditions are not so much limitations on the scope of treatment as sophisticated attempts to avoid liability for obvious malpractice, which should be void as against public policy. Furthermore, since plaintiff had no choice but to accept these conditions if she wanted medical treatment, courts should scrutinize the conditions carefully to make sure they were not unfair to the plaintiff. Any agreement by which a patient gives up her right to be told all the available options at some future time during the course of medical care should be considered fundamentally unfair and unenforceable. A pregnant woman may very easily say, at the beginning of an apparently normal pregnancy, that she would not consider abortion except to save her own life, yet later decide to abort when told that the fetus has Down's syndrome. To take the initial statement as a blanket consent to an unusually limited undertaking without further discussion of the eugenic abortion option when it becomes a critical choice simply ignores the fact that people often chance their minds about abstract ethical questions when faced with the realities of choice in a real-life situation.

However, viewed as a question of traditional contract law, this argument is unpersuasive. One of the purposes of a system of contract is to allow people to control the future by making legally-binding choices today about options that may become 'critical' tomorrow. But traditional contract principles may not be relevant when the agreement restricts the scope of medical advice. Concern for personal autonomy in decisions about what is done to one's own body would seem to preclude application of traditional contract principles here.[132] But the obstetrician opposed to abortion who finds his patient equally opposed to it agrees to the limitation on the scope of treatment in the interests of the unborn child. In treating the patient under the assumption that she would not choose eugenic abortion, the doctor protects the life of the unborn child while protecting the mother from the temptation to act against her conviction that the unborn child, whether sound or defective, is an independent human being deserving protection. For the court to hold that this agreement is legally ineffective because the only interest at stake is the mother's interest in deciding what happens to her own body would be for the state to choose one theory of the beginning of human life and impose it by sanctions on those who disagree. This is exactly what the Court in *Roe v. Wade* said the state could not do in principle at least.

Under the third option, the obstetrician could tell the patient his moral and professional views on abortion. He would also tell her that he planned to disclose fully all relevant information about the probabilities of birth defects and the alternatives available at each stage of pregnancy, but that in explaining the available options he would try to persuade her not to choose any option that would involve an abortion. The obstetrician would explain that because of his professional and moral opposition to abortion he would frankly oppose this option.

This third approach seems an improvement over the second. Its use would not tend to polarize the practice of obstetrics; it preserves

218

the moral integrity of the physician while respecting the moral autonomy of the patient. Nothing is hidden from the patient during the course of treatment.

The third option can be attacked from two different directions. The first objection to this approach is that respect for the patient's moral autonomy requires "non-directive," completely value-free counseling.[134] The informed consent standard, which enshrines this principle of respect for the patient's autonomy supports imposing a legal requirement of non-directive counseling when the decision, such as the decision to undergo a eugenic abortion, is a moral rather than a medical one. A patient goes to a physician for medical, not moral advice. Physicians who *press* their own moral views on their patients violate the expectations of their patients and engage in the practice of sectarian medicine contrary to the canons of Medical Ethics.[135]

However, this argument for a legally enforced standard of non-directive counseling is unpersuasive, the ideal assumptions underlying the argument are unsound, and the consequences of adopting such a standard would be unfortunate. The psychology assumed by the proponents of non-directive counseling is false to our basic experience as social and moral beings. They seem to assume that appropriate moral choices will be made if the patient is given a complete and completely value-free statement of all relevant empirical facts. The patient will then choose consistently with his deep-seated preferences, which cannot be changed by reasoned argument. Under this model, respect for the moral autonomy of another requires non-directive counseling. All the moral agent needs are the empirical facts. But if man is a rational and a social being, respect for the moral autonomy and responsibility of another may require that we witness to our moral convictions to guide him in forming and evaluating his, and that we buttress our witness by rational argument. If this is done without fraud or coercion we can claim to have acted with respect for his moral autonomy.

Moreover, if man is a rational and a social being, purely non-directive counseling may be impossible. Each of us expects others to have social, ethical and professional standards. In dealing with others, we constantly search for clues to their opinions about how we should behave. Regardless of how careful one is to assume an air of neutrality, the other will reach some conclusion about one's opinion and the depth of his commitment to it. Ordinarily, the most likely effect of one's studied attempt to remain 'neutral' while discussing basic ethical choices is that the other will infer that one does not distinguish between the possible choices on a moral basis. The strength of this inference may be affected by the context of the discussion. If one is a professional such as a doctor or a lawyer, the client, it is true, may attribute the air of neutrality to a professional's effort to avoid imposing moral values rather than personal moral indifference. Nonetheless, as the widespread reputation of lawyers as amoral 'hired guns' attests, ordinary people have difficulty divorcing the person as an independent moral agent from the person as a 'disinterested' professional, and assume that the professional has, at least, no moral objections to client choices that he helps implement.

The 1973 Supreme Court decisions on abortion left the physician-counselor in a curious position in relation to abortion choices. On the one hand, the Court nearly deified physicians as wise counselors who could exercise sound medical judgment based on all the factors — "physical, emotional, psychological, familial, and the woman's age"[136] — relevant to what was supposedly a purely medical abortion decision. On the other hand, the Court recognized the deep division in our society and within the medical profession on the question of whether abortion is the deliberate killing of an innocent defenseless human being.[137] According to the court, the state cannot interfere with the abortion decision by officially adopting one theory of the beginning of human life.[138] The question of whether the unborn child is a human being deserving respect and protection is then necessarily one of a set of questions the pregnant woman must answer in deciding whether to abort. To say that the question of the unborn child's status is a purely personal question on which the physician-counselor's advice is unneeded and unwelcome, then, is to deny one or the other of two apparent premises of the Court's argument — (1) that the abortion decision is a purely medical question to be resolved by the pregnant woman in consultation with her physician, and (2) that the question of when human life begins is a controverted question that the Court cannot decide. (But, in fact, it did. The Court decided in effect that human life does not begin at conception.)*

Under the above analysis, outlawing the third option by adopting a legally-enforced standard of 'non-directive' counseling seems

---

*Editor's note

unwise. It would deny the physician-counselor opposed to abortion the freedom to speak out and counsel against it, an infringement of the first amendment rights of doctors seemingly recognized in *Roe v. Wade* and *Doe v. Bolton.* It would deprive patients of information relevant to the abortion decision. Moreover, it is not supportable by analogy to the informed consent cases. All those cases require is that the physician explain the prospects and material risky of the proposed treatment together with the prospects and material risks of alternative courses of treatment.[139] Courts have not required doctors to present the alternatives without recommending any.

On the other hand, the third option protects both the moral and professional autonomy of the physician-counselor and the personal antonomy of the patient. It cannot be attacked as inconsistent with the expectations of the patient because it is a means of clarifying and structuring those very expectations.

Beyond the whole objection to the third option based on the opposition to directive counseling, another objection may be considered. It comes from those opposed to abortion who believe that a physician employing this approach may provide a patient with information leading to an abortion that would not have been performed had the physician kept quiet. Because his information may become the occasion of a decision to abort, the physician would be morally responsible for the death of the unborn child. The third option would thus not preserve the moral integrity of the physician.

This objection is not persuasive. First, the argument assumes that we are morally responsible, regardless of our intentions, for any death that would not have happened had we acted differently. This radical equivalence of means is a prominent feature of the utilitarian ethic, but has no place in traditional concepts of personal moral responsibility.[140] Under those traditional concepts it is hard to see how one can be morally responsible for an abortion when one has counselled against it. The critical question in assessing moral responsibility would be whether the counselor had a justifiable reason for giving the patient the information that ultimately led to the abortion. Arguably at least, there are good reasons for this. In our society after *Roe* and *Doe,* abortion on demand is a well-known fact of life. To ignore the abortion option completely in counseling would undermine one's effectiveness as a counselor, breach the faith of the patient, and place the counselor in the dubious position of attempting to hide what is common knowledge. Forthright discussion of available alternatives may be the price a counselor must pay to operate professionally in our society. If this discussion is accompanied by counsel against abortion, the counselor avoids personal moral responsibility for abortion by his patients.

Deliberate or Intentional Breach of Duty

The part just concluded has dealt with exploring the standard of care for a genetic counselor, that is, the scope of the counselor's duty. In the present part, the legal aspects of a breach of duty will be considered especially with regard to a breach of confidence and the concealment of the diagnosis.

A number of situations may arise in the course of genetic counseling that present conflicts of interests. The counselee's interest may conflict with society's interest, or the interest of third parties, or the counselor's personal interests. These three conflict situations have been discussed in the legal literature on genetic counseling. In each case, the counselor must make a deliberate choice to favor one interest over another. That puts these cases into the category of intentional torts for purposes of technical analysis. In professional malpractice, however, the differences between unintended and intended breach of duty may be analytically irrelevant. The result should depend on the nature of the genetic counselor's undertaking, the reasonable expectations of the counselees, customary practice of genetic counselors, and the consequences of recognizing a particular cause of action. These four analytical tools will be used to explore the three conflict of interest problems discussed in the literature.

Breach of Confidence and the Duty to Warn

In the following hypothetical case there is a serious conflict of interest between the counselor's patient and the patient's relatives:

> The counselor discovers that his patient is a carrier of a particular genetic defect, and the likelihood is high that the patient's brothers and sisters are either carriers or affected. The patient refuses to inform her brothers and sisters of the diagnosis, and forbids the counselor to inform them. Would the counselor be liable for damages for breach of confidence if he tells the brothers and sisters over the patient's objections? Would the counselor be liable for damages to a brother or sister if he fails to communicate the

diagnosis and a child with genetic defect is subsequently conceived and born?

Legal anaysis of this hypothetical case requires a look at the general question whether courts should recognize a cause of action for a physician's unauthorized disclosure of confidential communications. Five courts have recognized such a cause of action;[141] two have rejected it.[142] In most states the question has not been decided. The reasons for recognizing such a cause of action are persuasive. Given the professional ethical standard requiring confidentiality[143] and the general public understanding of that standard, patients can reasonably expect that their communications with physicians and the resulting medical diagnoses will be kept confidential.[144] The patient's interests in privacy and freedom from mental distress by disclosure of embarrassing personal details are substantial. Furthermore, the societal interest in public health requires open communication between patients and physicians, which might be jeopardized without assurances of confidentiality.[145] Given the importance of the patient's interest and the reasonable expectations of the patient, the physician who intentionally reveals confidential information has seriously wronged his patient. Courts have noted that such conduct is clearly reprehensible — contrary to professional[146] and community standards.[147] The case for recognizing a cause of action for intentional disclosure of confidential information thus seems strong. The remaining problem is that of determining what conditions justify or excuse such disclosure.

Courts have recognized a number of exceptions to the confidentiality rule. It has been held that a physician may, without liability: (1) disclose the fact that the patient is suffering from a contagious disease to those likely to be exposed to the disease by the patient;[148] (2) disclose complete information about the patient's physical condition to preclude misinterpretation of a patient-requested partial disclosure;[149] (3) disclose medical information relating to a claim that would have been discoverable had the claim resulted in litigation;[150] and (4) disclose medical information to the husband about his wife, even though the wife consulted the physician while separated from the husband and the husband intended to use the information in divorce proceedings.[151] The last three exceptions recognize a right of the physician to choose whether to disclose the information, without liability whichever way he chooses. The first exception, however, presents a special case in which the physician not only has a right to convey the diagnosis but also has a duty to warn those foreseeably endangered by his contagious patient. Failure to warn will result in liability to those unwarned who contract the disease.[152] Recently the California Supreme Court has extended this duty to warn. In *Tarasoff v. Board of Regents*[153] the court held that a therapist who determines (or should determine by use of ordinary skill and care of ordinary reputable therapists) that his patient presents a serious danger of violence to another has a legal duty to warn the intended victim of the danger.

The hypothetical case of warning siblings about a counselee's genetic defect outlined above (p. 224) is easily distinguished from *Tarasoff* and the contagious disease cases. In this case, the doctor's patient does not herself pose any risk of harm to others. Therefore, a secondary duty to warn cannot be derived from a primary duty to control the patient's movements by quarantine or commitment. The physician's relationship with the patient may thus not be sufficient in the hypothetical case to overcome the law's general reluctance to impose duties to take affirmative action to protect a stranger from foreseeable harm.

If the counselor does not have a duty to disclose genetic risks to the patient's relatives, does he nevertheless have a right to do so free from liability for breach of confidence? One could argue that disclosure is legally justified. The interest protected by confidentiality here is not as weighty as the interest protected by disclosure. The patient wants to avoid possible embarrassment and mental anguish from disclosure of his or her genetic status only to those who may share the same status. Disclosure, on the other hand, might help prevent the conception or birth of a child with a *serious* hereditary disorder. The interest in avoiding the great economic and emotional harm from such a birth is surely just as great as the interest in avoiding physical harm to those potentially exposed to a contagious disease. The relatives' interests thus should count as a "supervening interest"[154] sufficient to justify a breach of confidentiality under the general standards announced in prior cases.

The patient could argue, however, that there is no effective confidentiality requirement if breach of confidence may be justified in individual cases by balancing the interests served by confidentiality against the interests served by disclosure. The cases that purport to recognize the confidentiality obligation while approving disclosure must therefore be read as interpretations of the patient's reasonable expectations about the scope of confidentiality in the physician-patient relationship. Careful examination shows that in each case in which the court recognized an exception to the confidentiality requirement, previously recognized legal rights or duties of the doctor made the expectation of complete confidentiality unreasonable. Thus, public health laws allowing or requiring physicians to quarantine cases of contagious disease limit the confidentiality of certain diagnoses, as do mental health laws providing for the commitment of mentally ill patients posing a danger to themselves or others. The physician's legal obligation to avoid fraudulent and misleading statements makes it unreasonable for the patient to expect his doctor to give only a partial, misleading statement of the case at the patient's request. In the hypothetical case (p. 224), however, the genetic counselor could keep the genetic risk information confidential without breaching any previously imposed legal obligation. Hence one could argue that the patient's expectations of confidentiality are reasonable and should be enforced.

As the above arguments suggest, the legal result in the hypothetical case is far from certain. The genetic counselor might be well-advised to avoid situations in which he has to choose between two alternatives, each of which poses a significant threat of liability. He can do this by making clear at the outset (preferably both orally and in writing) that he will convey any genetic diagnosis directly affecting the interests of blood relatives to those relatives. If the patient agrees to genetic counseling under these conditions, the genetic counselor would be protected from liability for subsequently informing the blood relatives; the patient could not reasonably have expected the physician to keep that information secret.

Concealing the Diagnosis: Protecting the Marriage

The following hypothetical case presents a conflict of interest between the husband and the wife who seek genetic counseling:

Husband and wife come to a genetic counselor because they have a child with a serious genetic defect and want to know what the chances are of producing another such child. After testing the husband, the wife, and the child, the counselor determines that the husband could not have been the father of the child, and that the husband and wife have no chance of producing another child with similar defect, although the wife and her partner in adultery have a high probability of producing another child with similar defect. Would the counselor be liable in tort for damage to the wife (divorce, refusal to support the affected child) caused by revealing this diagnosis to the husband? Would the counselor be liable in tort to the husband for concealing the diagnosis?

The most important consideration in this hypothetical case is the reasonable expectations of the parties. This breaks down into two sub-questions: (1) "Who is the counselor's patient?" and (2) "What does the patient expect from the counselor?" In the ordinary case, when nothing is said about whether the husband or the wife or both are the patients, and when tests are conducted on both husband and wife, the natural conclusion would be that both husband and wife are the counselor's patients. Ordinarily, a physician is liable for concealing a diagnosis from his patient.[155] The only defense the courts have recognized is therapeutic privilege: the physician will not be liable for withholding the diagnosis if conveying the diagnosis would seriously threaten the health of the patient. The therapeutic privilege would not seem applicable in the second hypothetical case (p. 227), however, since the patients are not suffering from any disease and came to the counselor for information, not therapy.[156] The problem is that the information sought tends to sever the assumed community of interests between the two patients, not that it impairs the health or well-being of one of the patients. Unless this information was not part of the data sought by the couple who are both his patients, the counselor would seem to be obligated to inform both the husband and the wife.

The counselor might be tempted to define narrowly the information sought by the couple to justify concealing from the husband the fact that he was not the father of the affected child. The narrowest definition of the information sought would be "the probability that *this couple* would produce another child with the same or similar defect." In many cases, even this narrow definition of the information sought would not justify concealing the fact of non-paternity. If the affected child's defect were something like an autosomal recessive trait and the father was not a carrier or if the defect is only transmissible by a genetic defect in the true father (a defect the husband does not have), the genetic counselor would have to tell the couple that *their* chances of producing another child with similar defect were zero. This would inform all but the densest husband that the affected child was not his.

The situation is different when the affected child's defect is such that the husband could father a similarly defective child, but the genetic counselor discovers that the husband was not this child's father. If the fact of fathering one such defective child does not increase the probability of subsequently fathering another child with similar defect,[157] the narrow definition of the information sought would seem to justify concealing the fact of non-paternity from the husband. If the fact of fathering one such defective child does increase the probability of subsequently fathering another child with similar defect, however, the narrow-definition ploy runs into trouble. It can, of course, be applied to justify concealing the fact of non-paternity from the husband: the couple together could be told the probability of *their* producing another child with similar defect. But the counselor would then seem to be obliged to inform the wife secretly that she and her partner in adultery have a higher probability of producing such a child. The necessity for the second conference suggests that the narrow definition of the information sought may not be true to the normal expectations of the parties. What the couple ordinarily seeks is all the information relevant to their future reproductive decisions. Furthermore, the whole counseling process in this last case borders on deliberate misrepresentation by omission. It could, of course, be argued that in this last case the counselor is justified, because of concerns for family harmony and the best interests of the child, in concealing the fact of non-paternity from the husband when he can do so without outright misrepresentation, but the risks of frustrating the actual expectations of the parties and misleading the husband by omission are great and troubling.

The above discussion suggests that both marriage partners would ordinarily be deemed to be the genetic counselor's patients. In the highly unusual case in which it is clear that only one of the marriage partners is the counselor's patient, the counselor could confine his counseling just to that patient. The two cases decided on the issue held that a physician could not be held liable for breach of confidentiality when he tells the husband the medical facts about the wife.[158] These cases plus the cases requiring warning to those endangered by the patient[159] suggest that at the very least the counselor would not be liable for disclosing to the other marriage partner the risks of producing a defective child, and the counselor might well be liable for failure to warn the marriage partner who is not his patient. This reasoning would not justify telling the non-patient husband that he is not the father of the affected child, however, since the critical need justifying breach of confidentiality is the need to warn of the danger of producing a defective child. If there is no increased danger (because, *e.g.,* the husband was not the father of an affected child with autosomal recessive defect), no warning is needed, and if the danger is less with the husband than with the wife's lover, simple warning of the actual danger would be sufficient. As a practical matter, since the counselor ordinarily must test both husband and wife, the counselor could assume that only one of the two was his patient only if there were an explicit agreement to that effect prior to genetic testing and counseling. The problem we have been discussing here, while obviously a serious threat to the marital relationship of some small minority of couples referred to a genetic counselor because of an affected child, may not be so common a problem as to justify requiring every couple who comes to a genetic counselor to designate one only as the patient.

Concealing the Diagnosis: Protecting the Near-Normal or Normal Child

The following hypothetical case, discussed at length in the literature, presents a conflict of interest between the parents and the normal or near-normal child:

> In the course of genetic analysis of the fetus following amniocentesis the genetic counselor always discovers the sex of the child. Furthermore, he may discover certain genetic abnormalities that have questionable or relatively unimportant effects, such as XYY trait (questionably associated with anti-social behavior) and Klinefelter's Syndrome (XXY trait, resulting in sterile male with some feminine characteristics, otherwise normal). Is the genetic counselor legally justified in withholding information about the sex of the fetus, and whether it is affected with XYY or XXY trait, on the grounds that the decision to abort should not be based on these grounds?

Legal analysis of this hypothetical case requires a look at the reasonable expectations of the parties and the interests at stake. Since patients would ordinarily expect their counselor to inform them of any increased risk of genetic defect discovered in the course of the genetic investigation, the counselor would have the obligation to report all such increased risks. Thus, if the patient comes to the counselor worried specifically about the risk of producing a Down's syndrome child, and the counselor discovers the patient has Huntington's disease, the counselor would have a legal obligation to inform the patient of that diagnosis. Furthermore, as noted above, the counselor's claim to a therapeutic privilege to withhold a diagnosis is not very strong, given the purely diagnostic setting in which he ordinarily works. The mother could reasonably expect that the counselor would explain all genetic abnormalities discovered, however minor. She could also reasonably expect that the sex of the fetus would be disclosed, at least on request, since that information is necessarily generated by the diagnostic procedure and the genetic counseling undertaking is purely diagnostic. The counselor who undertook amniocentesis with selective abortion of a seriously defective, untreatable fetus in mind may have a hard time asserting a therapeutic privilege on behalf of the normal or near-normal fetus. Amniocentesis in that case was not, after all, provided in order to provide therapy for the unborn child. The counselor could argue that the underlying purpose of amniocentesis is, whenever possible, to assure a mother at high risk of producing a defective child that her child is normal and hence to save the normal child from abortion solely because of the risk. Granted that that may be the underlying purpose, the question remains whether the patient or the counselor gets to define what is normal. The patient could argue that, since she has the legal right to abort for any reason whatsoever, she may decide that a child is abnormal for any reason whatsover.[160]

The genetic counselor may have two ways out of this problem. First, because of the nature of the parent's interest in such cases, the threat of liability for failing to disclose this kind of information, as a practical matter, is minimal. A jury would be likely to find no damages when faced with a claim for damages by a couple who wanted a boy and wound up with a girl. Similarly, a couple claiming damages because they bore an otherwise-normal child with XYY or XXY traits could expect little sympathy and a minimal damage award from a jury. Adoption of the Texas or Wisconsin position on recovery for 'wrongful birth' would virtually insure this result: there could be no recovery for a normal child of the 'wrong' sex, and recovery in the case of the XYY or XXY child would be limited to the special expenses caused by the defect.'[161]

The lack of an effective sanction for violating the patient's expectations does not justify the violation, however. The second and preferable way out of this problem for the genetic counselor would be to agree with the patient before amniocentesis what kinds of information from the karyotyping will be discussed. In that way, subsequent non-disclosure of sex, or XYY or XXY trait would not violate the patient's expectations, and the risk of tort liability would be minimized.

Conclusion

Scientists and physicians have provided us with sophisticated tools for determining the risks of hereditary disorders and, in some cases, diagnosing certain genetic defects in the unborn child. The existence of these tools in a society that accepts both contraception and abortion gives rise to a number of difficult questions: who should be responsible for providing genetic counseling that brings these tools to those faced with practical childbearing decisions? When should such counseling be provided? In deciding questions of tort liability for failure to provide genetic counseling, or failure to provide adequate genetic counseling, common law courts may answer these questions. In the absence of other, more direct controls, tort law may by default be the principal legal control over the application of modern genetic theory and technology to human affairs. One may recognize the important social consequences of particular tort rules, however, without admitting that the choice between different rules ought to be based solely on those consequences. In particular, if one sees tort law as a highly-developed system of corrective justice, considerations of the parties' reasonable expectations and of the possible injustices from adoption of particular rules may weigh more heavily than the comparative social utilities of the alternative rules.

The two most difficult problems encountered in applying traditional tort doctrines of corrective justice to genetic counseling problems have been reviewed here. They are, first, whether the courts should recognize the proposed wrongful birth cause of action, and second, if they do, whether they should impose liability on obstetricians for failure to provide pregnant patients with genetic risk information that could prompt eugenic abortion. The commentators have been virtually unanimous in answering yes to both questions, arguing that basic negligence principles support recognizing a cause of action when defendant's negligence inflicts an unwanted or unplanned baby on the plaintiffs and that under certain circumstances obstetricians who fail to provide information about increased genetic risks and the availability of prenatal diagnostic techniques fail to get the patient's informed consent to continuation of the pregnancy and breach their duty to provide competent obstetrical care.

The courts, on the other hand, have been reluctant to accept commentators' arguments fully, and the analysis in this paper suggests possible reasons for that reluctance. Recognizing the wrongful birth cause of action may cause more injustice than it cures. The courts have therefore looked for compromise positions that accommodate the competing claims of justice. Unresolved questions about the scope of the obstetrician's undertaking make the question of obstetrician's liability a difficult one. In resolving these two difficult questions, courts should apply basic corrective justice principles with a sensitivity to the claims to personal dignity of all the affected parties — parents, children, genetic counselor and physicians.

NOTES

[1]Several commentators have already discussed the application of tort principles to genetic counseling. Annas, *Problems of Informed Consent and Confidentiality in Genetic Counseling, in* GENETICS AND THE LAW 111 (A. Milunsky & G. Annas eds. 1976); Annas & Coyne, *"Fitness" for Birth and Reproduction: Legal Implications of Genetic Screening,* 9 FAM. L.Q. *463 (1975);* Capron, *Informed Decisionmaking in Genetic Counseling: A Dissent to the "Wrongful Life" Debate,* 48 Ind. L. J. 581 (1973); Friedman, *Legal Implications of Amniocentesis,* 123 U. Pa. L. Rev. 92 (1974); Milunsky, *Medico-Legal Issues in Prenatal Genetic Diagnosis, in* GENETICS AND THE LAW 53 (A. Milunsky & G. Annas, eds. 1976); P. Reilly, GENETICS, LAW AND SOCIAL POLICY 163-75 (1977); Reilly, *Genetic Counseling and the Law,* 12 HOUS. L. REV. *640 (1975);* Waltz, *The Liability of Physicians and Associated Personnel for Malpractice in Genetic Screening, in* GENETICS AND THE LAW 139 (A. Milunsky & G. Annas, eds. 1976); Waltz & Thigpen, *Genetic Screening and Counseling: The Legal and Ethical Issues,* 68 Nw. U. L. REV. 696 (1973). The best and most recent discussion of the issues is in Note, *Father and Mother Know Best: Defining the Liability of Physicians for Inadequate Genetic Counseling,* 87 YALE L. J. 1488 (1978).

[2] Although this terminology has not been accepted by everyone [*See* Kass & Shaw, *The Risk of Birth Defects: Jacobs v. Theimer and Parents' Right to Know,* 2 AM. J. L. & MED. 213 at 241-243 (1976)], most commentators use this terminology. *See, e.g.,* Note, *Wrongful Birth in the Abortion Context – Critique of Existing Case Law and Proposal for Future Actions,* 53 DEN. L. J. 501 (1976); Comment, Parents of a Child Born with a Fatal Genetic Disease, That Could Have Been Detected When the Wife Had an Unqualified Right to Abort the Pregnancy, Have No Cause of Action for Emotional Trauma Sustained Against the Doctor Who Negligently Failed to Advise Them of the Situation, 41 ALB. L. REV. 162 (1977). *See also* Sherlock v. Stillwater Clinic, Minn., 260 N. W. 2d 169, 172 n. 3 (1977).

[3] *See* Christensen v. Thornby, 192 Minn. 123, 255 N.W. 620 (1934).

[4] See cases cited notes 15-16, 29 and 8-9, *infra.*

[5] *See, e.g.,* Gleitman v. Cosgrove, 49 N. J. 22, 227 A. 2d 689 (1967); Jacobs v. Theimer, 519 S. W. 2d 846 (Tex. 1975); Stewart v. Long Island College Hosp., 35 App. Div. 2d 531, 313 N. Y. S. 2d 502 (1970), *aff'g,* on wrongful life issue, 58 Misc. 2d 432 (Sup. Ct. 1968), 296 N. Y. S. 2d 41, *aff'd,* 30 N. Y. 2d 695, 283 N. E. 2d 661, 332 N. Y. S. 2d 640 (1972).

[6] *See* Stills v. Gratton, 55 Cal. App. 3d 698, 127 Cal. Rptr. 652 (1976).

[7] *See* Renslow v. Mennonite Hosp., 40 Ill. App. 3d 234, 351 N.E. 2d 870 (1976).

[8] Stills v. Gratton, 55 Cal. App. 3d 698, 127 Cal. Rptr. 652 (1976); Pinkney v. Pinkney, 198 So. 2d 52 (Fla. Dist. Ct. App. 1967); Zepeda v. Zepeda, 41 Ill. App. 2d 240, 190 N. E. 2d 849 (1963); Gleitman v. Cosgrove, 49 N. J. 22, 227 A. 2d 689 (1967); Stewart v. Long Island College Hosp., 35 App. Div. 2d 531, 313 N. Y. S. 2d 502 (1970), *aff'd,* 30 N. Y. 2d 695, 283 N. E. 2d 661, 332 N. Y. S. 2d 640 (1972); Williams v. State, 18 N. Y. S. 2d 481, 223 N. E. 2d 343, 276 N. Y. S. 2d 885 (1966); Dumer v. St. Michael's Hosp., 69 Wis. 2d 766, 233 N. W. 2d 373 (1975).

[9] Park v. Chessin, 88 Misc. 2d 222, 387 N. Y. S. 2d 204 (Sup. Ct. 1976), *aff'd,* 60 App. Div. 2d 80, 400 N. Y. S. 2d 110 (1977); Becker v. Schwartz, App. Div. 2d, 400 N. Y. S. 2d 119 (1977) (following *Park*).

[10] Tedeschi, *On Tort Liability for "Wrongful Life,"* 1 Israel L. Rev. 513 (1966).

[11] Compare the following analysis by Bernard Williams in *The Makropolous Case: Reflections on the Tedium of Immortality,* published in B. WILLIAMS, PROBLEMS OF THE SELF 82, 87 (1973):

> None of this — including the thoughts of the calculative suicide — requires my reflection on a world in which I never occur at all. In the terms of "possible worlds" (which can admittedly be misleading), a man could, on the present account, have a reason from his own point of view to prefer a possible world in which he went on longer to one in which he went on for less long, or — like the suicide — the opposite; but he would have no reason of this kind to prefer a world in which he did not occur at all. Thoughts about his total absence from the world would have to be of a different kind, impersonal reflections on the value *for the world* of his presence or absence: of the same kind, essentially, as he could conduct (or, more probably, not manage to conduct) with regard to anyone else. While he can think egoistically of what it would be for him to live longer or less long, he cannot think egoistically of what it would be for him never to have existed at all. Hence the sombre words of Sophocles "Never to have been born counts highest of all . . ." are well met by the old Jewish reply — "how many are so lucky? Not one in ten thousand."

[12] Tedeschi, *On Tort Liability for "Wrongful Life,"* 1 Israel L. Rev. 513, 530 (1966).

[13] Capron, *Informed Decisionmaking in Genetic Counseling: A Dissent to the "Wrongful Life" Debate,* 48 IND. L. J., 581 (1973). In addition to the problems discussed in the text, Professor Capron's basic argument for recognizing the parent's "right" to full information from the genetic counselor seems to be just a subtle form of bootstrapping. Basically, Professor Capron first argues *by analogy* to the informed consent to treatment cases that there *is* a "right" to be an informed decisionmaker, and that that

right should be recognized in genetic counseling cases. He then turns around and argues that legal recognition of that right is "just" because it treats similar cases similarly. By deriving his proposed rule from a right generalized from other kinds of cases, Professor Capron avoids the onerous task of justifying an argument by analogy. Ordinarily, in legal arguments from analogy one identifies the basic principles behind analogous cases and then focuses on the factual differences between the present case and the allegedly analogous cases to see whether competing principles implicated by the different facts support a different result in the present case. Professor Capron avoids this by talking in terms of a 'rights' formulated in terms general enough to apply to both cases. This boils down to the simple reassertion that the cases are similar.

[14] Park v. Chessin, 46 N. Y. 2d 401, 386 N. E. 2d 807 (1978).

[15] *See* Troppi v. Scarf, 31 Mich. App. 240, 187 N. W. 2d 511 (1971).

[16] *See, e.g.,* Christensen v. Thornby, 192 Minn. 123, 255 N.W. 620 (1934); Bowman v. Davis, 48 Ohio St. 2d 41, 356 N.E. 2d 496 (1976).

[17] *See* C. McCormick, Handbook on the Law of Damages 560-62 (1935).

[18] *See* J. Stein, Damages and Recovery: Personal Injury and Death Actions 16-17 (1972).

[19] *See* T. Sedgwick, 1 A Treatise on the Measure of Damages 98 (9th ed. A. Sedgwick & J. Beale 1912).

[20] *See* Restatement of Torts § 920 (1939); C. McCormick, Handbook on the Law of Damages 146-48 (1935).

[21] Gleitman v. Cosgrove, 49 N. J. 22, 227 A. 2d 689 (1967).

[22] 31 Mich. App. 240, 187 N. W. 2d 511 (1971).

[23] This problem vanishes, of course, if one identifies a legal right — the right to choose whether to abort an unborn child, or to choose whether to employ contraceptive measures — that is impaired by the negligence of the defendant in a wrongful birth case. *See* Note, *Wrongful Birth in the Abortion Context – Critique of Existing Case Law and Proposal for Future Actions,* 53 Den L. J. 501 (1976). One can then deem any interference with that right a harm. The traditional justification for letting the jury assign values to intangibles would then apply. This analytical ploy seems suspect however. Regardless of the interest affected by defendant's conduct, the only "right" protected by the traditional negligence cause of action is the right to be free from negligent infliction of actual physical or economic damage. The proposed exception to this general rule for negligent impairment of a woman's reproductive choices, then, would have to be based on constitutional grounds. The constitutional argument for recognizing a cause of action for wrongful birth is very weak.

[24] *See, e.g.,* Terrell v. Garcia, 496 S. W. 2d 124 (Tex. Ct. App. 1973).

[25] *See* Troppi v. Scarf, 31 Mich. App. 240, 256-57, 187 N. W. 2d 551, 518-519 (1971); Kass & Shaw, *The Risk of Birth Defects: Jacobs v. Theimer and Parents' Right to Know,* 2 AM. J. L. & MED. 213, 227-234 (1976-77); Note, *Wrongful Birth in the Abortion Context – Critique of Existing Case Law and Proposal for Future Actions,* 53 DEN. L. J. 501, 516-18 (1976).

[26] This problem was clearly seen by the court in Rieck v. Medical Protective Co., 64 Wis. 2d 514, 219 N. W. 2d 242 (1974). After rejecting a proposed wrongful life action by plaintiff parents against their obstetrician for negligent failure to diagnose pregnancy in time for a safe abortion, the court added the following note, apparently addressed to the child:

> Since the child involved might someday read this decision as to who is to pay for his support and upbringing, we add that we do not understand this complaint as implying any present rejection or future strain upon the parent child relationship. Rather we see it as an endeavor on the part of clients and counsel to determine the outer limits of physician liability for failure to diagnose the fact of pregnancy. *Id.* at 520, 219 N. W. 2d at 245-46.

The same problem troubled the Minnesota court in Sherlock v. Stillwater Clinic, Minn., 260 N. W. 2d 169 (1977). Although the court felt "compelled" by "obedience to the rule of law" to recognize the parents' cause of action for wrongful birth, the court added that "we are not unmindful of the deep and often times painful ethical problem that cases of this nature will continue to pose for both the courts and litigants. It is therefore our hopes that future parents and attorneys will give serious reflection to the silent interests of the child and, in particular, the parent-child relationship that must be sustained long after legal controversies have been laid to rest." *Id* at 176-77.

[27] 327 A. 2d 757 (Del. Super. Ct. 1974), *aff'd.* 349 A. 2d 8 (Del. 1975).

[28] *Id.*

[29] Troppi v. Scarf, 31 Mich., App. 240, 187 N.W. 2d 511 (1971); Custodio v. Bauer, 251 Cal. App. 2d 303, 59 Cal. Rptr. 463 (1967); Anonymous v. State, 33 Conn. Sup. 126, 366 A. 2d 204 (Conn. Super. Ct. 1976); Stills v. Gratton, 55 Cal. App. 2d 698, 127 Cal. Rptr. 652 (1976); Jackson v. Anderson, 230 So. 2d 503 (Fla. Dist. Ct. App. 1970); Betancourt v. Gaylor, 136 N. J. Super, 69, 344 A. 2d 336 (Super. Ct. 1975); Ziemba v. Sternberg, 45 App. Div. 2d 230, 357 N. Y. S. 2d 265 (1974); Bowman v. Davis, 48 Ohio St. 2d 41, 356 N. E. 2d 496 (1976).

[30] *See* Kass & Shaw, *The Risk of Birth Defects: Jacobs v. Theimer and Parents' Right to Know,* 2 AM. J. L. & MED. 213 (1976-77); Thayer, *Liability to a Family For Negligence Resulting in the Conception and Birth of a Child,* 14 ARIZ. L. REV. 181 (1972); Comment, *Busting the Blessing Balloon: Liability for the Birth of an Unplanned Child,* 39 ALB. L. REV. 221 (1975); Note, *Misfeasance in the Pharmacy: A Bundle of "Fun, Joy and Affection?",* 8 CAL. W. L. REV. 341 (1972); Note, *Birth of Healthy But Unplanned Child Due to Pharmacist's*

Negligence Held a Compensable Injury, 3 SETON HALL L. REV. 492 (1972); Note, *Recovery of Child Support for "Wrongful Birth,"* 47 TULANE L. REV. 225 (1972), Note, *Negligently Filled Prescription for Birth Control Pill Results in Recovery for Birth of Normal Child,* 40 U.M.K.C.L. REV. 264 (1971-72); Comment, *A Married Couple Can Recover Damages for the Birth of a Healthy Child Which Resulted From a Pharmacist's Negligent Filling of the Couple's Prescription for Oral Contraceptive,* 38 BROOKLYN L. REV. 531 (1971); Comment, *Parents Allowed Recovery of Expenses in Having and Rearing an Unwanted Child Where Pharmacist Negligently Dispensed Birth Control Pills,* 3 CUM.-SAM. L. REV. 220 (1972); Comment, *Cause of Action for Birth of Unwanted Child Due to Negligent Dispensing of Oral Contraceptives,* 76 DICK. L. REV. 402 (1972); Comment, *Damage Suits Against Pharmacists and Physicians Based on Negligence in Birth Control Treatments,* 13 WM. & MARY L. REV. 666 (1972); Note, *Wrongful Birth in the Abortion Context – Critique of Existing Case Law and Proposal for Future Actions,* 53 DEN. L. J. 501 (1976).

[31] 327 A. 2d 757 (Del. Super. Ct. 1974), *aff'd,* 349 A. 2d 8 (Del. 1975).

[32] Minn., 260 N. W. 2d 169 (1977).

[33] The *Troppi* court dealt with similar issues in rejecting the defendant's argument that plaintiffs should have mitigated damages by abortion or giving up the child for adoption. Troppi v. Scarf, 31 Mich. App. 240, 257-60, 187 N. W. 2d 511, 519-20 (1971). As a practical matter, the arguments may be the same, but the court's argument in Coleman seems properly understood as one of estoppel, since it argues that plaintiffs keeping the child evidences a judgment that benefits outweigh detriments, not that plaintiffs should have mitigated damages by aborting or placing the child for adoption.

[34] Compare the similar argument against the mitigation claim in Troppi v. Scarf, 31 Mich. App. 240, 257-60, 187 N.W. 2d 511, 519-20 (1971).

[35] Restatement of Torts § 920 and, comment b (1939).

[36] Thus, the Troppi court, which rejected the estoppel argument under the guise of mitigation of damages interpretation, had little trouble in also rejecting the separable interest argument, arguing "Since pregnancy and its attendant anxiety, incapacity, pain and suffering are inextricably related to child bearing, we do not think it would be sound to attempt to separate those segments of damage from the economic costs of an unplanned child in applying the 'same interest' rule." 31 Mich. App. at 255, 187 N. W. 2d at 518.

[37] Comment b to Restatement § 920 contains no reference to cases, and the Reporter published no commentary on this section. Professor Seavey was the Reporter for this section. In his personal copies of preliminary drafts of this section, preserved at Harvard Law School's Library, there are a number of typed and scribbled citations. Preliminary Draft #1, Group 5 — Damages, (dated 13, 1937) and Preliminary Draft #3, Group 5 — Damages (dated March 21, 1938). Adoption of the "interest" language at the time of the third

draft probably reflects the influence of Dean Pound's "jurisprudence of interest" on the Harvard contingent.

[38] Ewing v. City of Louisville, 140 Ky. 726, 131 S. W. 1016 (1910); Harvey v. Georgia S. & Fla. R. R., 90 Ga. 66, 15 S. E. 783 (1892); Marcy v. Fries, 18 Kan. 353 (1877); Brown v. Virginia-Carolina Chem. Co., 162 N. C. 83, 77 S. E. 1102 (1913).

[39] Terrell v. Garcia, 496 S. W. 2d 124 (Tex. Ct. App. 1973); Hays v. Hall, 477 S. W. 2d 402 (Tex. Ct. App. 1972), *rev'd on other grounds,* 488 S. W. 2d 412 (Tex, 1972); Rieck v. Medical Protective Co., 64 Wis. 2d 514, 219 N. W. 2d 242 (1974).

[40] Jacobs v. Theimer, 519 S. W. 2d 846 (Tex. 1975); Dumer v. St. Michael's Hosp., 69 Wis. 2d 766, 233 N. W. 2d 372 (1975).

[41] Dumer v. St. Michael's Hosp., 69 Wis. 2d 766, 233 N. W. 2d 372 (1975). The court merely noted this factual difference between this case and the prior case: "[In Rieck, plaintiffs] sought to recover this entire expense of raising a normal, healthy but claimed unwanted child during its dependency. Here the parents sue only for the expense occasioned by the congenital defects." *Id.* at 795, 233 N. W. 2d at 376.

[42] Jacobs v. Theimer, 519 S. W. 2d 846, 849 (Tex. 1975).

[43] *Id.*

[44] Kass & Shaw, *The Risk of Birth Defects: Jacobs v. Theimer and Parents' Right to Know,* 2 AM. J. L. & MED. 213, 234-39 (1976-77); Note, *Wrongful Birth on The Context of Abortion – Critique of Existing Case Law and Proposal for Future Actions,* 53 DEN. L. J. 501, 511 (1976).

[45] The dissenting judge in the Wisconsin case attacked the majority for adopting a legal distinction between the normal and the defective that "smacks too much of a Hitlerian 'elimination of the unfit' approach." Dumer v. St. Michael's Hosp., 69 Wis. 2d 766, 780, 233 N. W. 2d 372, 379 (1975).

[46] *See generally* Morris, *Punitive Damages in Tort Cases,* 44 HARV. L. REV. 1173 (1931); Note, *Exemplary Damages in the Law of Torts,* 70 (HARV. L. REV. 517 (1957).

[47] *See generally* McCoid, *The Care Required of Medical Practitioners,* 12 VAND. L. REV. 549, 550-57 (1959).

[48] 410 U. S. 113 (1973).

[49] 410 U. S. 179 (1973).

[50] *See* Stewart v. Long Island College Hosp., 35 App. Div. 2d 531, 313 N. Y. S. 2d 502 (1970), *aff'd,* 30 N. Y. 2d 695, 283 N. E. 2d 661, 332 N. Y. S. 2d 640 (1972); Gleitman v. Cosgrove, 49 N. J. 22, 227 A. 2d 689 (1967) (policy recognized, but not tied to abortion statute).

[51] *See* Jacobs v. Theimer, 519 S. W. 2d 846, 850-51 (Tex. 1975) (dissent); Gleitman v. Cosgrove, 49 N. J. 22, 48, 227 A. 2d 689, 703 (1967) (concurrence).

[52] *See* L. AREY, DEVELOPMENTAL ANATOMY 58 (6th ed. 1954).

[53] Compare Williams, *Personal Identity and Individuation and Bodily Continuity and Personal Identity,* in B. WILLIAMS, PROBLEMS OF THE SELF 1 and 19 (1973).

[54] 410 U. S. 113 (1973).

[55] 410 U.S. 179 (1973).

[56] *See, e.g.,* Kass & Shaw, *The Risk of Birth Defects: Jacobs v. Theimer and Parents' Right to Know,* 2 Am. J. L. & Med. 213, 220 (1976-77); Note, *Wrongful Birth in the Abortion Context – Critique of Existing Case Law and Proposal for Future Actions,* 53 DEN. L. J. 501 (1976).

[57] *Cf.* Gleitman v. Cosgrove, 49 N. J. 22, 227 A. 2d 689 (1967) (3 out of 4 judges in majority assumed that plaintiff's mother could somehow have obtained an abortion, yet rely on public policy against abortion to support rejecting proposed wrongful birth cause of action); Jacobs v. Theimer, 519 S. W. 2d 846 (Tex. 1975) (since plaintiffs' allegations of proximate cause not contested at summary judgment stage, court would assume that plaintiff's wife would have obtained legal abortion somewhere had defendant physician informed her of birth defect risk).

[58] 432 U. S. 464 (1977).

[59] Note, *Wrongful Birth on the Abortion Context – Critique of Existing Case Law and Proposal for Future Actions,* 53 DEN. L. J. 501 (1976).

[60] Bowman v. Davis, 48 Ohio St. 2d 41, 356 N. E. 2d 496 (1976). Sherlock v. Stillwater Clinic, Minn., 260 N. W. 2d 169 (1977). *See also* Troppi v. Scarf, 31 Mich. App. 240, 253, 187 N. W. 2d 511, 517 (1971) (Relying on *Griswold* to support constitutional right to wrongful birth cause of action for failed contraception).

[61] 381 U. S. 479 (1965).

[62] 410 U. S. 113 (1973).

[63] 410 U. S. 179 (1973).

[64] 428 U. S. 52 (1976).

[65] 42 U.S. C. § 1985 (1970).

[66] *See* Griffin v. Breckenridge, 403 U. S. 88 (1971). The *Griffin* court interpreted 42 U. S. C. § 1985 (3) to reach private conduct, but only when that conduct involved a specific intent to deprive Plaintiff of his rights, based on "some racial, or perhaps otherwise class-based, invidiously discriminatory animus." 403 U. S. at 102. In the ordinary wrongful birth case based on a negligence theory, the defendant would neither have the requisite intent nor the invidiously-discriminatory animus, and there would be no conspiracy (as required by the statute).

[67] *See* Bowman v. Davis, 48 Ohio St. 2d 41, 356 N. E. 2d 496 (1976); Troppi v. Scarf, 31 Mich. App. 240, 187 N. W. 2d 511 (1971).

[68] See, *supra,* pp. 181ff.

[69] 432 U.S. 464 (1977).

[70] Somewhat surprisingly, in light of the prior opinion in *Roe v. Wade,* the Court found constitutionally-permissible the purpose to encourage childbirth over abortion. *Id.* 475-77.

[71] *See* Epstein, *Medical Malpractice: The Case for Contract,* 1976 Am. B. Foundation Research J. 87, 141-47, Keeton, *Compensation for Medical Accidents,* 121 U. Pa. L. Rev. 590, 597 (1973); King, *In Search of a Standard of Care for the Medical Profession: The "Accepted Practice" Formula,* 28 Vand. L. Rev. 1213, 1224 (1975).

[72] *See* 1 Interagency Task Force on Product Liability, Product Liability: Final Report of the Insurance Study, ES, 3-7; ch. 2, 13-22; ch. 3, 4-14 (1977).

[73] Professor Calabresi has recognized this problem of providing the appropriate incentives to optimal medical care as the central problem in advocating a no-fault system for medical malpractice. Calabresi, *The Problem of Malpractice: Trying to Round out the Circle,* 27 U. Toronto L. J. 131 (1977); Professor Calabresi's "solution," presented ostensibly as a joke, would require mandatory participation in Health Maintenance Organizations that must include, as part of the HMO package, mandatory life insurance and wage maintenance insurance. Professor Calabresi attempts to disarm us by clucking over the extremely high economic costs and interference with individual liberty his "joke" would necessarily entail, but ultimately the joke is on us for Professor Calabresi evidently seriously supports this proposal. *Id.* at 141.

[74] *See* Epstein, *supra* note 71, at 105.

[75] *See* Prosser 143.

[76] *See generally* J. Eddy, Professional Negligence (1955); Professional Negligence (T. Roady & W. Anderson eds. 1960); Restatement (Second) of Torts § 299A (1965) Comment, *Professional Negligence,* 121 U. Pa. L. Rev. 627 (1973).

[77] *See generally* authorities cited in note 76 *supra.*

[78] L. Regan, Doctor and Patient and the Law 17 (3rd ed. 1956), quoted in McCoid, *The Care Required of Medical Practitioners,* 12 Van. L. Rev. 549, 558 (1959). Some states have eliminated the limitation to physicians in the same or similar localities, adopting instead the general standard of the profession. *E.g.,* Speed v. State, 240 N. W. 2d 901 (Iowa, 1976); Blair v. Eblen, 461 S. W. 2d 370 (Ky. 1970).

[79] P. Reilly, Genetics, Law and Social Policy 175-89 (1977).

[80] Reilly, *Genetic Counseling and the Law,* 12 Hous. L. Rev. 640, 641 (1975).

[81] *See* Fraser, *Counseling in Genetics: Its Intent and Scope in Genetic Counseling* 7, (National Foundation-March of Dimes, Birth Defects: Original

Article Series, Vol. VI, No. 1, 1970); Sly, *What is Genetic Counseling?*, in CONTEMPORARY GENETIC COUNSELING 5, 7 (National Foundation-March of Dimes, Birth Defects: Original Article Series, Vol. IX, No. 4, 1973). *See generally* P. REILLY, GENETICS, LAW & SOCIAL POLICY 152-166 (1977) (historical analysis of concept of genetic counseling). *See also* K. LUDMERER, GENETICS AND AMERICAN SOCIETY: A HISTORICAL APPRAISAL 165-193 (1972) (relationship between modern genetic counseling and eugenics movement).

[82] Compare the elaborate attempt by Professor Capron to derive the genetic counselor's legal duty solely from philosophical principles of personal autonomy in Capron, *Informed Decision making in Genetic Counseling: A Dissent to the "Wrongful Life" Debate,* 48 IND. L. J. 581 (1973).

[83] For a discussion of a number of diagnosis cases, *see* A. HOLDER, MEDICAL MALPRACTICE LAW 71-96 (2d ed. 1978).

[84] See J. WALTZ & F. INBAU, MEDICAL JURISPRUDENCE 96-97 (1971).

[85] *See* Johnson v. Yeshiva U. Hosp., 42 N. Y. 2d 818, 364 N. E. 2d 1340, 396 N. Y. S. 2d 647 (1977) (physician did not depart from standard medical practice in failing to suggest amniocentesis to detect chromosomal abnormality: holding based on state of the art in 1969); Park v. Nissen, No. 190033 (Cal. Super. Ct., Orange County, Dec. 13, 1974), reported in CITATION, June 1, 1975, at 38 (standard community medical practice did not require physician to offer amniocentesis to detect chromosomal abnormality in fetus).

[86] For a similar argument stressing the consensual basis for the malpractice standard case, *see* Epstein, *Medical Malpractice: The Case for Contract,* 1976 AM. B. FOUNDATION RESEARCH J. 87.

[87] *See generally* McCoid, *The Care Required of Medical Practitioners,* 12 VAN L. REV. 549, 605-09 (1959).

[88] For discussion of similar problems in application of the "informed consent" doctrine, *see* Meisel, *The Expansion of Liability for Medical Accidents: From Negligence to Strict Liability by Way of Informed Consent,* 56 NEB. L. REV. 51, 113-23 (1977).

[89] 53 App. Div. 2d 420, 386 N. Y. S. 2d 460 (1976); *aff'd,* 42 N. Y. 2d 109, 366 N. E. 2d 64, 397 N. Y. S. 2d 363 (1977).

[90] P. REILLY, GENETICS, LAW, AND SOCIAL POLICY 10 (1977); L. REISMAN & A. MATHENEY, GENETICS AND COUNSELING IN MEDICAL PRACTICE 164-65 (1969).

[91] The Court of Appeals affirmed solely on this basis. 42 N. Y. 2d 109, 336 N. E. 2d 64, 397 N. Y. S. 2d 363 (1977). Judge Cooke in dissent rightly attacked this theory. The majority relied on *Tobin v. Grossman,* 24 N. Y. 2d 609, 249 N. E. 2d 419, 301 N. Y. S. 2d 554 (1969). In *Tobin,* plaintiff mother sued to recover damages for mental anguish caused by witnessing the suffering of her child who was physically injured by defendant's negligence.

In rejecting the mother's claim, the Court reasoned that there was no logical or principled way to limit recovery by third parties — grandparents, aunts, bystanders — who might suffer mental anguish because of another's injury. The law should therefore limit recovery to the one directly harmed by defendant's negligence; otherwise potential liability for any one wrong would be unduly burdensome. The Court said: "It is enough that the law establishes liability in favor of those directly or intentionally harmed." *Id.* at 619, 249 N. E. 2d at 424, 301 N. Y. S. 2d at 562. In *Howard,* however, the parents claimed that defendant obstetrician breached a duty owed directly to them. The *Tobin* court's fears of potentially unlimited liability for any one wrong thus are not applicable to the *Howard* facts. Moreover, application of the *Tobin* reasoning to *Howard* requires one to assume that the child, suffering from a genetic disorder that defendant obstetrician could neither cure nor prevent, was directly injured by the obstetrician's conduct, an assumption contrary to the reasoning of the courts that reject that wrongful life cause of action. For similar criticism of the *Howard* decision, see Note, *Father and Mother Know Best: Defining the Liability of Physicians for Inadequate Genetic Counseling,* 87 YALE L. J. 1488, 1514 (1978).

The parties' litigation strategies that ultimately produced such a strange result were brilliant. Plaintiffs brought only two causes of action: a claim for mental distress and emotional disturbance caused by observing the child suffer and die, and a claim for medical and funeral expenses — for the child incurred by the parents. Plaintiff's attorney may well have left out the ordinary claim for pain and expense of childbirth for good reason. Under compensatory damage theories, those damages would have to be reduced by the pain and expense of the amniocentesis and abortion necessary to have prevented the childbirth. That would have included in the damage claim a reminder to the jury that plaintiffs claim they would have aborted the affected child. By focusing instead only on the damages to them as loving, grieving parents, the plaintiffs enhance their jury appeal. Secondly, the damages claimed are arguably only those specially occasioned by the child's defect. Thus, even if the court adopted the Texas-Wisconsin limitation on damages in wrongful birth cases, both claims might survive. [Although the Texas court in *Jacobs v. Theimer* refused to allow recovery for the plaintiffs' mental anguish, one could argue that that limitation is inconsistent with the argument for allowing as compensable damages those specially caused by the child's defect.] The defense attorney cleverly attacked only the first cause of action, leaving out an appeal the plaintiff's claim showing an obvious direct injury from defendants' alleged breach of duty, thus making the *Tobin* argument seem more plausible. Plaintiffs' attorney voluntarily dismissed the second cause of action in order to make the order of the intermediate appellate court a final order appealable to the Court of Appeals. May 24,

1978 letter from Alfred S. Julien to Patrick J. Kelley, in author's files. After the adverse Court of Appeal's decision, plaintiffs' counsel reinstituted the second cause of action. Defendant's attorney then moved to dismiss, the motion was granted, and the ruling is currently on appeal. *Id.*

[92] 53 App. Div. 2d at 424, 386 N. Y. S. 2d at 462.

[93] 60 App. Div. 2d 80, 400 N. Y. S. 2d 110 (1977).

[94] The case report does not give the technical medical term for the disease. It was probably cystinosis, an autosomal recessive defect in the renal transport mechanism. *See* L. REISMAN & A. MATHENY, *supra* note 90, at 160-61.

[95] 60 App. Div. 2d at 80, 400 N. Y. S. 2d at 112.

[96] The literature contains reports of gross diagnostic failures in some cases. Reisman and Matheny reported the following case:

> Consider the case of the family who came to the birth defects center with an almost helpless young child found to be profoundly retarded. The previous medical contacts made by this family on the child's behalf had consisted of numerous visits to the family pediatrician and to various specialists, including an orthopedist, a general surgeon, and an allergist. Prior to the family's visit to the center, medical attention had apparently been paid mostly to the surgical removal of extra digits on the child's hands and feet. The family had finally come to the center because it had become obvious that the child's progress was markedly delayed — yet in all those numerous visits to different physicians, the parents had never been told that their child was profoundly retarded or that there might be a genetic problem involved, despite the fact that such a condition was obvious from birth. In fact, the child was found to have a translocation type of D-trisomy abnormality, and the father to be the carrier of the abnormal translocation chromosome. Imagine the spiritual as well as the economic bankruptcy of this family by the time they learned that the surgical procedures had not much more than cosmetic value, and that much more serious problems were involved.

L. REISMAN & A. MATHENY, *supra* note 90, at 27-28.

[97] *See generally id.* at 75-77. Not all translocation cases come from carrier mothers, so discovery of the translocation defect should trigger chromosomal tests on the mother to determine carrier status.

[98] One proposed measure of sound medical practice that a court accepting this argument might look to is contained in Milunsky & Atkins, *Prenatal Diagnosis of Genetic Disorders,* in THE PREVENTION OF GENETIC DISEASE AND MENTAL RETARDATION 221, 221-23 (A. Milunsky ed. 1975). The authors listed the following "indications" that a pregnant woman should consider amniocentesis: (1) Maternal age over 40, (2) either parent carrier of chromosomal abnormality, (3) prior pregnancy with autosomal trisomy, and (4) "Amniocentesis is recommended where there is evidence of possible

transmission of an autosomal or X-linked recessive condition where the disease is detectable *in utero* and where the affected offspring will suffer from severe disease, congenital malformation, or mental retardation. In the case of X-linked conditions leading to severe disease, where the disease is not detectable *in utero,* amniocentesis is justified in order to determine the sex of the fetus: male fetuses will have a high chance of being affected and could be aborted should the parents so elect." *But cf. infra,* text accompanying notes 122-128.

[99] A leading obstetrics textbook published in 1961 defined the aim of obstetrics as follows:

> *Aim of Obstetrics.* The transcedent objective of obstetrics is that every pregnancy culminates in a healthy mother and healthy baby. It strives to reduce to a very minimum the number of women and infants who die as a result of the reproductive process or who are left injured therefrom. It aims further to minimize the discomforts of pregnancy, labor, and the puerperium and at the same time so to safeguard and ease the whole course that both mother and child will conclude the experience in a healthy state, both physically and mentally.

N. EASTMAN & L. HELLMAN, WILLIAMS' OBSTETRICS 1-2 (12th ed. 1961).

> The aims of antepartum care in respect to the mother are: (1) to maintain the health and peace of mind of the pregnant woman; (2) to reduce the complications of the antepartum course; (3) to increase the safety of delivery; (4) to produce better health postpartum; and (5) to insure the ability to care for all requirements of the fetus. The aims with regard to the fetus are: (1) reduction of prematurity, stillbirth, and neonatal mortality rates and (2) optimal health in the newborn.

Id. at 338.

> An obstetrics textbook published in 1974 echoed that understanding:
> There can be no doubt whatsoever that the objectives of obstetrics must be to ensure that every child will develop to the fullest measure the potential with which he was endowed at conception. . . .
> The single, pervading objective of obstetrics, as stated earlier, is to minimize maternal risks inherent in pregnancy, while at the same time optimizing fetal outcome to produce a healthy, living infant that will have the capability to attain the full potential he was endowed with at the moment of conception. A physician's management of pregnancy, therefore, has the dual objective of a healthy mother and a healthy baby.

J. B. GREENHILL & E. FRIEDMAN, BIOLOGICAL PRINCIPLES AND MODERN PRACTICE OF OBSTETRICS, 1, 2-3 (1974).

[100] *See* Mohr v. Williams, 95 Minn. 261, 104 N. W. 12 (1905); *see generally* Plante, *An Analysis of "Informed Consent,"* 36 FORDHAM L. REV. 639

244

(1968).

[101] *See* authorities cited in note 100 *supra.*

[102] *See* Natanson v. Kline, 186 Kan. 393, 350 P. 2d 1093 (1960); *see generally* Katz, *Informed Consent – A Fairy Tale? Law's Vision,* 39 U. PITT. L. REV. 137 (1977); Riskin, *Informed Consent: Looking for the Action,* 1975 U. ILL. L. F. 580.

[103] *See* Natanson v. Kline, 186 Kan. at 410, 350 P. 2d at 1106. Professor Jay Katz rejects this assumption. *See* Katz, *supra* note 102, at 148, 151-53 (criticizing *Natanson*).

[104] *See, e.g.,* Canterbury v. Spence, 464 F. 2d 772 (D. C. Cir. 1972) (*overruled sub silentio,* Haven v. Randolph, 494 F. 2d 1069 (1974)); Cobbs v. Grant, 8 Cal. 3d 229, 502 P. 2d 1, 104 Cal. Rptr. 505 (1972); Scaria v. St. Paul Fire & Marine Ins. Co., 68 Wis. 2d 1, 227 N. W. 2d 647 (1975). The informed consent doctrine. *See* Note, *Father and Mother Know Best: Defining the Liability of Physicians for Inadequate Genetic Counseling,* 87 YALE L. J. 1488, 1506-08 (1978).

[105] The influence of Jay Katz has been so strong in the commentary that one is almost tempted to talk of the Yale School of Informed Consent. *See* J. KATZ & A. CAPRON, CASTASTROPHIC DISEASES: WHO DECIDES WHAT? A Psychosocial and Legal Analysis of the Problems Posed by Hemodialysis and Organ Transplantation 82-90 (1975); Capron, *Informed Consent in Catastrophic Disease Research and Treatment,* 123 U. PA. L. REV. 340 (1974); Katz, *Informed Consent – A Fairy Tale? Law's Vision,* 39 U. PITT. L. REV. 137 (1977); Meisel, *The Expansion of Liability for Medical Accidents: From Negligence to Strict Liability by Way of Informed Consent,* 56 NEB. L. REV. 51 (1977); Riskin, *Informed Consent: Looking for the Action,* 1975 U. ILL. L. F. 580; Note, *Restructuring Informed Consent: Legal Therapy for the Doctor-Patient Relationship,* 79 YALE L. J. 1533 (1970); Note, *Informed Consent and the Dying Patient,* 83 YALE L. J. 1632 (1974).

[106] *See, e.g.,* Friedman, *Legal Implications at Amniocentesis,* 123 U. Pa. L. Rev. 92, 147 (1974); Annas, *Problems of Informed Consent and Confidentiality in Genetic Counseling,* in GENETICS AND THE LAW 111, 116-17 (A. Milunsky & G. Annas eds. 1976). The author of the Note, *Father and Mother Know Best: Defining the Liability of Physicians for Inadequate Genetic Counseling,* 87 YALE L. J. 1488 (1978) recognized that the argument from informed consent is only an argument by analogy, and not a simple application of the informed consent doctrine.

[107] 519 S. W. 2d 846, 848 (Tex, 1975).

[108] 53 App. Div. 2d, at 425-27, 386 N. Y. S. 2d at 463-64.

[109] In *Beal v. Doe,* 432 U. S. 438, 445-48 (1977), the United States Supreme Court rejected a similar argument equating childbirth and abortion as alternative "treatments" of pregnancy. Compare Mr. Justice Brennan's

dissent in that case. *Id.* at 448-54.

[110] 57 App. Div. 2d 73, 394 N. Y. S. 2d 933 (1977).

[111] No further definition of the deformity is given in the reported decision.

[112] 57 App. Div. 2d at 82, 394 N. Y. S. 2d at 939.

[113] New York Public Health Law (McKinney) § 2805-d (2) (1977) limiting informed consent doctrine to those cases involving "(a) non-emergency treatment, procedure or surgery, or (b) a diagnostic procedure which involved invasion or disruption of the integrity of the body."

[114] Annas, *supra* note 106, at 116.

[115] *Id.*

[116] Note, *Father and Mother Know Best: Defining the Liability of Physicians for Inadequate Genetic Counseling,* 87 YALE L. J. 1488, 1505 (1978).

[117] 60 App. Div. 2d 80, 400 N. Y. S. 2d 110 (1977) (recognizing wrongful life cause of action).

[118] It is surprising that the author of the Yale Note accepted this argument about the obstetrician's undertaking while rejecting the similar argument for recognizing the wrongful life cause of action. *Supra* note 116, at 1501, note 54.

[119] *See* authorities cited *supra* note 99.

[120] *Compare* Coleman v. Garrison, 327 A. 2d 757 (Del. Super. Ct. 1974), *aff'd* 349 A. 2d 8 (Del. 1975), discussed *supra* in text accompanying notes 31 and 32.

[121] *See generally* Prosser, 250-70.

[122] *See* Milunsky & Atkins, *supra* note 98 at 221-63, quoted in P. REILLY, GENETICS, LAW, AND SOCIAL POLICY 25 (1977).

[123] MILUNSKY & ATKINS, *supra* note 98 at 221-23.

[124] *See supra* note 116, at 1505.

[125] *See* Note, *Abortion Conscience Clauses,* 11 COLUM. J. L. & SOC. PROB. 571, 577-79 (1975).

[126] *See supra* note 116, at 1510-12.

[127] *Id.* at 1496-99.

[128] *See generally* Epstein, *Medical Malpractice: The Case for Contract,* 1976 AM. B. FOUNDATION RESEARCH J. 87; Miller, *The Contractual Liability of Physicians and Surgeons,* 1953 (WASH. U. L. Q. 413.

[129] *Cf.* U. C. C. § 1-205 (2) & (3) (1957 version):

A usage of trade is any practice or method of dealing having such regularity of observance in a place, vocation or trade as to justify an expectation that it will be observed with respect to the transaction in question. The existence and scope of such a usage are to be proved as facts. If it is established that such a usage is embodied in a written trade code or similar writing the interpretation of the writing is for the court.

A course of dealing between parties and any usage of trade in the vocation or trade in which they are engaged or of which they are or should be aware given particular meaning to and supplement or qualify terms of an agreement.

[130] *Supra* note 116, at 1496-99.

[131] The Court in Hume v. United States, 132 U. S. 406, 410 (1889) stated that an unconscionable agreement is one "such as no man in his senses and not under delusion would make on the one hand, and as no honest and fair man would accept on the other." The unconscionability provision of Uniform Commercial Code would not apply directly to doctor-patient agreements, since they are not transactions in goods within U. C. C. § 2-102. Courts have, however, carried over the notion of unconscionability into the general law of contracts in situations not directly governed by the Code. *See generally,* J. CALAMARI & J. PERILLO, THE LAW OF CONTRACTS 322-23 (2d ed. 1977).

[132] *But cf.* Epstein, *supra* note 128 at 102-08.

[133] 410 U. S. 113, 160-63 (1973).

[134] This argument was made by Professor Annas in his paper, *Problems of Informed Consent and Confidentiality in Genetic Counseling,* in GENETICS AND THE LAW 114 (A. Milunsky and G. Annas, eds. 1976). The 1973 Maryland statute creating a state Commission on Hereditary Disorders set out, as one of a number of principles to guide the Commission in developing rules and regulations, the following: "That counseling services for hereditary disorders be available to all persons involved in screening programs, that such counseling be non-directive; and that such counseling emphasize informing the client and not require restriction of childbearing." Md. Ann. Code art. 43, § 818 (G) (Cum. Supp. 1977).

[135] See Pilpel, *A Non-Catholic Lawyer's View,* in 1 ABORTION IN A CHANGING WORLD 157, 158-59 (R. Hall ed. 1970).

[136] Doe v. Bolton, 410 U. S. at 191. *See also* Roe v. Wade, 410 U.S. at 153. *See generally* Marcin & Marcin, *The Physician's Decision-Making Role in Abortion Cases,* 35 JUR. 66 (1975).

[137] Roe v. Wade, 410 U.S. at 116.

[138] *Id.* at 162.

[139] What is deemed a material risk may differ depending on whether the court has adopted a medical practice standard or a reasonable patient standard of disclosure. Under the first standard, material risks are those which ordinary reputable physicians would disclose under the circumstances. *See, e.g.,* Riedisser v. Nelson, 111 Ariz. 542, 534 P. 2d 1052 (1975). Under the second, material risks are those which an ordinary reasonable patient would consider relevant in deciding whether to consent to the proposed treatment. *See, e.g.,* Canterbury v. Spence, 464 F. 2d 772 (D. C. Cir. 1972).

The reasonable patient standard adopted in *Canterbury v. Spence* has been accepted by courts in a number of states, including California, Rhode Island, Washington, and Wisconsin. Cobbs v. Grant, 8 Cal. 3d 229, 502 P. 2d 1, 104 Cal. Rptr. 505 (1972); Wilkenson v. Vesey, 110 R. I. 606, 295 A. 2d 676 (1972); Hunter v. Brown, 4 Wash. App. 899, 484 P. 2d 1162 (1971); Trogun v. Fruchtman, 58 Wis. 2d 596, 207 N. W. 2d 297 (1973). Courts in Arizona, Delaware, Illinois, and Virginia have specifically rejected the *Canterbury* standard and reaffirmed the medical practice disclosure standard. Riedisser v. Nelson, 111 Ariz. 542, 534 P. 2d 1052 (1975); Wagner v. Olmedo, 365 A. 2d 643 (Del. 1976); Miceikis v. Field, 37 Ill. App. 3d 763, 347 N. E. 2d 320 (1976); Bly v. Rhoads, 216 Va. 645, 222 S. E. 2d 783 (1976).

[140] *See generally* Bernard Williams' critique of utilitarianism in J. C. SMART & B. WILLIAMS, UTILITARIANISM: FOR AND AGAINST (1973).

[141] *See* Horne v. Patton, 291 Ala. 701, 287 So. 2d 824 (1973); Simonsen v. Swenson, 104 Neb. 224, 177 N. W. 831 (1920); Hague v. Williams, 37 N. J. 328, 181 A. 2d 345 (1962); Clark v. Geraci, 29 Misc. 2d 791, 208 N. Y. S. 2d 564 (Sup. Ct. 1960); Schaffer v. Spicer, 215 N. W. 2d 134 (S. D. 1974).

[142] Collins v. Howard, 156 F. Supp. 322 (S. D. Ga. 1957) (applying Georgia law); Quarles v. Sutherland, 215 Tenn. 651, 389 S. W. 2d 249 (1965).

[143] *See* American Medical Association Judicial Council, OPINIONS AND REPORTS OF THE JUDICIAL COUNCIL 53-55 (1971).

[144] *See* Hague v. Williams, 37 N. J. 328, 181 A. 2d 345 (1962); Clark v. Geraci, 29 Misc. 2d 791, 208 N. Y. S. 2d 564 (Sup. Ct. 1960).

[145] Some courts recognizing a cause of action for breach of confidence have relied on the doctor-patient testimonial privilege, which is based on this rationale. *See* Schaffer v. Spicer, 215 N. W. 2d 134 (S. D. 1974). *But cf.* Simonsen v. Swenson, 104 Neb. 224, 117 N. W. 831 (1920) (testimonial privilege irrelevant when disclosure made out of court).

[146] Courts and commentators have noted that disclosure of confidential communications is prohibited by the Hippocratic Oath and the ethical principle adopted by the American Medical Association. *See* Clark v. Geraci, 29 Misc. 2d 791, 208 N. Y. S. 2d 564 (Sup. Ct. 1960); Green & Capron, *Issues of Law and Public Policy in Genetic Screening,* in ETHICAL, SOCIAL AND LEGAL DIMENSIONS OF SCREENING FOR HUMAN GENETIC DISEASE 57, 60-62 (D. Bergsma ed. 1974).

[147] Courts have referred to licensing statutes making breach of confidence grounds for revocation and to testimonial privilege statutes to buttress the conclusion that breach of confidence is contrary to community standards. *See* Clark v. Geraci, 29 Misc. 2d 791, 208 N. Y. S. 2d 546 (Sup. Ct. 1960); Schaffer v. Spicer, 215 N. W. 2d 134 (S. D. 1974).

[148] Simonsen v. Swenson, 104 Neb. 224, 177 N. W. 831 (1920).

[149] Clark v. Geraci, 29 Misc. 2d 791, 208 N. Y. S. 2d 564 (Sup. Ct. 1960) ("partial waiver" held to be complete waiver so physician could avoid misrepresentation).

[150] Hague v. Williams, 37 N. J. 328, 181 A. 2d 345 (1962). *Cf.* Quarles v. Sutherland, 215 Tenn. 651, 389 S. W. 2d 249 (1965).

[151] Pennison v. Provident Life & Accident Ins. Co., 154 So. 2d 617 (La. Ct. App. 1963), *writ refused,* 244 La. 1019, 156 So. 2d 226 (1963); Curry v. Corn, 52 Misc. 2d 1035, 277 N. Y. S. 2d 470 (Sup. Ct. 1966).

[152] *See, e.g.,* Hofmann v. Blackmon, 241 So. 2d 752 (Fla. Dist. Ct. App. 1970); Skillings v. Allen, 143 Minn. 323, 173 N. W. 663 (1919); Jones v. Stanko, 118 Ohio St. 147, 160 N. E. 456 (1928).

[153] 17 Cal. 3rd 425, 551 P. 2d 334, 131 Cal. Rptr. 14 (1976).

[154] *See* Hague v. Williams, 37 N. J. 328, 181 A. 2d 345 (1962) (question is whether "supervening interests of society" justify disclosure of confidential information).

[155] *See, e.g.,* Dietze v. King, 184 F. Supp. 944 (E. D. Va. 1960); Doty v. Lutheran Hosp. Ass'n., 110 Neb. 467, 194 N. W. 444 (1923); Martisek v. Ainsworth, 459 S. W. 2d 679 (Tex. Ct. App. 1970).

[156] *See generally* Green & Capron, *Issues of Law and Public Policy in Genetic Screening,* in ETHICAL, SOCIAL, AND LEGAL DIMENSIONS OF SCREENING FOR HUMAN GENETIC DISEASE 57 (D. Bergsma ed. 1974).

[157] For example, if the child has a sex-linked defect transmitted by the mother's X-chromosome, the genetic make-up of the father is irrelevant.

[158] *See* cases cited *supra* note 152.

[159] *See* cases cited *supra* notes 153 — 154.

[160] *But cf.* Delgado & Keyes, *Parental Preferences and Selective Abortion: A Commentary on Roe v. Wade, Doe v. Bolton, and the Shape of Things to Come.* 1974 WASH. U. L. Q. 203. (Arguing that state could constitutionally prohibit abortion for 'frivolous' reasons such as the sex of the fetus).

[161] *See* text accompanying notes 39 to 47, *supra.*

EPILOGUE

Looking back over the material presented in the three parts and the appendix of this book, the reader may wonder about the future of those who are, or will be, born afflicted with some genetic or congenital defect. In brief there appears to be two main attitudes towards such individuals. One posture which has been labelled as representative of secular humanism looks at the human race in its temporal dimension as the ultimate value by which all other goods are to be judged. From that perspective individual life is ultimately subordinated to the welfare of the human species. Consequently, the tendency of those in a decision-making position will be to promote the physical, mental and social well-being of human persons in so far as such is in the best interests of the human race. In some instances that will mean preventing couples from procreating who are at high risk for conceiving a child with a significant genetic defect. In other cases, coercive limitation will encourage or require the aborting of fetuses diagnosed to have a specified genetic disease. To what extent the reproductive freedom of couples will be coercively limited remains to be seen. But early signs of such are already beginning to appear in medical and ethical literature as well as in legal decisions and discussions.

The other main attitude towards the issue of those handicapped by a genetic defect is that of the Christian and of those who hold similar values regarding the human person. In this posture all is subordinated to God. The human race collectively, and humans individually, find their meaning and worth in the relationships they have to the Supreme Being, their Creator and Redeemer. Consequently, humans, individually and collectively, enjoy only a delegated dominion over the world and their own bodies. The responsible exercise of that dominion requires a thorough understanding of the relevant natural forces and laws as well as a prayerful perception of God's revelation to the human race as recorded in the sacred scriptures, reflected on by theologians and taught authoritatively by the magisterium of the Church.

Furthermore, the Christian is aware of the impact of sin on human affairs as well as the reality and meaning of suffering. The latter is not an unmitigated evil. Through the suffering, death and resurrection of Jesus Christ, the Christian is able to perceive the role of suffering in human life. Evil in whatever form must be resisted but only by means

251

which themselves are not morally evil. The suffering visited upon an individual, a family, or a society because of a genetic defect is not lightly borne. When possible it is to be avoided by morally legitimate means which in light of the constant teaching of the Church's magisterium excludes the use of artificial contraceptives and direct sterilization. If a living fetus is detected to have a serious genetic defect, abortion may not be employed but the child must be allowed to come to term. When born, such a child is to be treated with all the care a non-afflicted child would receive and even more because of its greater need. Through the eyes of faith, such a child can be the occasion for evoking even greater love from the parents and siblings. Yet the parents need the emotional and economic support of the society which has a responsibility to provide care for its needy members.

The Church has a challenge to provide leadership in the care and concern which these handicapped persons receive. This is due to them not only out of love but even from justice. In addition, the Church needs to encourage, promote and when possible even financially support research in the diagnosis and treatment of these genetic conditions.

There is hope. Many advances have taken place in the past 20 years. Many more can occur as our understanding of the causes and nature of genetic defects are better understood. Some treatment is now possible for a few conditions such as PKU and galactosemia. But these only treat the condition symptomatically. Public understanding of what can be done to maximize the available capacities of afflicted individuals is still relatively poor. In one way public opinion and emphasis on the mentally and physically "perfect" human person has laid an additional burden on handicapped persons. Public attitudes, as reflected in and shaped by the mass media, need to be modified to meet the reality. Ultimately, a balanced Christian optimism needs to be stressed along with the realization that God's love for us is unconditional. Even what physical or moral evil befalls us is an occasion for the concerned individual to respond with an unconditional love for the other.

INDEX